Frederick Adolf Paola, MD, JD
Professor, Health Professions Division, Nova Southeastern University and
Professore a contratto, Department of Molecular Medicine,
Universita' degli Studi di Pavia and Professore a contratto, Department of Medicine,
Università degli Studi di Padova

ETHICAL & LEGAL ASPECTS OF HEALTH CARE PRACTICE

FIRST EDITION

JONES & BARTLETT
LEARNING

World Headquarters
Jones & Bartlett Learning
25 Mall Road
Burlington, MA 01803
978-443-5000
info@jblearning.com
www.jblearning.com

Jones & Bartlett Learning books and products are available through most bookstores and online booksellers. To contact Jones & Bartlett Learning directly, call 800-832-0034, fax 978-443-8000, or visit our website, www.jblearning.com.

Substantial discounts on bulk quantities of Jones & Bartlett Learning publications are available to corporations, professional associations, and other qualified organizations. For details and specific discount information, contact the special sales department at Jones & Bartlett Learning via the above contact information or send an email to specialsales@jblearning.com.

Production Credits
Vice President, Product Management: Marisa R. Urbano
Vice President, Content Strategy and Implementation: Christine Emerton
Director, Product Management: Matthew Kane
Director, Content Management: Donna Gridley
Manager, Content Strategy: Carolyn Pershouse
Product Manager: Bill Lawrensen
Content Strategist: Carol Brewer Guerrero
Content Coordinator: Samantha Gillespie
Director, Project Management and Content Services: Karen Scott
Manager, Project Management: Jackie Reynen
Project Manager: John Coakley
Senior Digital Project Specialist: Angela Dooley
Marketing Manager: Mark Adamiak
Content Services Manager: Colleen Lamy
Vice President, Manufacturing and Inventory Control: Therese Connell
Composition: Straive
Project Management: Straive
Cover Design: Briana Yates
Text Design: Briana Yates
Media Development Editor: Faith Brosnan
Rights & Permissions Manager: John Rusk
Rights Specialist: Liz Kincaid
Cover Image (Title Page, Part Opener, Chapter Opener):
© Agsandrew/Shutterstock
Printing and Binding: McNaughton & Gunn

Library of Congress Cataloging-in-Publication Data
Names: Paola, Frederick A., author.
Title: Ethical and legal aspects of health care practice / Frederick Adolf Paola, MD, JD, Professor, Health Professions Division, Nova Southeastern University and Professore a contratto, Department of Molecular Medicine, Universita' degli Studi di Pavia and Professore a contratto, Department of Medicine, Università degli Studi di Padova.
Description: Burlington, Massachusetts : Jones & Bartlett Learning, [2023] | Includes bibliographical references and index. | Summary: "This book is designed to help students work through the ethics of clinical cases. It is a survey of legal and ethical issues intended for health profession. As students, it covers various approaches to ethical analysis, illustrates their application through the use of cases, and surveys important substantive topics in the field of medical ethics"– Provided by publisher.
Identifiers: LCCN 2022038598 | ISBN 9781284178395 (paperback)
Subjects: LCSH: Medical care–Law and legislation–United States. | Medical ethics.
Classification: LCC KF3821 .P36 2023 | DDC 344.7304/1–dc23/eng/20220930
LC record available at https://lccn.loc.gov/2022038598

6048

Printed in the United States of America
26 25 24 23 22 10 9 8 7 6 5 4 3 2 1

Brief Contents

Contents

Foreword

I've found that teaching healthcare ethics can be a tricky task. Health professions students must learn a complex and difficult new language en route to achieving their goal. This isn't just a matter of memorizing thousands of new words and their meanings. They also need to understand the language's syntax and grammar before they can become fluent speakers and fully integrated into the culture of health care. Human anatomy provides part of the vocabulary, as do physiology, biochemistry, pathology, and several other sciences. But it's only when students begin to interact with patients in the hospital or clinic under the supervision of experienced clinicians that they learn to integrate vocabulary, grammar, syntax, and culture in order to use the language effectively.

Ethics is another discipline that contributes essential concepts to the language of medicine. Yet I'm often surprised when teaching healthcare ethics to medical students to find that many of them reveal a serious gap between their assessment of how important moral issues are in medicine (very) and their willingness to grapple with basic ethical concepts in reasoning about them. Such students may engage in animated discussion, clearly airing their opinions on moral dilemmas, but eventually conclude, "It's all a matter of what you believe. There's no right or wrong answer." Others avoid the discussion phase entirely by raising the question, "What does the law say?" Since ethics is purely subjective, they assert, why do we need to reason about this case at all? A third group may avoid thoughtful analysis by employing the old, "We need more information" gambit. No matter how much information is provided in the case study, they prefer to discuss what additional tests or consultations we might order for the patient before being in a position to resolve an ethical dilemma, thereby not having to commit themselves.

Of course, I'm exaggerating. In fact, the vast majority of my students take very seriously their commitment to health care and the relief of suffering. They are by no means insensitive to real-life moral dilemmas. And yet students often have some difficulty understanding the need to learn certain elements of the language of ethics before beginning to care for patients, much as they need to internalize physiological principles.

There is a complicating factor. Clinicians, as well as many educators, point out that there is much more to the moral practice of health care than basic concepts like autonomy, beneficence, justice, informed consent, and so forth. The good practitioner must also integrate empathy, communication, culture, and narrative into their practice. Unquestionably true, but students need to begin with the basics. The beauty of *Ethical and Legal Aspects of Health Care Practice* is the clarity and elegance with which it does just that.

Take professionalism, for example. In the last 20 years, health profession schools have placed an increasing emphasis on creating explicit curricula on professional virtue and duty. Most curricula now include discussion of issues like duty to treat, professional boundaries, or conflict of interest, which can be lively, but not necessarily grounded in an underlying conceptual framework. Chapter 2 of *Ethical and Legal Aspects of Health Care Practice* presents a concisely structured account of the goals of medicine, legitimate and illegitimate means of achieving those goals, goal-means disparity or conflict, and the definition and assessment of futility. The chapter includes learning objectives, illustrative cases, and as is characteristic of the book, it concludes with review questions and case analyses.

I've worked as a teacher and consultant in clinical ethics for 40 years and read many—perhaps too many!—ethics textbooks for physicians, nurses, and other healthcare professionals. Some were broadly discursive with philosophical subtlety. Others consisted of series of academic articles on various cases or topics. Still others were structured around some sort of analytic system. In its concision and clarity, Frederick Paola's *Ethical and Legal Aspects of Health Care Practice* is arguably the most useful text I've seen for a basic course in healthcare ethics.

—Jack Coulehan, MD, MPH, FACP
Emeritus Professor of Medicine
Senior Fellow, Center for Medical Humanities,
Compassionate Care, and Bioethics
Stony Brook University

Preface

What Is a Health Professional?

This book is about ethics and law as they relate to health professionals (HPs). Seems straightforward enough, but what is ethics, what does it have to do with law, and what is an HP? We shall take up the first two questions in Chapter 1. For now, let's take up the third question—what is an HP?

The answer is that it depends to some extent on whom you ask.[1] While a fuller discussion of the concept of a *professional* is deferred to Chapter 2, by health professional we intend healthcare workers with special education/knowledge and/or training/skill. The term traditionally included physicians and surgeons,[2] but now includes physician assistants (PAs); pharmacists and pharmacy technicians; nurses and nurse practitioners; dentists; midwives; psychologists and psychiatrists;[3] and physical therapist (PTs), occupational therapist (OTs), respiratory therapists (RTs), or others

---

1 For example, the National Health Service (NHS) in the United Kingdom lists 14 so-called "allied health professions": art therapists, drama therapists, music therapists, chiropodists/podiatrists, dietitians, occupational therapists, operating department practitioners, orthoptists, osteopaths, paramedics, physiotherapists, prosthetists and orthotists, radiographers, and speech and language therapists. (See, The 14 allied health professions. https://www.england.nhs.uk/ahp/role/ Accessed January 16, 2021.) In contrast, the Association of Schools of Allied Health Professions (ASAHP) has adopted the definition used in the Federal Code:

> Title 42, Chapter 6A, Subchapter V, Part F, Sec. 295p of the Federal Code states that the term "allied health professionals" means a health professional (other than a registered nurse or physician assistant) who has not received a degree of doctor of medicine, a degree of doctor of osteopathy, a degree of doctor of dentistry or an equivalent degree, a degree of doctor of veterinary medicine or an equivalent degree, a degree of doctor of optometry or an equivalent degree, a degree of doctor of podiatric medicine or an equivalent degree, a degree of bachelor of science in pharmacy or an equivalent degree, a degree of doctor of pharmacy or an equivalent degree, a graduate degree in public health or an equivalent degree, a degree of doctor of chiropractic or an equivalent degree, a graduate degree in health administration or an equivalent degree, a doctoral degree in clinical psychology or an equivalent degree, or a degree in social work or an equivalent degree or a degree in counseling or an equivalent degree.

See, What is Allied Health? https://www.asahp.org/what-is. Accessed January 15, 2021.

2 Along with divinity and law, medicine was one of the three original "learned professions." See, Fisher R, ed. Statistics of the State of New-York. *Fisher's National Magazine and Industrial Record*. 1846;3(3):234.

3 We exclude veterinarians, veterinary technicians, and veterinary assistants only because our focus in this text is on human patients.

who perform services in the so-called allied health professions (AHPs).[4]

This book intends, and is written for, HPs in this broad and inclusive sense. That's a pretty large and diverse audience[5] and precludes an in-depth treatment of any one type of HP in this book. Rather, the cases and examples that have been chosen for discussion have been chosen for their broad applicability to HPs in general. No doubt, they reflect in part the background of the authors as well.

How to Use—and How Not to Use—This Book

It is a truism that one can't please all the people all the time. The best one can hope for is to please some of the people all of the time, or all of the people some of the time. More probably, some of the people some of the time.

And so it goes with this book. As stated in *What Is a Health Professional?*, the audience this book is trying to reach is broad and diverse and includes persons with varying academic and professional goals and no doubt with diverse personal beliefs and values. As we shall see in Chapter 1, there are many moral questions for which morality provides a definitive answer. For example, may I kill someone because I don't like the way he drives?[6] No. But there are some moral questions for which morality arguably does not provide a definite answer. One such question might be, Is it morally permissible to abort a fetus before the point of viability? How should a book such as this, targeted at a broad and diverse audience, handle such controversial questions?

One option would be to simply avoid them and avoid offending anyone in the process. This book rejects that option, for the following reasons.

---

4 Colloquially the term "allied health professional" is used in a broad sense, and includes the following:

> . . . many of the well-known non-nurse, non-physician health care providers including audiologists and speech language pathologists; physical therapists, occupational therapists and respiratory therapists; diagnostic medical personnel (medical laboratory scientists, cytogenetic technologists, diagnostic molecular scientists, histotechnologists, and pathologists' assistants); imaging specialists (radiographers, nuclear medicine technologists, and sonographers); nutritionists and dietitians; and physician assistants. Others often included in allied health include dental personnel (dental hygienists and dental assistants); emergency medical personnel (EMTs, paramedics); exercise science professionals (athletic trainers, exercise physiologists, kinesiotherapists); health information technologists; health educators (asthma educators, diabetes educators); counselors (genetic counselors, mental health counselors, family therapists); specialists in cancer diagnosis and treatment (medical physicists, medical dosimetrists, and radiation therapists); pharmacy personnel (pharmacy technicians and assistants) and other healthcare providers and support personnel, such as medical assistants.

See, What is Allied Health? https://www.asahp.org/what-is. Accessed January 15, 2021.

5 Reportedly, there are about five million AHPs alone working in more than 80 fields and constituting 60% of healthcare providers. (See, Allied Health Professions Overview, https://explorehealthcareers.org/field/allied-health-professions/#:~:text=There%20are%20five%20million%20allied,of%20all%20health%20care%20providers. Accessed January 19, 2021.) If my math is correct, that works out to greater than eight million HPs in the United States.

6 Consider that the female protagonist of the Bruce Springsteen song From Small Things (Big Things One Day Come) is alleged to have shot her lover dead on a sunny Florida road because she could not stand the way he drove. From Small Things (Big Things One Day Come). Springsteenlyrics.com. https://www.springsteenlyrics.com/lyrics.php?song=fromsmallthings. Accessed February 2, 2021.

First, avoidance of controversial topics is the coward's way out,[7] and it would be ironic for a book about ethics to adopt such a vicious[8] approach to the subject.

Second, omitting controversial topics would do a disservice to the subject matter of ethics, suggesting as it would that topics about which we disagree are somehow outside of ethics, beyond its purview. They are not.

Third, it's important and good that reasonable persons be able to discuss matters on which they reasonably disagree. Choosing the path of avoidance of controversy starts us down a very slippery slope. If we only discuss matters on which we all agree, then we can never hope to reach agreement on matters on which we disagree. And what happens when we identify a small area of disagreement concerning a matter on which we had previously agreed? We stop talking about it, to avoid controversy! You see where this is going?

So this book does not shy away from controversial topics. It accepts that there are some issues on which reasonable persons can disagree. When a decision must be made in such cases, it may come down to which side is able to make the more persuasive argument.

We don't pretend that the analyses of the cases in this text are the only right answers to the questions posed. It might be that they aren't even the best answers possible. The analyses offered are examples of how to approach the cases presented, and we hope that they are useful in this regard. If you disagree with the analysis of a particular case—if you think the book "got it wrong"—use the error as a teaching tool. And let us know about it.

And one more thing, some might be asking: What's with all the quotes at the start of the chapters, and the references to popular music in the text? Bioethics and the medical humanities have long been joined at the hip.[9] The humanities are "a group of academic subjects [including but not limited to art, film studies, and literature] united by a commitment to studying aspects of the human condition and a qualitative approach that generally prevents a single paradigm from coming to define any discipline."[10] It is this broader, more qualitative approach espoused by the humanities—their tendency to oppose more narrow, reductive, and minimalist approaches such as the legal approach—that makes them so valuable in the study of ethics.

—Fred Paola

---

7 As Sean Connery's character, Jim Malone, says in the 1957 book *The Untouchables*, "Well, the Lord hates a coward." Ness, Eliot and Fraley, Oscar. *The Untouchables*. New York: Julian Messner, 1957.

8 The operative vice is, of course, cowardice. We shall discuss the vices in Chapter 1.

9 American Society for Bioethics and Humanities. https://asbh.org. Accessed May 9, 2021.

10 Charon R, Trautmann Banks J, Connelly JE, et al. Literature and medicine: contributions to clinical practice. *Annals of Internal Medicine*. 1995;122(8):599–606.

Walkthrough

This survey of legal and ethical issues for health professions students covers various approaches to ethical analysis, illustrates their application through the use of cases, and discusses important substantive, relevant topics in the field of medical ethics.

Case Studies and Analyses: Worktext Format

This work-text—a combination workbook and textbook—is designed to help students work through the ethics of clinical cases. Real and fictitious cases are presented throughout each chapter. The reader is challenged to apply moral and ethical principles to make a substantive analysis of each case.

Each chapter concludes with case analyses, serving as examples of arguments that could be used to work through the particular case.

CASE 5.B

A video posted on YouTube in April 2008 showed a raucous Philippine operating room full of doctors and nurses laughing and cheering during an operation to remove a canister of perfume from the rectum a 39-year-old male patient.

> The unauthorized nearly 3-minute video of a noisy operating room shows doctors and nurses laughing, giggling and cheering. At one point, a hand appears with a cell phone camera taking a close-up picture of the surgery. As a doctor gingerly pulls out the 6-inch long canister from the male patient's rectum, someone shouts, "Baby

The video was apparently shot by one of the student nurses.[58] Whose conduct was blameworthy? Why? What should the consequences have been for those involved?

Analysis: ______________________________

____

____

____

____

____

Case 5.B Analysis

Multiple health professionals and health professionals-in-training breached their professional fiduciary duties to the patient in question. The health professionals responsible for precepting and serving as role models for the medical and nursing students involved failed miserably. Just as a health professional's access to a patient and his or her medical record is on a "need to know" basis,[48] access to the operating room in this case should have been restricted by the surgeon and nurse in charge to those persons who had legitimate patient-care or pedagogical reasons to be there. The presence of superfluous personnel was an invasion of the patient's privacy (intrusion). The Reportedly, 12 other health professionals "faced an administrative case for grave misconduct."[49] Had this occurred in the United States, consequences might have included (1) discipline of the medical and nursing students involved, up to and including expulsion; (2) professional disciplinary actions against the involved licensed health professionals; (3) administrative action against the involved hospital; and (4) a private cause of action for monetary damages against any/all of the above.

CASE 8.C: *Yorston v. Penell*[43]

The plaintiff Yorston accidentally shot himself in the leg with a nail gun. He was brought to the hospital and became a patient of Dr. Pennell, an attending surgeon on the medical staff but NOT a hospital employee. Also involved in the care of the patient were Dr. Hatemi, the surgical resident, and Mr. Rex, a surgical subintern [usually a third or fourth year medical student], both of whom were hospital employees. Mr. Rex was instructed to do the admitting history and physical examination (H&P) by Dr. Hatemi. During the course of the exam, the patient advised Mr. Rex that he was allergic to penicillin, but Mr. Rex neglected to note this in his written H&P. Subsequently, Dr. Hatemi, on the instructions of Dr. Pennell, operated on Yorston. Postoperatively, in reliance

Case 8.C Analysis

One possibility is that Dr. Pennell is being held liable by the court for failing to adequately supervise Rex and Hatemi. That would be a form of *derivative liability*, but in fact the case was not submitted to the jury on that theory. It turns out that Dr. Pennell's liability is completely divorced from any wrongdoing on his part. His liability is said to be vicarious; the negligence of someone else (Rex) is being imputed to him. Pennell's liability is not contingent upon any wrongful act or omission of his own, but rather on the wrongful act(s) or omission(s) of other healthcare providers.

High-Level Discussions of Critical Content

Grounded in more than 27 years of experience teaching medical ethics and legal medicine, the author presents a framework from which students can effectively analyze difficult and critical topics relevant to healthcare practice now and as laws evolve, an essential foundation in the principles and practice of medical ethics for any healthcare professional.

3. Analysis of Precedent: Analogy and Distinction[18]

Here I mean to discuss the process of looking at previously decided similar cases (*precedent*) to facilitate moral decision-making and moral justification. In the legal context, this is referred to as *common law analysis*. Because our focus here is on morality rather than law, we will use the term *analysis of precedent*.

Any analysis of precedent should begin with a thorough understanding of each one of the previously decided similar cases—including the relevant facts, as well as the reasons and policy considerations implicated. (For the sake of simplicity, the illustrative hypothetical cases employed next are rather spartan and do not lend themselves to such in-depth understanding.)

Consider the following short series of hypothetical legal cases, which we will use to illustrate the process of analyzing precedent.

Case 1: Dr. X learns that his promiscuous single patient, John Doe, is HIV+. Dr. X cautions Doe re: transmissibility of HIV but does not inquire further into his (Doe's) sex life. Doe has sex with and infects his girlfriend, Jane Q-Public. Q-Public sues Dr. X, arguing that he should have warned her. The court holds (decides) that there was no duty to warn under the circumstances.

Case 2: Dr. Y learns that his married patient, Joe Doakes, is HIV+. He fails to warn Doakes' wife,

5.1. Disclosure of COIs

COI policies typically require that a covered clinician or researcher disclose to his or her institution the existence of outside relationships giving rise to secondary interests. Some policies also require that financial secondary interests be disclosed to others who might be affected—e.g., research subjects, journal readers, students, or patients.

Besides organizational COI policies, the law has a role to play as well. For example, the Physician Payment Sunshine Act, part of the 2010 Affordable Care Act, requires all drug and device companies to publicly report their payments to healthcare providers. (A search tool used to search payments made by drug and medical device companies to physicians and teaching hospitals is available at https://openpaymentsdata.cms.gov/.) ProPublica[44] has been tracking drug company payments to doctors since 2010 through a project known as Dollars for Docs.[45] Consider the following piece, published in 2016:

> **Now There's Proof: Docs Who Get Company Cash Tend to Prescribe More Brand-Name Meds**
> by Charles Ornstein, Mike Tigas, and Ryann Grochowski Jones
> March 17, 2016, 5 a.m. EDT

Glossary of Legal Terms

The text concludes with a Glossary of Legal Terms for student familiarization and study of these important concepts.

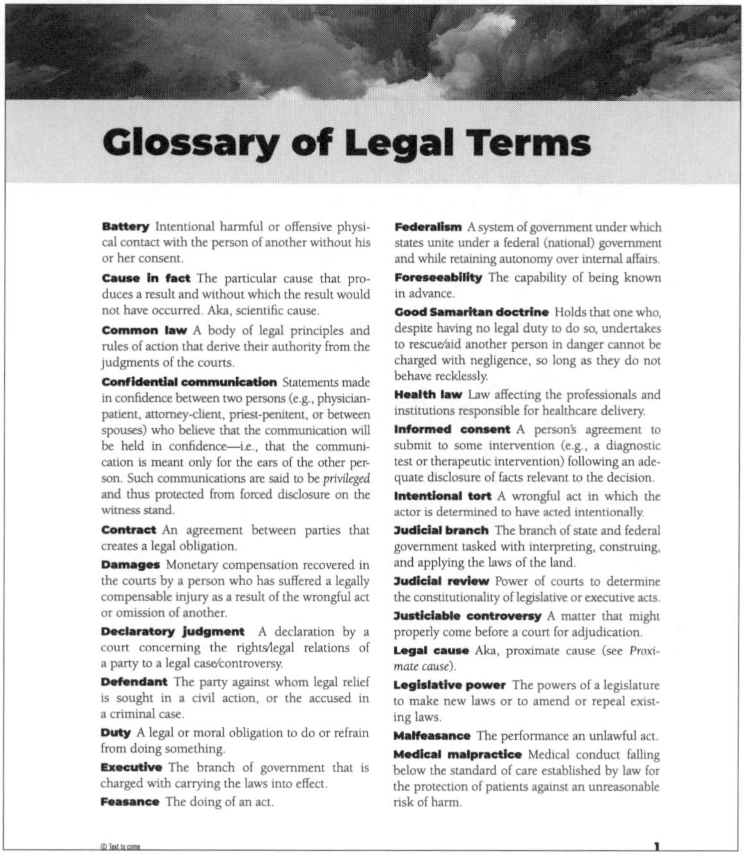

Glossary of Legal Terms

Battery Intentional harmful or offensive physical contact with the person of another without his or her consent.

Cause in fact The particular cause that produces a result and without which the result would not have occurred. Aka, scientific cause.

Common law A body of legal principles and rules of action that derive their authority from the judgments of the courts.

Confidential communication Statements made in confidence between two persons (e.g., physician-patient, attorney-client, priest-penitent, or between spouses) who believe that the communication will be held in confidence—i.e., that the communication is meant only for the ears of the other person. Such communications are said to be *privileged* and thus protected from forced disclosure on the witness stand.

Contract An agreement between parties that creates a legal obligation.

Damages Monetary compensation recovered in the courts by a person who has suffered a legally compensable injury as a result of the wrongful act or omission of another.

Declaratory judgment A declaration by a court concerning the rights/legal relations of a party to a legal case/controversy.

Defendant The party against whom legal relief is sought in a civil action, or the accused in a criminal case.

Duty A legal or moral obligation to do or refrain from doing something.

Executive The branch of government that is charged with carrying the laws into effect.

Feasance The doing of an act.

Federalism A system of government under which states unite under a federal (national) government and while retaining autonomy over internal affairs.

Foreseeability The capability of being known in advance.

Good Samaritan doctrine Holds that one who, despite having no legal duty to do so, undertakes to rescue/aid another person in danger cannot be charged with negligence, so long as they do not behave recklessly.

Health law Law affecting the professionals and institutions responsible for healthcare delivery.

Informed consent A person's agreement to submit to some intervention (e.g., a diagnostic test or therapeutic intervention) following an adequate disclosure of facts relevant to the decision.

Intentional tort A wrongful act in which the actor is determined to have acted intentionally.

Judicial branch The branch of state and federal government tasked with interpreting, construing, and applying the laws of the land.

Judicial review Power of courts to determine the constitutionality of legislative or executive acts.

Justiciable controversy A matter that might properly come before a court for adjudication.

Legal cause Aka, proximate cause (see *Proximate cause*).

Legislative power The powers of a legislature to make new laws or to amend or repeal existing laws.

Malfeasance The performance an unlawful act.

Medical malpractice Medical conduct falling below the standard of care established by law for the protection of patients against an unreasonable risk of harm.

© Text to come 1

Instructor Resources

An extensive collection of instructor resources to accompany *Ethical and Legal Aspects of Health Care Practice* includes the following, which are available to qualified instructors:

- Answer Key to Chapter Review Questions
- Instructor Case Studies – with critical thinking questions and analyses of each case study
- Slides in PowerPoint format
- Test bank – also available in LMS-compatible formats

- Remediation Test Bank – comprehensive examination questions suitable for remediation
- Supplementary Chapters
  - The Role of the Physician Assistant in the Modern U.S. Healthcare System
  - The Role of the Physician Assistant in Mode rn Global Healthcare
  - The Role of the Respiratory Therapist in the Modern U.S. Healthcare System
- Sample Syllabi
  - One-credit course
  - Two-credit course
  - Three-credit course

Navigate eBook

A Navigate eBook is available for separate purchase and can be read online or offline through the Navigate app.

Acknowledgments

Contributors

Stephanie Lolita Anderson, MD, JD
Assistant Professor
Nova Southeastern University
Fort Myers, Florida

Jack Coulehan, MD, MPH, FACP
Emeritus Professor of Medicine
Senior Fellow, Center for Medical Humanities, Compassionate Care, and Bioethics
Stony Brook University
Stony Brook, New York

Katheryn Knutson, DHSc, PA-C
Assistant Professor
Florida Gulf Coast University
Fort Myers, Florida

Eugene M. Macogay, MSc, RRT, RRT-ACCS
Director of Clinical Education, Respiratory Care
St. Petersburg College
St. Petersburg, Florida

Janet K. Sparker, EdD, RN, PA-C
Associate Professor
Nova Southeastern University
Fort Myers, Florida

Robert M. Walker, M.D., FACP, FAAHPM
Affiliate Associate Professor of Medicine
USF Morsani College of Medicine
Division of Hospice and Palliative Medicine
Tampa, Florida

Reviewers

Abdullah Alismail, PhD(c), M.S, RRT-NPS, RRT-SDS, FCCP
Assistant Professor of Cardiopulmonary Sciences and Medicine
Department of Cardiopulmonary Sciences, School of Allied Health Professions
Department of Medicine, School of Medicine
Loma Linda University
Loma Linda, California

Hope Appelbaum, MEd, RRT
Director of Clinical Education for the Respiratory Program
Kettering College
Kettering, Ohio

Earlene Avalon, PhD, MPH
Associate Teaching Professor and Lead Faculty
Northeastern University
Boston, Massachusetts

Karen Berg, PT, DPT
Board Certified Orthopedic Clinical Specialist
Clinical Assistant Professor and Co-Associate Director of Clinical Education
University of Michigan—Flint Physical Therapy Department
Flint, Michigan

Hannah C. Beriault, MPH, RRT
Director of Clinical Education
Georgia Southern University—Armstrong Campus
Savannah, Georgia

Nicole Bougie, MS, CCC-SLP
Instructor/Clinical Supervisor
Eastern New Mexico University
Portales, New Mexico

Elizabeth Brownlee, MPAS, PA-C, DFAAPA
Assistant Professor, Director of Didactic Education
University of Florida, School of PA Studies
Gainesville, Florida

Kevin E. Brueilly, PT, PhD
Professor
Charleston Southern University
Charleston, South Carolina

Larry Chinnock, PT, EdD, MBA
Chair, Department of Physical Therapy
School of Allied Health Professions
Loma Linda University
Loma Linda, California

Kelly L. Colwell, EdD, MRC, RRT, RRT-NPS, CPFT, AE-C
Graduate and Undergraduate Program Director, Respiratory Care and Polysomnography Programs
Youngstown State University
Youngstown, Ohio

Linda D'Silva, PT, PhD
Assistant Professor
University of Kansas Medical Center
Kansas City, Kansas

Denise Finch, OTD, OTR/L, CHT, FAOTA
Assistant Professor
Occupational Therapy
MCPHS University
Manchester, NH

Tim Gilmore, PhD, RRT, RRT-NPS, RRT-ACCS, CPFT, AE-C
Program Director, Associate Professor
Cardiopulmonary Science Program
Louisiana State University Health
Shreveport, Louisiana

G. Scott Gravlee, PhD
Associate Professor of Philosophy
Department of Philosophy and Religious Studies
College of Arts and Humanities
University of Mount Union
Alliance, Ohio

Kimberly Haley, MEd, BSRT, RRT
Respiratory Therapy Clinical Director
Carlow University
Pittsburgh, Pennsylvania

Robert Hawkes, MSPA, PA-C
Physician Assistant Program Director
Florida Gulf Coast University
Fort Myers, Florida

Jill Heitzman, PT, DPT, PhD, GCS, NCS, CWS, CEEAA/ACEEAA
Program Director, Physical Therapy
Maryville University
St. Louis, Missouri

Patrick Helton, DHEd, RRT, RRT-NPS, RPFT, AE-C, CHES
Adjunct Professor
Midwestern State University
Wichita Falls, Texas

Albert J. Heuer, PhD, MBA, RRT-ACCS, FAARC
Professor, Rutgers School of Health Professions
Newark, New Jersey

Erica Judie, DHSc, RRT-ACCS
Assistant Professor, Respiratory Care
Midwestern State University
Wichita Falls, Texas

Russ Kauffman, MPAS, PA-C
Assistant Professor
University of North Dakota
Grand Forks, North Dakota

Aleko Kimbouris, MSHS, MPH, PA-C
Assistant Professor
Center for Physician Assistant Studies
Johnson & Wales University
Providence, Rhode Island

Vicki LaFay, PT, DPT, PhD
Program Director/Chair, Department of Physical Therapy
Clarkson University
Potsdam, New York

Melanie D. Lambert, PT, DPT
Board-Certified Clinical Specialist in Orthopaedic Physical Therapy
Assistant Professor
Marshall School of Physical Therapy
Huntington, West Virginia

Blanche Leeman, EdD, OTR/L, CHT
Assistant Professor 2
Stonybrook University
Stony Brook, New York

Fabian Lora, MSRC(c) RRT-NPS, C-NPT
Loma Linda University
Loma Linda, California

Kristin Lugo, PharmD
Director of Clinical Education
Assistant Clinical Professor
Ohio University, Division of Physician Assistant Practice
Dublin, Ohio

Deborah Matheron, PhD, CCC-SLP/L
Associate Professor
SUNY Cortland
Cortland, New York

Renee Mazurek, PT, DPT
Clinical Associate Professor
DPT Program
Department of Rehabilitation Sciences & Technology
College of Health Sciences
University of Wisconsin-Milwaukee
Milwaukee, Wisconsin

Kristen McHenry, EdD, RRT-ACCS
Assistant Professor, Degree Advancement Program
Boise State University
Boise, Idaho

Olaide Oluwole-Sangoseni, PT, Ph.D., DPT, MSc, FNAP
Associate Professor of Physical Therapy
Board-Certified Clinical Specialist in Geriatric Physical Therapy (GCS)
Advanced Master Clinician Orthopaedic Physical Therapy (MSc)
Certified Biomedical Dry Needling (Cert. BDN)
Distinguished Fellow of the National Academies of Practice (FNAP)
Maryville University of St. Louis
St. Louis, Missouri

Lee Anne Pate, MEd, RRT
Associate Professor
Director of Clinical Education
Respiratory Therapy Program
Allied Health Sciences Department
Shawnee State University
Portsmouth, Ohio

Laurie Ray, PT, PhD
Associate Professor & Consultant
UNC-Chapel Hill, DAHS, Division of Physical Therapy
Chapel Hill, North Carolina

Kelly Rose, MSHS, RRT, AE-C
Director of Clinical Education/Assistant Professor, Respiratory Therapy Program
Utah Valley University
Orem, Utah

Byron Russell, PT, PhD
Director, Physical Therapy Program
Midwestern University
Glendale, Arizona

Robert Sandstrom, PhD, PT
Professor
Department of Physical Therapy
Creighton University
Omaha, NE

Erica Sherman, PT, DPT, MBA
Co-Associate Director of Clinical Education and Assistant Professor
University of Michigan—Flint
Flint, Michigan

Erin Simunds, MS, PT
Assistant Professor of Physical Therapy
Concordia University
St. Paul, Minnesota

Stephen G. Smith, MPA, RT, RRT, FAARC
Clinical Associate Professor
Stony Brook University—RCP
Stony Brook, New York

Wendi C. Stewart, MS, PA-C
Program Director, Associate Professor
Mayborn College of Health Sciences
University of Mary Hardin-Baylor
Belton, Texas

Howell Tapley, PT, PhD
Professor and Program Director
Indiana State University
Terre Haute, Indiana

Adam Walsh, PT, DPT, OCS, SCS, FAAOMPT
Assistant Professor
University of New Mexico
Albuquerque, New Mexico

SECTION 1

Introduction to the Study of Ethics and Law for Health Professionals

The first four chapters of this book constitute an introduction to the material that follows. At this point the reader might reasonably ask, "Why is there a need for such an introduction? Why not delve directly into a discussion of the substance of ethics and law as they relate to health professionals?"

Simply stated, an introduction is necessary because it's not possible to apply ethical and legal tenets to the practice of health care without first introducing those tenets. We could not discuss the ethical and legal aspects of healthcare practice without reference to ethical and legal norms. This introduction provides a framework and a vocabulary for that application and discussion.

One can talk/think about ethics on a variety of levels. In Chapter 1 we do so—Chapter 1 discusses approaches to ethics at the level of *theory*, at the level of *principles*, and at the level of *rules* and *ideals*. Health care providers are probably most familiar with the language of principles, thanks in no small measure to the influence of the classic text *Principles of Biomedical Ethics*[1] by Beauchamp and Childress, and the book you are reading addresses ethical principles in some detail. Nevertheless, I also devote significant space to Bernard Gert's formulation of the rules and ideals, for three reasons. First, unlike the four-principles approach of Beauchamp and Childress, Gert's formulation of the moral rules and ideals (and virtues) is part of a comprehensive moral theory (Gert's formulation of common morality), and so ties in nicely with our multi-level approach to ethics. Second, from its fourth edition on, Beauchamp and Childress' text introduced the issue of common morality in part in response to criticism by Gert et al.[2] Third and perhaps most importantly, because the moral rules are more specific action guides than are moral principles, I suspect that many students will find them easier to work with.

Chapter 2 explores what it means to be a good (i.e., "ethical") health professional. It does so by considering the role-specific duties of the health professional (health care's so-called *internal morality*). This chapter also explores the concept of *professionalism*, which may be thought of as the character-based analog of the duties corresponding to the aforementioned internal morality.

Chapter 3 is a how-to chapter—how to apply the concepts discussed in Chapters 1 and 2 in the making of individual moral judgments in real-life scenarios.

Chapter 4 is a brief introduction to U.S. law as it relates to health professionals.

1 Beauchamp TL, Childress JF. *Principles of biomedical ethics*. 5th ed. Oxford: Oxford University Press, 2001.

2 Letícia Erig Osório de A, Volnei G. The common morality theory in the work of Beauchamp and Childress. *Revista Bioética*. 2015; 23(3): 634–644. https://dx.doi.org/10.1590/1983-80422015233100.

CHAPTER 1

Theory, Principles, and Rules in Ethics

LEARNING OBJECTIVES

1. Define *ethics* and *morality.*
2. Explain how the *moral rules*, *moral ideals*, and *moral virtues* relate to morality.
3. Explain how *moral decisions, moral rules, moral principles,* and *ethical theory* relate to one another.
4. Recognize and distinguish *deontology*, *consequentialism*, and *virtue ethics*.
5. List and explain the *principles of biomedical ethics.*
6. Recognize and distinguish *nonmaleficence* and *beneficence.*
7. Explain the *rule of the double effect* and recognize instances in which it does and does not apply.
8. Recognize and distinguish *specific* and *general beneficence.*
9. Recognize and distinguish *obligatory beneficence* and *ideal beneficence.*
10. Define *paternalism.*
11. State the *formal principle of justice.*
12. List several *material principles of justice.*
13. Explain how *utilitarian*, *egalitarian*, and *libertarian* theories of justice differ.

I'm not a judge or jury. But I can tell you this: he won't sell anybody out to buy his future!! And that, my friends, is called integrity! That's called courage! Now that's the stuff leaders should be made of. Now I have come to the crossroads in my life. I always knew what the right path was. Without exception, I knew. But I never took it. You know why? It was too damn hard. Now here's Charlie. He's come to the crossroads. He has chosen a path. It's the right path. It's a path made of principle—that leads to character. Let him continue on his journey.[3]

—**Lieutenant Colonel** Frank Slade, in *Scent of a Woman*

3 Scent of a woman. American Rhetoric Movie Speeches. https://www.americanrhetoric.com/MovieSpeeches/specialengagements/moviespeechscentofawoman.html. Accessed March 13, 2019.

This book is about law and ethics as they relate to health professionals. Seems straightforward enough, but what is ethics, and what does it have to do with law?

1. Ethics and Morality

Simply stated, ethics refers to moral philosophy,[4] or the philosophy of morality. Morality, in turn, has been defined by Bernard Gert as "an informal public system applying to all rational persons, governing behavior that affects others, and includes what are commonly known as the moral rules, [the moral] ideals, and [the moral] virtues and has the lessening of evil or harm as its goal."[5] Let's take a closer look at this definition.

Morality exists to minimize harm to others, specifically to members of the group protected by morality. One of the issues about which people disagree is, who belongs to the protected group? So, for example, are all humans entitled to the protection of the moral rules, or does such protection only apply to humans already born? Do the moral rules protect humans who are no longer sentient (think patients in permanent vegetative state)? Do the moral rules protect animals? Plants? Since our concern herein is with the practice of health care, we shall focus on humans as the protected "others."

Morality minimizes harm to protected group members by governing the behavior of those to whom morality applies—so-called *moral agents*. Moral agents are persons who are responsible for and held accountable for their actions. Rational persons—persons capable of acting rationally—are moral agents.

Morality governs the behavior of moral agents by prohibiting them from violating the *moral rules*, by encouraging them to further the *moral ideals*, and by encouraging their cultivating the *moral virtues*. We shall have more to say about the moral rules, ideals, and virtues shortly.

Now, what does Bernard Gert mean by an "informal public system"? By categorizing morality as a "public system," Gert means that all persons whose behavior is to be judged morally (moral agents) know the general kinds of actions that morality prohibits, requires, discourages, encourages, and allows. Note that this represents a critical difference between morality and law. The legal principle "ignorantia legis non excusat"[6] means that ignorance of the law is not an excuse. A person who breaks a law will not escape legal liability merely because he/she was unaware of that law.

Gert's characterization of the public system that is morality as "informal" means that "it has no authoritative judges and no decision procedure that provides a unique guide to action in all situations, or that resolves all disagreements. [In contrast, to] say that a public system is formal is to say that it has one or both of these things (Gert 2005: 9)."[7] This represents a second important difference with the law.

2. The Substance of Morality

According to Bernard Gert's theory of common morality, a complete account of morality includes the *moral rules*, the *moral ideals,* and the *moral virtues*.

2.1. The Moral Rules

The moral rules as formulated by Gert are easy to remember—10 of them, like the Commandments:

- Do not kill.
- Do not cause pain/suffering.

4 Internet Encyclopedia of Philosophy. https://www.iep.utm.edu/ethics/. Accessed February 14, 2019.
5 Gert B. *Morality: Its Nature and Justification*. New York, NY: Oxford University Press; 1998:13.
6 The Law Dictionary, https://thelawdictionary.org/ignorantia-legis-non-excusat/. Accessed February 18, 2019.
7 The definition of morality. Stanford Encyclopedia of Philosophy. https://plato.stanford.edu/entries/morality-definition/#DescDefiMora. Accessed February 14, 2019.

- Do not disable.
- Do not deprive of freedom.
- Do not deprive of pleasure.
- Do not deceive.
- Do not break your promise.
- Do not cheat.
- Do not break the law.
- Do not neglect your duty.

The first five moral rules prohibit actions that directly cause others to suffer some harm (death, pain/suffering, disability, loss of freedom, or loss of pleasure); the second five prohibit actions that generally increase the risk that others will suffer one of the first five harms. Most of the rules are straightforward, but the following points bear mentioning here.

Morality prohibits the violation of any moral rule *unless that violation can be justified*. When, you might ask, is a moral rules violation justified? Gert has written that a violation is justified when an "impartial rational person" can advocate that the violation be publicly allowed. Consider CASE 1.A.

CASE 1.A

It is 1942. The Nazis knock on your door in the middle of the night, inquiring as to whether there are any Jews on the premises. In fact, your Jewish neighbors are hiding in your attic. Telling the truth will result in suffering and death. Should you tell the truth?

Explain your answer in terms of the moral rules.

Analysis: ______________________________

____

____

____

____

____

____

____

____

____

2.1.1. Do Not Break the Law

Consider the ninth rule above, under which breaking the law is a *prima facie*[8] moral rules violation. This rule provides an explicit nexus between morality and the law—an answer to the question, "What does ethics have to do with law?" Keep in mind, however, two qualifications. First, a violation of the moral rule against lawbreaking is no more absolute than any other moral rule; such a violation is justified when an impartial rational person can advocate that the violation be publicly allowed. Second, the law creates no corresponding moral duty when the law is itself immoral; hence the natural law dictum, "lex iniusta non est lex."[9]

2.1.2. Do Not Neglect Your Duty

Finally, consider the tenth rule, which prohibits neglect of duty. This rule is a source of moral duties that derive from our societal roles and is of special importance to healthcare practice.

Health professionals, like everyone else, must obey the moral rules as they relate to patients and nonpatients alike; however, by virtue of their role as healthcare providers, health professionals owe duties to their patients beyond those they owe to

8 Prima facie means "at first appearance" or "at first view" See Dictionary.com. https://www.dictionary.com/browse/prima-facie. Accessed July 8, 2019.

9 Natural law theories. Stanford Encyclopedia of Philosophy. https://plato.stanford.edu/entries/natural-law-theories/#LexIniNonEstLexDoSerUnjLawBinLeg. Accessed February 18, 2019.

nonpatients. These role-related duties derive from the fact that the provider–patient relationship is a fiduciary one, in which the health professional is obligated to protect and further the patient's best healthcare interests. "Fiduciary principles impose a special measure of loyalty and devotion on . . . [health professionals] by virtue of their control over an important subject matter, [and] the vulnerability of their . . . [patients] . . . ."[10]

One can conceptualize these special duties in terms of the moral rules. Applying the general moral rules previously listed (do not kill, etc.) to healthcare practice yields ethical rules specific to the care of patients such as, for example, the rule of confidentiality:

> In medicine, the need for the physician to obtain information from the patient, in addition to the fact that people generally do not want information about themselves to be revealed, in conjunction with the general moral not to cause pain generates the medical ethical rule "Do not breach confidentiality."[11]

2.2. The Moral Ideals

While the moral rules convey what morality requires and prohibits, the moral ideals convey what morality encourages. While "people can be punished for not following [the] moral rules, . . . not following moral ideals does not warrant punishment;"[12] consider that it would be impossible to follow the moral ideals with regard to everyone else at all times even if one were so inclined.

For each of the 10 moral rules listed above, one can articulate a corresponding moral ideal:

- Preserve life.
- Relieve pain/suffering.
- Prevent/lessen disability.
- Prevent the loss of freedom.
- Prevent the loss of pleasure.
- Prevent deceiving.
- Prevent promise-breaking.
- Prevent cheating.
- Prevent law-breaking.
- Prevent the neglect of duty.

Being a health professional involves devotion to the moral ideals (preserve life, relieve pain/suffering, prevent/lessen disability) as they relate to one's patients. Stated otherwise, it is a health professional's duty to follow certain moral ideals as they relate to his/her patients.

2.3. The Moral Virtues/Vices

While the focus of the moral rules and ideals is on acts, the focus of the *moral virtues* is on moral agents and their character.[13]

One's character is composed of *character traits*. Character traits are dispositions to have certain kinds of behavioral responses in certain circumstances. Character traits are influenced by *personality traits*, which are "dispositions to have certain kinds of emotional responses in certain general kinds of circumstances,"[14] but are also influenced by the teaching and training we receive from mentors and are strengthened or weakened by one's own behavior.

> Those character traits that . . . all impartial rational persons judge in the same way, like courage and cruelty, are called virtues and vices. But not all character traits are virtues or vices; some . . . like ambition are such that rational persons disagree about whether they should be cultivated. With regard to the virtues and vices, rational people agree that they want all the personal virtues [e.g., courage,

---

10 Hall MA, Bobinski MA, Orentlicher D. *Health Care Law and Ethics*. 6th ed. Aspen Publishers, NY; 2003:163.
11 Gert B, Culver CM, Danner CK. *Bioethics: A Systematic Approach*. New York, NY: Oxford University Press;1997:62.
12 Gert B. *Morality: Its Nature and Justification*. New York, NY: Oxford University Press; 1998:248.
13 See the quote from *Scent of a Woman* that opens the chapter.
14 Gert B. *Morality: Its Nature and Justification*. New York, NY: Oxford University Press; 1998:279.

temperance, and prudence] themselves and want everyone else to have all the moral virtues.[15]

The *moral virtues* comprise a subset of character traits that involve "justifiably following the moral rules and ideals significantly more than most people do; moral vice involves acting contrary to . . . morality significantly more than most people do."[16] In Gert's formulation of the moral virtues, there is a moral virtue and a moral vice corresponding with each of the indirect (second five) moral rules (see **Table 1.1**) that involve acting either in accordance with (virtue) or contrary to (vice) the dictates of morality significantly more than most people do. Sometimes, these five moral virtues are collectively referred to as *justice*.

Regarding the direct (first five) moral rules, the situation is different (see **Table 1.2**). First, note that there is only a single moral virtue (*kindness*) that encompasses all these rules. Second, unlike the other moral virtues, *kindness* refers not to a disposition to obey the direct moral rules, but rather to "a disposition to follow the direct moral ideals."[17] We don't describe as kind/virtuous someone who refrains from killing, causing pain, etc.; we describe as kind/virtuous someone who acts to preserve life, relieve pain/suffering, etc. Finally, note that there are two vices corresponding to the direct (first five) moral rules—cruelty and callousness. Cruelty refers to "unjustifiable violations of any of the first five rules . . . . [i]f a person never unjustifiably causes harm, but also never acts to prevent or relieve it when he has an opportunity to do so, he may be regarded as callous."[18]

Table 1.1 The Second Five Moral Rules and Their Corresponding Moral Virtues and Vices

Second Five Moral Rules	Corresponding Moral Virtue	Corresponding Moral Vice
Do not deceive.	Truthfulness	Deceitfulness
Do not break your promise.	Trustworthiness	Untrustworthiness
Do not cheat.	Fairness	Unfairness
Do not break the law.	Honesty	Dishonesty
Do not neglect your duty.	Dependability	Undependability

Table 1.2 The First Five Moral Rules and Their Corresponding Moral Virtues and Vices

First Five Moral Rules	Corresponding Moral Virtue	Corresponding Moral Vice
Do not kill.	Kindness	Cruelty/Callousness
Do not cause pain/suffering.	Kindness	Cruelty/Callousness
Do not disable.	Kindness	Cruelty/Callousness
Do not deprive of freedom.	Kindness	Cruelty/Callousness
Do not deprive of pleasure.	Kindness	Cruelty/Callousness

15 Gert B. *Morality: Its Nature and Justification.* New York, NY: Oxford University Press; 1998:282.
16 Gert B. *Morality: Its Nature and Justification.* New York, NY: Oxford University Press; 1998:283.
17 Gert B. *Morality: Its Nature and Justification.* New York, NY: Oxford University Press; 1998:285.
18 Gert B. *Morality: Its Nature and Justification.* New York, NY: Oxford University Press; 1998:285.

3. The Ethics Pyramid

We can talk about ethics at various levels, from the abstract to the concrete. Imagine ethics as a pyramid. At the apex of our metaphorical pyramid, we have *ethical theory*. At this level, we deal with ethics in the abstract. Gert's theory of common morality, superficially sketched previously, is an example of an ethical theory, one which he described as a natural law theory;[19] competing ethical theories include, for example, virtue ethics, utilitarianism, and Kantianism.

As we move down the pyramid, we consider ethics in increasingly concrete or specific ways—at the level of *moral principles*, then at the level of *moral rules*, and finally at the level of moral decisions in individual cases.

We generally think about ethics in two contexts—either we are engaged in the retrospective process of explaining why something someone did was (or was not) morally proper ("moral justification"), or we are engaged in the prospective process of deciding how to proceed morally under the circumstances ("moral decision-making").[20]

3.1. Ethical Theory

There are three major theoretical approaches to deciding how one ought to act, morally speaking: *deontology*, *consequentialism*, and *virtue ethics*.[21] The first two approaches focus on the act in question; virtue ethics, in contrast, focuses on the character of the actor rather than on the act.

3.1.1. Deontology

Deontologists, like consequentialists but unlike virtue ethicists, are concerned with what we ought to do. Unlike consequentialists, however, deontologists believe that the morality of an act depends not on the consequences of that act, but rather on the act's conformity with moral norms. Hence, deontologic ethical theories (e.g., Kantianism) emphasize duties or rules. This explains the adage that for deontologists, the Right is prior to the Good.[22]

3.1.2. Consequentialism

Consequentialism (e.g., utilitarianism) holds that "whether an act is morally right depends, not on the intrinsic nature of that act, but rather "only on the consequences of that act *or of something related to that act* . . . . [italics added]."[23] This definition of consequentialism allows for different types of consequentialism. So, *act consequentialism* holds that whether an act is morally right depends on the consequences of that act itself. In contrast, *rule consequentialism* holds that whether an act is morally right depends on the consequences not of the act but of a rule related to the act. "*[P]ublic acceptance rule consequentialism* . . . [is one type of rule consequentialism holding that] an act is morally wrong if and only if it violates a rule whose public acceptance maximizes the good."[24]

CASE 1.B

Consider the following:

> Imagine that each of five patients in a hospital will die without an organ transplant. The patient in Room 1 needs a heart, the patient in Room 2 needs a liver, the patient in Room 3 needs a kidney, and so on. The person in Room 6 is

---

19 Gert B. *Morality: Its Nature and Justification.* Revised ed. New York, NY: Oxford University Press; 2005: xiii-xiv.

20 Gibson J. Thinking about the "ethics" in bioethics. In: Furrow BR, Greaney TL, Johnson SH, Jost TS, Schwartz RL, eds. *Bioethics: Health Care Law and Ethics.* 5th ed. St. Paul, MN: Thomson; 2001:1–5.

21 Common morality is probably best thought of as a mix of these.

22 Deontological ethics. Stanford Encyclopedia of Philosophy. https://plato.stanford.edu/entries/ethics-deontological/#DeoThe. Accessed March 16, 2019.

23 Consequentialism. Stanford Encyclopedia of Philosophy. https://plato.stanford.edu/entries/consequentialism/#WhaCon. Accessed March 18, 2019.

24 Consequentialism. Stanford Encyclopedia of Philosophy. https://plato.stanford.edu/entries/consequentialism/#WhaCon. Accessed March 18, 2019.

in the hospital for routine tests. Luckily (for them, not for him!), his tissue is compatible with the other five patients, and a specialist is available to transplant his organs into the other five. This operation would save their lives, while killing the "donor." There is no other way to save any of the other five patients.

Is the operation morally permissible according to consequentialism?[25]

Analysis: ______________________________

____

____

____

____

____

____

____

____

____

3.1.3. Virtue Ethics

Virtue ethics represents a third approach to ethics, one that focuses on "'the virtuous individual and on those inner traits, dispositions, and motives that qualify her as being virtuous rather than on acts themselves or consequences."[26] In the Beatles song "She Loves You," the girl, it turns out, is a virtue ethicist, focused as she is on the character of the one she loves rather than on his transgression(s); for her lover is not "the hurting kind" even though he "hurt her so."[27]

As we saw previously in our discussion of common morality, virtue ethics is not the only approach that has something to say about the virtues. The term *virtue theory* "includes accounts of virtue within other approaches," including, for example, common morality; but for the virtue ethicist, the virtues are central.

It is in the context of virtue ethics that an agent's motives (something we haven't discussed until now) become relevant, although we shall see that virtue ethicists disagree amongst themselves as to why those motives matter.

Under Gert's formulation of common morality, which accommodates virtue theory, a "motive does not determine whether the action is morally acceptable . . . . The motive, at most, determines the moral worth of the action, that is, how much it indicates about the moral character of the agent."[28]

Similarly, on an Aristotelian view of virtue ethics, "the rightness of an action is . . . ultimately *independent* of the motives of the person who performed the action."[29] In contrast, for agent-based virtue ethicists, the motives of the actor determine the rightness of an action.

> For . . . [some] what matters are *this particular agent's actual motives and dispositions*. The goodness of action A, for example, is derived from the agent's actual motives when she performs A. If those motives are good then the action is good, if not then not. On . . . [others'] account, by contrast, a good or bad, right or wrong action is defined not by this agent's actual motives but rather by whether this is the sort of action

25 Consequentialism. Stanford Encyclopedia of Philosophy. https://plato.stanford.edu/entries/consequentialism/#WhaCon. Accessed March 28, 2019.

26 Brady MS. Against agent-based virtue ethics. *Philosophical Papers* 2004;33(1):1–10.

27 She loves you," The Beatles Lyrics. https://www.azlyrics.com/lyrics/beatles/shelovesyou.html.

28 Gert B, Culver CM, Clouser KD. *Bioethics: A Return to Fundamentals.* New York, NY: Oxford University Press; 1997:286.

29 Brady MS. Against agent-based virtue ethics. *Philosophical Papers*. 2004;33(1):2.

a virtuously motivated agent would perform.[30]

3.2. Moral Principles

Principles, like rules, are action guides, although the guidance they provide is more general than that provided by rules. Gert et al. have written, "*principles* . . . are action guides that summarize and encapsulate a whole [moral] *theory* and thus, in a shorthand manner, assist a moral agent in making a moral decision."[31] (Italics added.) Thus, deciding which moral principle(s) to invoke as an action guide will depend on the moral theory or theories to which one subscribes. So, for the Kantian the fundamental principle of morality is the *categorical imperative*, which Kant formulated as "act only in accordance with that maxim through which you can at the same time will that it become a universal law."[32] An alternative formulation of the same principle states that "we should never act in such a way that we treat humanity, whether in ourselves or in others, as a means only but always as an end in itself."[33] For the utilitarian, on the other hand, the fundamental principle of morality is the *greatest happiness principle*, which "holds that actions are right in proportion as they tend to promote happiness; wrong as they tend to produce the reverse of happiness. By happiness is intended pleasure and the absence of pain; by unhappiness, pain and the privation of pleasure."[34]

The moral principles with which practicing health professionals are most familiar are in fact not part of any ethical theory. I refer here to the four-principles approach espoused by Beauchamp and Childress in their classic textbook, *Principles of Biomedical Ethics*.[35] Those principles are *respect for autonomy, nonmaleficence, beneficence,* and *justice*. Because this probably represents the dominant approach to bioethics, we shall discuss it here.

3.2.1. Respect for Autonomy/Persons

The principle of respect for autonomy/persons asserts, "First, that individuals should be treated as autonomous agents, and second, that persons with diminished autonomy are entitled to protection."[36] To treat individuals as autonomous agents means to allow them to exercise their right of self-determination, "free from both controlling interference by others and from limitations, such as inadequate understanding, that prevent meaningful choice."[37] Thus, respect for autonomy entails both *negative* obligations (that autonomous choices not be constrained) and positive obligations (that adequate information relevant to the choice be disclosed, and that autonomous decision-making be fostered).

The *principle of respect for autonomy* evokes the moral rule, "Do not deprive of freedom."[38]

3.2.2. Nonmaleficence

The Hippocratic imperative, "Bring benefit and do no harm," expresses the twin principles of

30 Virtue ethics. Stanford Encyclopedia of Philosophy. https://plato.stanford.edu/entries/ethics-virtue/. Accessed July 8, 2019.

31 Gert B, Culver CM, Clouser KD. *Bioethics: A Return to Fundamentals*. New York, NY: Oxford University Press; 1997:75.

32 Kant's moral philosophy. Stanford Encyclopedia of Philosophy. https://plato.stanford.edu/entries/kant-moral/#ForUniLawNat. Accessed February 21, 2019.

33 Kant's moral philosophy. Stanford Encyclopedia of Philosophy. https://plato.stanford.edu/entries/kant-moral/#ForUniLawNat. Accessed February 21, 2019.

34 Mill's moral and political philosophy. Stanford Encyclopedia of Philosophy. https://plato.stanford.edu/entries/mill-moral-political/#UtiStaCon. Accessed February 21, 2019. See also: Utilitarianism [U] (1861) [CW X]. References by chapter and paragraph number. II 2.

35 Beauchamp TL, Childress JF. *Principles of Biomedical Ethics*. 5th ed. Oxford, UK: Oxford University Press; 2001.

36 The Belmont Report: Ethical principles and guidelines for the protection of human subjects of research. https://www.hhs.gov/ohrp/regulations-and-policy/belmont-report/read-the-belmont-report/index.html. Accessed June 25, 2022.

37 Beauchamp TL, Childress JF. *Principles of Biomedical Ethics*. 5th ed. Oxford, UK: Oxford University Press; 2001:58.

38 Gert B, Culver CM, Clouser KD. *Bioethics: A Return to Fundamentals*. New York, NY: Oxford University Press; 1997:75.

nonmaleficence ("do no harm") and *beneficence* ("bring benefit").[39]

The *principle of nonmaleficence* states, "One ought not to inflict evil or harm,"[40] where harm refers to an adverse effect on one's interests. It underlies the medical maxim *primum non nocere:* "Above all [or first] do no harm."[41]

Regarding the relationship between this principle and the moral rules, Gert has suggested that the principle of nonmaleficence is "most reasonably interpreted as . . . summarizing . . . the moral rules 'Don't kill,' 'Don't cause pain,' . . . 'Don't disable,' . . . and probably the rule 'Don't deprive of pleasure' as well."[42]

The principle of nonmaleficence prohibits not all harmful acts, but rather unjustifiably harmful acts. A harmful act is justifiable if there is a legitimate reason for it. Thus, opening an anesthetized patient's abdomen with a scalpel is harmful (one can expect postoperative pain and perhaps psychic suffering related to the appearance of a scar), but justified (and hence not wrongful) in the patient with acute appendicitis who has consented to an appendectomy.

3.2.2.1. The Rule of the Double Effect. The *rule of the double effect (RDE)*—sometimes referred to as the *principle of the double effect (PDE)*—helps us apply the principle of nonmaleficence in cases in which a single action will produce two inseparable effects, one good and one harmful. Consider the following scenario:

> Denise is a passenger on an out-of-control trolley. The conductor has fainted, and the trolley is headed toward five people walking on the tracks; the banks are so steep that they will not be able to get off the track in time. The track has a side track heading off to the left, and Denise can turn the trolley onto it. There is, however, one person on the left-hand track. Denise can turn the trolley, killing the one; or she can refrain from flipping the switch, letting the five die. Is it morally permissible for Denise to flip the switch, turning the trolley onto the side track?[43]

Flipping the switch produces two inseparable effects—the rescue of the five and the death of the one. Under the RDE,

> A person may licitly perform an action that he foresees will produce a good effect and a bad effect provided that four conditions are verified at one and the same time:
>
> 1. that the action in itself from its very object be good or at least indifferent;
> 2. that the good effect and not the evil effect be intended;
> 3. that the good effect be not produced by means of the evil effect;
> 4. that there be a proportionately grave reason for permitting the evil effect.[44]

Flipping a switch is a morally indifferent act, satisfying condition one. Since Denise's intention is to save the five and not to kill the one, condition two is satisfied. Saving the five is not dependent on the death of the one—if the side track were empty, flipping the switch would have the same life-saving effect—so condition three is met as well. Finally, preventing the death of five persons would seem to be a proportionately grave reason for allowing the death of one. Therefore, it is arguably morally permissible for Denise to flip the switch.

The RDE seems to be of legal as well as moral significance. In 1997, in the companion cases

---

39 Jonsen AR, Siegler M, Winslade WJ. *Clinical Ethics.* 6th ed. New York, NY: McGraw-Hill; 2006:18.

40 Beauchamp TL, Childress JF. *Principles of Biomedical Ethics.* 5th ed. Oxford, UK: Oxford University Press; 2001:116

41 Beauchamp TL, Childress JF. *Principles of Biomedical Ethics.* 5th ed. Oxford, UK: Oxford University Press; 2001:113.

42 Gert B, Culver CM, Clouser KD. *Bioethics: A Return to Fundamentals.* New York, NY: Oxford University Press; 1997:76.

43 Hauser, MD. *Moral Minds: The Nature of Right and Wrong.* New York, NY: HarperCollins Publishers; 2006:115.

44 Doctrine of Double Effect. Stanford Encyclopedia of Philosophy. https://plato.stanford.edu/entries/double-effect/. Accessed December 24, 2018.

Washington v. Glucksberg[45] and *Quill v. Vacco*,[46] the U.S. Supreme Court held that state prohibitions of assisted suicide do not violate the U.S. Constitution. In her concurring opinion,

> Justice O'Connor found it relevant that in New York and Washington, a patient who is suffering and terminally ill encounters "no legal barriers to obtaining medication, from qualified physicians, to alleviate that suffering, even to the point of causing unconsciousness and hastening death."[47] Apparently, for Justice O'Connor the availability of legal alternatives such as . . . exploitation of the double-effect principle means that a prohibition of physician-assisted suicide does not prevent the exercise of the putative right of the suffering, terminally ill patient to control the circumstances of his or her death.[48]

CASE 1.C

Consider the following:

> Frank is on a footbridge over . . . trolley tracks. He knows trolleys and can see that the one approaching the bridge is out of control, with its conductor passed out. On the track under the bridge there are five people; the banks are so steep that they will not be able to get off the track in time. Frank knows that the only way to stop an out-of-control trolley is to drop a very heavy weight into its path. But the only available, sufficiently heavy weight is a large person also watching the trolley from the footbridge. Frank can shove the large person onto the track in[to] the path of the trolley, resulting in [the] death [of one]; or he can refrain from doing this, letting the five die.[49]

Is it morally permissible for Frank to shove the large person onto the tracks? Why or why not?

Analysis: ______________________________

3.2.3. Beneficence

The *principle of beneficence* "asserts the duty to help others further their important and legitimate interests."[50] Unlike the negative obligations of *nonmaleficence, beneficence* imposes positive obligations upon those to whom it applies. In other words, obeying the dictates of *beneficence* may require that I act.

Beauchamp and Childress distinguish between *specific beneficence* and *general beneficence*.

Specific beneficence is obligatory beneficence. It refers to the duty to further the important and legitimate interests of select others with whom we are in some special relationship. Health professionals owe a duty of *specific beneficence* to their patients. Thus, the principle of nonmaleficence prohibits them from harming their patients and the principle

45 *Washington v. Glucksberg*, 117 S.Ct. 2258 (1997).
46 *Vacco v. Quill*, 117 S.Ct. 2293 (1997)
47 *Washington v. Glucksberg*, 117 S.Ct. 2258 (1997).
48 Hauser, MD. *Moral Minds: The Nature of Right and Wrong*. New York, NY: HarperCollins Publishers; 2006:115.
49 Paola F. How dead is the federal constitutional right to assisted suicide? *Am J Med*. 1998;104:565–568.
50 Beauchamp TL, Childress JF. *Principles of Biomedical Ethics*. 2nd ed. New York, NY: Oxford University Press; 1983.

of beneficence requires them to act affirmatively in their patients' best healthcare interests.

General beneficence "is directed beyond those special relationships to all persons."[51] On the whole, *general beneficence* is ideal beneficence. Like the moral ideals discussed previously, general beneficence encourages us to help all others but does not require that we do so.[52]

3.2.3.1. Paternalism. Beauchamp and Childress define paternalism as "the intentional overriding of one person's known preferences . . . by another person, where the person who overrides justifies the action by the goal of benefiting or avoiding harm to the person whose preferences . . . are overridden."[53] Stated otherwise, paternalism consists in the judgment that the principle of beneficence trumps the principle of respect for autonomy. While historically the principle of beneficence was thought to express the primary obligation of healthcare providers, nowadays the principle of respect for autonomy is ascendant; consequently, the term paternalism is most often used pejoratively.

Beauchamp and Childress distinguish between weak and strong versions of paternalism.

> In weak paternalism, an agent intervenes on grounds of beneficence . . . only to prevent substantially [nonautonomous] conduct . . . . [Such conduct] include[s] cases of consent or refusal that is not adequately informed, severe depression that precludes rational deliberation, and addiction that prevents free choice and action. . . . Strong paternalism, by contrast, involves interventions intended to benefit a person, despite the fact that the person's risky choices . . . are informed, voluntary and autonomous.[54]

3.2.4. Justice

The *principle of justice* attempts to answer the question, how should society distribute benefits and burdens?

The Aristotelian *principle of formal justice* is common to all theories of justice. It holds that justice requires that we treat equals equally and unequals unequally, but in proportion to their relevant inequalities. When, then, is an inequality relevant? The *material principles of distributive justice* provide answers to this question.

> Philosophers . . . have proposed each of the following principles as a valid material principle of distributive justice . . . .
>
> 1. To each person an equal share
> 2. To each person according to need
> 3. To each person according to effort
> 4. To each person according to contribution
> 5. To each person according to merit
> 6. To each person according to free-market exchanges[55]

Which material principle of justice one applies depends upon the theory of justice to which one subscribes.

---

51 Beauchamp TL, Childress JF. *Principles of Biomedical Ethics.* 5th ed. Oxford, UK: Oxford University Press; 2001:169.

52 I say "for the most part" because Beauchamp and Childress argue that, even absent the existence of any special relationship, a person X owes an *obligatory* duty of beneficence toward a person Y if each of the following conditions is true:

- Y is at risk of significant loss of or damage to life or health or some other major interest;
- X's action is needed (singly or in concert with others) to prevent this loss or damage;
- X's action (singly or in concert with others) has a high probability of preventing it;
- X's action would not present significant risks, costs or burdens to X; and
- the benefit that Y can be expected to gain outweighs any harms, costs, or burdens to X that is likely to occur.

(Beauchamp TL, Childress JF. *Principles of Biomedical Ethics.* 5th ed. Oxford, UK: Oxford University Press; 2001:171.)

53 Beauchamp TL, Childress JF. *Principles of Biomedical Ethics.* 5th ed. Oxford, UK: Oxford University Press; 2001:178.

54 Beauchamp TL, Childress JF. *Principles of Biomedical Ethics.* 5th ed. Oxford, UK: Oxford University Press; 2001:181.

55 Beauchamp TL, Childress JF. *Principles of Biomedical Ethics.* 5th ed. Oxford, UK: Oxford University Press; 2001:228.

Let's look briefly at three different theories of justice.

3.2.4.1. Utilitarian Theories of Justice. Under *utilitarian* theories, a just distribution of benefits and burdens would be one that produces the most overall happiness. For the utilitarian, "Whatever does the greatest overall good will be 'just.'"[56]

3.2.4.2. Egalitarian Theories of Justice. Egalitarianism holds that persons should receive an equal distribution of goods. The extreme egalitarian view is that equality is the sole aim of justice. More moderate forms of egalitarianism—*qualified egalitarianism*—require only certain basic equalities among individuals but permit inequalities that benefit those who are worst off.[57] (Italics added.) In other words, qualified egalitarians believe that equality is *an* aim of justice, but not *the sole* aim. John Rawls's description of justice as fairness in his work *A Theory of Justice* is an example of qualified egalitarianism. Rawls argues that the principles of justice are those principles that would be agreed upon by persons establishing a society from behind a metaphorical "veil of ignorance"—that is, persons who "would not know their own race, sex, degree of wealth, or natural abilities."[58] According to Rawls, those principles are:

> First: each person is to have an equal right to the most extensive basic liberty compatible with a similar liberty for others.
>
> Second: social and economic inequalities are to be arranged so that they are both (a) reasonably expected to be to everyone's advantage, and (b) attached to positions and offices open to all.[59]

3.2.4.3. Libertarian Theories of Justice—Nozick. Libertarian theories of justice emphasize procedural fairness. Robert Nozick's libertarian theory of justice—so-called "entitlement theory"—is described in his work *Anarchy, State and Utopia*. Nozick argues that whether any particular distribution of good among individuals depends not upon how much of the good each individual has, but upon how that distribution came about. Nozick distinguishes between *unhistorical* (or end-result) theories of justice (such as utilitarian justice or egalitarian justice), and *historical* theories.[60] According to Nozick,

56 Lebacqz, K. *Six Theories of Justice*. Minneapolis, MN: Augsburg Publishing House; 1987:21.

57 Beauchamp TL, Childress JF. *Principles of Biomedical Ethics*. 5th ed. Oxford, UK: Oxford University Press; 2001:233.

58 Rawls J. A theory of justice. In: Sher G, ed. *Moral philosophy*. New York, NY: Harcourt, Brace, Jovanovich; 1987:457.

59 Rawls J. A theory of justice. In: Sher G, ed. *Moral philosophy*. New York, NY: Harcourt, Brace, Jovanovich; 1987:450.

60 The following excerpt illustrates how one's past actions can influence his or her present entitlements:

> Ordinary prudence . . . require(s) that a (driver) be prepared to stop short . . . if by doing so he can avoid death or injury to another person. Let it be conceded also that a person need not in general take an action sacrificing his own life in order to avert a grave risk to another. Now let us imagine the case where A loads his truck with heavy steel pipe in such a way that if he stops short [the pipe] will shift forward and is very likely to crush him. . . . A, thus laden, sees B drive out of a side road into his path. If A stops short he will avoid hitting and perhaps killing B, but he will also risk being killed by the pipe stacked in his truck. It would seem that A had the right to impose no more than a certain level of risk on others in venturing out on the highway. If he stays within that level and . . . something goes wrong . . . he is not at fault . . . need not sacrifice his life to avoid taking the life of another person who is involved in the encounter. But since [A] ventured out bearing this particularly heavy and dangerous burden he forfeits that right. This argument makes the rightfulness of A's conduct depend on choices made on some distinct, earlier occasion. We can see this if we contrast A's situation with that of C, a hitchhiker who is a passenger [in] A's truck. C is not constrained to risk his life to save B. If A in a fit of cowardice had leapt from the cab leaving C at the controls, we feel that C would be justified in not stopping short. Yet at the moment of the crucial option—to stop or not to stop—the choice of risks presented to A or to C would be exactly the same. This must show that A's prior action in loading the truck in some way obligated him to drive so as to avert danger to person's in B's position, even at the risk of his own life.

See Fried C. Imposing Risks Upon Others. In: Sher G, ed. *Moral Philosophy*. San Diego: Harcourt Brace Jovanovich, 1987:453-472, p. 457.

"A distribution is just if everyone is entitled to the holdings they possess under the distribution."[61] Under Nozick's theory, there are three principles of justice: (1) the *principle of justice in acquisition,* which deals with the acquisition of goods that were previously unheld; (2) the *principle of justice in transfer,* which deals with the appropriation of goods from other persons; and (3) the *principle of rectification,* which addresses what may be done to rectify injustices (violations of the first two principles) that have shaped present holdings.[62]

CASE 1.D

A doctor believes that abortion is wrong, even in order to save the mother's life. A pregnant patient presents with aggressive uterine cancer. Would performing a hysterectomy, the aim of which is to save the woman's life, be morally prohibited? Frame your answer using the principles of biomedical ethics.

Analysis: ______________________________

CASE 1.E

Consider the following lifeboat ethics hypothetical:

> So here we sit, say 50 people in our lifeboat. To be generous, let us assume it has room for 10 more, making a total capacity of 60. Suppose the 50 of us in the lifeboat see 100 others swimming in the water outside, begging for admission to our boat . . . . [T]he boat has an unused excess capacity of 10 more passengers . . . .[63]

How should the "we" in the case proceed if we wish to do so in accordance with the principle of justice?

Analysis: ______________________________

---

61 Nozick R. *Anarchy, State, and Utopia.* New York, NY: Basic Books; 1974:151.

62 Nozick R. *Anarchy, State, and Utopia.* New York, NY: Basic Books; 1974:150–153.

63 Lifeboat Ethics. The Garrett Hardin Society. https://www.garretthardinsociety.org/articles/art_lifeboat_ethics_case_against_helping_poor.html. Accessed July 8, 2019.

CASE 1.F

Consider the following case.[64]

In December, 2020 Fountain Valley Regional Hospital & Medical Center respiratory therapists (RTs), faced with increasingly difficult work conditions and safety concerns associated with a rising COVID-19 patient census, reached out to the National Union of Healthcare Workers (NUHW) for assistance. In an email to the hospital CEO Kenneth McFarland, NUHW, requested a meeting to discuss "a very bad situation regarding patient safety." Receiving no response, NUHW sent a follow-up message and received a reply from Human Resources at Fountain Valley asking them to be patient and to put their concerns in writing.

The RTs complained that the recent explosion in the number of ventilated patients and the shortage of RTs caused by COVID-19 were pushing remaining RTs to the breaking point. Pre-pandemic, RTs usually worked 12-hour shifts during which they were assigned duties, each of which is associated with a point value. (For example, care of a patient on a ventilator counts for six to 10 points.) Normally, the workload of an RT is capped at 30 points, but during the recent COVID-19 upsurge, an RT might be assigned 100 points' worth of duties during a shift; further, RTs are having their normal 12-hour shift extended by up to eight hours.

RTs at Fountain Valley are reportedly taking care of three to four times the normal number of patients, and the patients they are caring for are sicker than usual. The RTs have stated that the staffing situation is contributing to patient mortality and is placing their (the RTs') licenses at risk.

Further complicating matters is a shortage of oxygen at the facility.

A hospital spokeswoman declined to respond directly to the claims of the RTs, saying only that their concerns were being reviewed and that the hospital was capable of safely caring for its patients in the current situation.

NUHW was urging the hospital to increase the number of RTs working, either through hiring additional RTs or incentivizing employees with extra shift bonuses. Fountain Valley Regional had begun offering nurses $2,000 per extra shift on top of regular pay.

Comment on the ethical issues raised, either in terms of theory or principles or rules.

Analysis: ____________________

64 Cardine S. Fountain Valley Regional respiratory therapists at epicenter of COVID-19 battle say they are burning out. *Daily Pilot* (Costa Mesa California). December 24, 2020. advance-lexis-com.ezproxylocal.library.nova.edu/api/document?collection=news&id=urn:contentItem:61KN-X2R1-DY8P-B21V-00000-00&context=1516831. Accessed January 17, 2021.

WRAP-UP

Chapter Summary

Ethics refers to the philosophy of morality. According to Gert, morality is a system, applying to all rational persons and governing behavior affecting others, the goal of which is to lessen harm. Gert's theory of *common morality* includes the *moral rules*, the *moral ideals*, and the *moral virtues*. Other ethical theories include *deontology* (e.g., Kantianism), *consequentialism* (e.g., utilitarianism), and *virtue ethics*. Like moral rules, *moral principles* are action guides, though more abstract, and there are principles associated with the various ethical theories. The *principles of biomedical ethics* described by Beauchamp and Childress are not part of any ethical theory, and include *respect for autonomy, nonmaleficence, beneficence*, and *justice*.

Review Questions

1. Define *ethics* and *morality*.
2. Explain the relationship between *morality* and *law*.
3. List the *moral rules*, the *moral ideals*, and the *moral virtues* as described by Bernard Gert.
4. Explain how Gert's first five and second five *moral rules* differ from each other.
5. Name the four *ethical theories* discussed in this chapter.
6. Explain the most important way in which *virtue ethics* differ from *deontology* and *consequentialism*.
7. List and explain the four *principles of biomedical ethics*.
8. What does the *principle of respect for autonomy* demand of us?
9. What does the *principle of nonmaleficence* demand of us?
10. What is the *rule of the double effect?* What elements must be present in order for it to apply?
11. What does the *principle of beneficence* demand of us?
12. What is the difference between *specific* and *general beneficence?* Between *obligatory* and *ideal beneficence?*
13. What is *paternalism?* Is it ever justified? When?
14. What does the *formal principle of justice* require?
15. What are the *material principles of justice* under utilitarian, egalitarian and libertarian views of justice?

Case Analyses

Case 1.A Analysis

No, morality does not require that you tell the truth under these circumstances. First, while deceiving the Nazi inquisitors is a *prima facie* (i.e., on its face, or at first glance) violation of the rule "Do not deceive," the violation is justified since an impartial rational person can advocate that the violation be publicly allowed, since answering truthfully would produce inordinate harm (loss of freedom, pain and suffering, possibly death for both the respondent and the persons he/she was hiding). Secondly (alternatively), one can argue that there is no moral rules violation because there is no duty to tell the truth under these circumstances. The question posed by the Nazi inquisitor is a so-called trap question, "a 'yes-no' or bivalent question forcing the respondent to reveal information on pain of lying. It is generally wrong to ask trap questions."[65]

Case 1.B Analysis

It depends. *Act consequentialism* holds that whether an act is morally right depends on the consequences of that act. In this case, the operation will result in the death (killing) of one patient but the saving of five others (net saving of four lives). So, for the act consequentialist, the operation is at least morally permissible. In contrast, *rule consequentialism* holds that whether an act is morally right depends on the consequences not of the act itself but of a rule related to the act. In this case, the rule in question is the so-called *dead donor rule*, which prohibits the taking of vital organs from living patients. While in this case obeying the rule will result in a net loss of four lives, the rule consequentialist might argue that having such a rule in place maximizes the good (by reassuring patients that they need not fear for their lives when they check into the hospital), and that therefore the operation is morally impermissible since it violates a rule that maximizes the good.

Case 1.C Analysis

No, it is not permissible to push the large person onto the tracks because doing so violates the principle of nonmaleficence. Furthermore, the RDE is not applicable in this case. The act of pushing the large person onto the tracks will again produce two inseparable effects—the rescue of five and the death of one; but if we try to apply the RDE, we see that Frank's action does not satisfy condition three, which requires that the good effect NOT be produced by means of the evil effect. In this case, the large person is harmed as a means to the end of saving the other five. Therefore, pushing the large person onto the tracks is morally impermissible, a violation of the nonmaleficence principle.

Case 1.D Analysis

No, a hysterectomy is not morally prohibited. The physician believes abortion to be wrong, presumably a violation of the nonmaleficence principle. However, under the rule of the double effect (RDE), when an action (in this case, hysterectomy) has two inseparable effects, one ethically permissible (the cure of the woman's uterine cancer) and the other ethically impermissible (the death of the fetus), the permissible effect may be pursued even though the impermissible effect will follow if (1) the action (hysterectomy, NOT abortion) is intrinsically good or indifferent, (2) the actor intends the good, not the evil, effect, (3) the good effect is not a result of the evil effect (note that saving the woman does NOT depend on the death of the fetus—imagine a case in which the fetus was viable), and (4) there is a proportionately grave reason for permitting the evil effect. In this case, the proportionately grave reason is the saving of the pregnant woman's life.

Case 1.E Analysis

Recall that justice is about distributing benefits and burdens. The benefit at stake here is a place in the lifeboat. Fundamentally, justice requires that we treat equals equally and unequals unequally, but in proportion to their relevant inequalities. The first issue is whether the 50 persons already in the lifeboat are entitled to remain therein (i.e., whether they are unequal to the 100 in the sea). Recall that under the entitlement theory of justice, a distribution is just if everyone is entitled to the holdings they possess under the distribution. Because we know nothing about how the current 50/100 distribution came about, we cannot say

65 McCarty R. The right to lie: Kantian ethics and the inquiring murderer. *American Philosophical Quarterly*. 2012;49(4):331–343.

whether it is just or not.[66] Let's assume for the sake of argument that the distribution is just, and that our task is to allocate the 10 remaining places in the lifeboat among the 100 survivors in the sea. If we employ a utilitarian theory of justice, we might prioritize the youngest, those with the most favorable survival prognosis, and those possessing some instrumental value (e.g., knowledge of the sea, rowing ability, or medical knowledge). Conversely, if we employ an egalitarian approach, we might employ a first-come, first-admitted-to-the-lifeboat approach, we might favor a lottery, or we might allocate the 10 places to the sickest in the sea.[67]

Case 1.F Analysis

The report raises a number of ethical issues. One way to make a start when faced with a complicated fact pattern like this is to identify the actors—the moral agents—involved. Here the agents include, obviously, the respiratory therapists (RTs) and the hospital administrators; but there are other, not so obvious moral agents involved as well, including (but not limited to) government actors responsible for the public response to the COVID pandemic (see Chapter 4). Since this book is about health professionals, let's focus on the RTs.[68] Regarding the RTs, the article is certainly laudatory, but is their behavior vis-à-vis the surplus patients an example of *ideal beneficence* or *obligatory beneficence*?[69] Is the surplus of patients simply "part of the job," analogous to the seasonal increases in patient census that one finds in states such as Florida that serve as winter havens for retired northerners? Or, given the size of the surplus and the transmissibility and potential severity of COVID-19, is it unfair to say that this is just "part of the job"? The article does not specify whether the RTs were ordered (or coerced) to take on the additional patient load, or whether they did so voluntarily. In any event, the article suggests that the relative shortage of RTs (each RT caring for more patients than he/she reasonably can) is adversely affecting patient care outcomes. To the extent that such a situation is avoidable (it may not always be avoidable in public health emergencies such as this one),[70] the principle of *nonmaleficence* is implicated. In this case, it appears that the RTs are doing all that they can to ameliorate the shortage. It should be noted, however, that offering "$2000 per extra shift plus pay" would not address the problem unless it induces RTs who are not currently taking shifts to do so—that is, unless it increases the number of RTs working at Fountain Valley Regional. Finally, it is worth noting that scarcity is a phenomenon that affects not only goods, such as oxygen and mechanical ventilators, but also human resources, such as person-hours (herein RT-hours).[71] This means that the principle of justice is implicated and decisions must be made about how best to allocate those resources.

---

66 If we were to decide that all 150 survivors have equal *a priori* claims to a place in the boat, we would need to decide how to allocate 50 places in the lifeboat among 150 survivors.

67 Krütli P, Rosemann T, Törnblom KY, Smieszek T. How to fairly allocate scarce medical resources: ethical argumentation under scrutiny by health professionals and lay people. *PLoS One*. 2016;11(7):e0159086.

68 But see footnote 6 in Chapter 3.

69 Drummond, D. Stop calling doctors heroes and saints: the case against altruism. *Medscape Internal Medicine*. November 24, 2020. https://www.medscape.com/viewarticle/941446. Accessed January 17, 2020.

70 Consider the "meatball surgery" for which M*A*S*H units were known. See, The Monster M*A*S*H Wiki. https://mash.fandom.com/wiki/Meatball_Surgery. Accessed January 18, 2021.

71 BoyceWire. https://boycewire.com/scarcity-definition/. Accessed January 18, 2021.

CHAPTER 2

Professionalism and the Internal Morality of Medicine[1]

LEARNING OBJECTIVES

1. Understand the *internal morality of medicine* concept and its relationship to the moral rules.
2. List six *goals of medicine*.
3. Explain what is meant by the *means of medicine*.
4. Apply the concepts of *goal illegitimacy*, *means illegitimacy* and *means-ends disjunction*.
5. Define *medical futility* and distinguish among the various subtypes of medical futility.
6. Define profession and *professionalism*.
7. List, recognize, distinguish and apply the tenets of professionalism.

More. *You want me to swear to the Act of Succession?*

Margaret. *"God more regards the thoughts of the heart than the words of the mouth." Or so you've always told me.*

More. *Yes.*

Margaret. *Then say the words of the oath and in your heart think otherwise.*

More. *What is an oath then but words we say to God?*

Margaret. *That's very neat.*

More. *Do you mean it isn't true?*

Margaret. *No, it's true.*

More. *Then it's a poor argument to call it "neat," Meg. When a man takes an oath, Meg, he's holding his own self in his own hands. Like water. [He cups his hands.] And if he opens his fingers then—he needn't hope to find himself again . . .* [2]

---

1 Some might argue that our referring to the "internal morality of medicine" here is allopathocentric (thanks to Dr. E. Marcolini, MD, for this word; see *Emergency Physicians Monthly,* available at https://epmonthly.com/article/crash-cart-honoring-covid-cleaners/). However, we employ that language because the literature uses that same terminology; had we substituted "health care" for "medicine," readers looking to the literature for an "internal morality of health care" would have been disappointed. Alternatively, we might have used the hybrid term "medicine/health care," but doing so repeatedly would have been cumbersome. When we refer to the "internal morality of medicine," we mean medicine in its broadest, most inclusive sense.

2 Bolt, Robert. A Man for All Seasons. London, 1960.

Chapter 1 included a discussion of the moral rules. In this chapter we explore more closely the last of the listed rules—"do not neglect your duty"—as it pertains to health professionals.

What is the nature of the duty that derives from the health professional role? You will recall the Hippocratic imperative that physicians "bring benefit and do no harm," and that they further their patients' medical interests.[3] But what does that mean? When is a patient's interest a *medical* interest, and by what means are health professionals supposed to further those interests?

Clearly not all acts performed by health professionals are medical or healthcare acts.[4] Legislating as a member of Congress[5] or saying Catholic mass after being ordained a priest[6] are not rendered healthcare acts simply because they are performed by health professionals. What makes an act arguably a healthcare act is that it is done *under color of healthcare authority*—meaning that there is a presumption of healthcare authority underlying the act. While a determination of the healthcare versus non-healthcare nature of an act depends on a multiplicity of factors, an act is *prima facie* done *under color of health care authority* (and hence arguably a health care act) when (1) it takes place in the context of a health professional-patient relationship, (2) ostensibly healthcare means (see following) are employed, or (3) ostensibly medical goals are pursued.[7]

1. The Internal Morality of Medicine

Brody and Miller have argued that the "goals and means of medicine constitute an internal morality," and that the "professional integrity of physicians is constituted by allegiance to this internal morality."[8] They and others they have argued that the goals of medicine are inherent and derive from the very nature of medical practice.[9,10,11,12] Consequently, acts promoting no medical goal contravene this *internal morality of medicine*; further, an act promoting a legitimate medical goal might still violate the internal morality of medicine because of the medical unacceptability of the means employed.

1.1. The Goals of Medicine

While some ethicists deny the existence of the goals of medicine, the majority position is that there are goals that mark the profession and that these goals are normative.[13] While a number of

3 Again, when we speak of the "internal morality of medicine," or "medical interests," or the "goals of medicine" in this chapter, we might as well have said the "internal morality of health care," or "health care interests," or the "goals of health care." We chose not to do so for the reasons we outlined in footnote 1. As it relates to their internal morality, most of the differences among the various healing arts revolve around the means they employ rather than their goals.

4 As mentioned previously, what most distinguishes the various healing arts are the diverse means that they employ in pursuit of what are by and large shared goals. Healthcare acts include medical acts (performed by, for example, MDs, DOs and PAs) and nonmedical healthcare acts (performed by, for example, PTs, RTs, OTs, SLPs and others).

5 https://pahx.org/assistants/bass-karen/

6 Two New Priests Ordained for Diocese of Scranton. Carbondale News. https://www.tricountyindependent.com/story/news/local/2016/06/16/two-new-priests-ordained-for/64908345007/. Accessed June 27, 2022.

7 Paola FA, Nixon LL, Walker R. Beyond medical futility: A proposed taxonomy of ultra vires acts in medicine. *Intern Emerg Med.* 2006;1(4):267–272.

8 Brody H, Miller FG. The internal morality of medicine: explication and application to managed care. *J Med Philosophy.* 1998;23:384–410.

9 Pellegrino ED, Thomasma DC. *A philosophical basis of medical practice: toward a philosophy and ethic of the healing professions.* New York: Oxford University Press, 1981.

10 Kass LR. Regarding the end of medicine and the pursuit of health. *Public Interest.* 1975 (Summer);40:11–42.

11 Kass LR. Ethical dilemmas in the care of the ill: I. What is the physician's service? *JAMA.* 1980;244(16):1811–1816.

12 Kass LR. Ethical dilemmas in the care of the ill: II. What is the patient's good? *JAMA.* 1980;244(17):1946–1949.

13 Rhodes R. Futility and the goals of medicine. *J Clin Ethics.* 1998;9(2):197–199.

formulations have been proposed,[14,15,16,17] we shall focus on those articulated by the 1996 Hastings Center's "Goals of Medicine" Project, in which representatives from 14 countries proposed four such goals: (1) the prevention of disease and injury and the promotion and maintenance of health; (2) the relief of pain and suffering caused by maladies; (3) the care and cure of those with a malady[18] and the care of those who cannot be cured; and (4) the avoidance of premature death and the pursuit of a peaceful death.[19]

Brody and Miller have importantly pointed out that a list of the goals of medicine must include the threshold goals of "diagnosing the disease or injury" (since appropriate treatment depends on proper diagnosis) and of "reassuring the 'worried well' who have no disease or injury."[20]

In cases where a health professional's action has more than one effect, the principle of the double effect may be applicable.[21] For example, it has been reported that patients receiving botox to smooth forehead wrinkles experienced relief from chronic headaches as an unanticipated side effect.[22] Assuming a restrictive formulation of the goals of medicine (one that excludes reversal of the signs of aging as a goal), one could argue that the medical legitimacy of the procedure—i.e., its consistency with the internal morality of medicine—depends on whether the health professional's intended goal was one of headache relief (legitimate) or cosmetic enhancement (illegitimate).

When the health professional is other than an MD, DO, or PA, do goals differ significantly? It does not appear so. For example, physical therapists (PTs) "examine each person and then develop[s] [*sic*] a treatment plan *to improve their ability to move, reduce or manage pain, restore function, and prevent disability*"[23] (italics added). The aim of respiratory therapy (RT) is "to improve breathing mechanics once the airway is blocked, or lung function is jeopardized."[24] The goal of occupational therapy (OT) is "to promote, maintain and/or restore functional independence in daily living skills."[25] Likewise, "the overall objective of speech-language pathology (SLP) services is to optimize individuals' abilities to communicate and to swallow, thereby improving quality of life."[26] Thus, it should be clear that all of the health professions or healing arts share the goals of preventing or curing or mitigating some harm (death, pain/suffering, disability, loss of freedom, loss of pleasure) caused by a malady.

---

14 Rhodes R. Futility and the goals of medicine. *J Clin Ethics*. 1998;9(2):194–205.

15 Nordin I. The limits of medical practice. *Theoretical Medicine and Bioethics*. 1999;20:105–123.

16 Brulde B. The goals of medicine: towards a unified theory. *Health Care Analysis* 2001;9:1–13.

17 Nordenfelt L. On the goals of medicine, health enhancement and social welfare. *Health Care Analysis*. 2001;9:15–23.

18 As defined by Clouser, Culver, and Gert, "a person has a malady if and only if he has a condition, other than his rational beliefs and desires, such that he is suffering, or is at increased risk of suffering, a harm or an evil (death, pain, disability, loss of freedom or opportunity, loss of pleasure) in the absence of a distinct sustaining cause." See, Clouser KD, Culver CM, Gert B. Malady: a new treatment of disease. *Hastings Center Report*. 1981; 11:29–37.

19 The goals of medicine: setting new priorities. *Hastings Center Report*. 1996;26(6):S9–S14.

20 Brody H, Miller FG. The internal morality of medicine: explication and application to managed care. *J Med Philosophy*. 1998;23:384–410.

21 Jonsen AR, Siegler M, Winslade WJ. *Clinical Ethics*. 6th ed. New York: McGraw-Hill, 2006:28.

22 Parker-Pope, T. Cosmetic surgery used to smooth foreheads might cure migraines. *Wall Street Journal*, December 1, 2000, B1.

23 APTA. https://www.apta.org/your-career/careers-in-physical-therapy/becoming-a-pt. Accessed May 18, 2021.

24 The Goal of a Respiratory Therapist. Distance Learning Systems (DLSI). https://dlsii.com/blog/thegoalofarespiratory therapist/#:~:text=The%20aim%20of%20respiratory%20therapy,to%20ease%20their%20breathing%20problem. Accessed May 18, 2021.

25 Occupational therapy: characteristics, goals, and functions. https://neuronup.us/cognitive-stimulation-news /occupational-therapy/occupational-therapy-characteristics-goals-and-functions/#:~:text=Occupational%20 therapy%20is%20a%20health,independence%20in%20daily%20living%20skills. Accessed May 18, 2021.

26 ASHA Scope of Practice in Speech-Language Pathology.: https://www.asha.org/siteassets/publications/sp2016-00343 .pdf. Accessed May 20, 2021.

1.2. The Means of Medicine

As noted previously, an act might promote the legitimate goals of medicine and yet, because of the unacceptability of the means being employed, violate the internal morality of medicine.

It should be understood that a means is unacceptable if it involves the unjustified violation of a moral rule. That aside, when is a means acceptable? When is a means a legitimate medical means?

We submit that insight into the nature of medical means can be gleaned from American medical malpractice case law. In *Pike v. Honsiger*, 155 N..Y. 201 (1898), the court expressed the standard of care as follows: "The physician is under an obligation to exercise the same degree of knowledge . . . [and] skill . . . that the ordinary competent practitioner would exercise under the same or similar circumstances." Knowledge is defined as "an organized body of information";[27] *medical* knowledge denotes the organized body of *medical* information. Such medical information includes the basic sciences (e.g., anatomy, embryology, physiology, biochemistry and molecular biology, histology, microbiology, pathology, and genetics) and the clinical sciences (e.g., internal medicine and its subspecialties, surgery and its subspecialties, obstetrics and gynecology, pediatrics, and psychiatry). Skill refers to "the ability to *do* something well,"[28] and in the medical context to the ability to do something *medical* well. Physical diagnosis requires medical skill, as does the performance of medical procedures (such as inserting a central venous catheter, performing a thoracentesis, or removing a gallbladder). Thus, a physician or PA[29] employs medical means when exercising medical knowledge and/or skill in the pursuit of some goal.

Analogously, nonphysician health professionals employ healthcare means when they exercise their special knowledge and/or skill in the pursuit of some goal. The specialized knowledge of a physical therapist (PT), for example, includes functional anatomy, biomechanics, applied physiology and electrotherapy.[30] Specialized skills of the PT include patient instruction, airway clearance techniques, application of assistive technology, functional training, manual therapy techniques, motor function training, and therapeutic exercise.[31] Similarly, RTs, OTs and OTAs, and SLPs[32] have their own specialized knowledge and skills that, when exercised in the pursuit of some goal, constitute the means of those professions.

1.3. The Means-Goal Fit

In their discussion of the internal morality of medicine, Brody and Miller discuss goals and means but do not explicitly discuss the nexus between the two—what I refer to here as the means-goal fit. However, their appreciation of the importance of the tightness of the means-goal fit is implicit when they write, "The physician must avoid harming the patient in any way that is out of proportion to expected benefit, and must seek to minimize the indignity and the invasion of privacy involved in medical examinations and procedures."[33]

---

27 Oxford American Dictionary. Eugene Ehrlich, Stuart Berg Flexner, Joyce M. Hawkins, Oxford American Dictionary (Heald Colleges Edition, 1980).

28 Oxford American Dictionary. Eugene Ehrlich, Stuart Berg Flexner, Joyce M. Hawkins, Oxford American Dictionary (Heald Colleges Edition, 1980).

29 Recall that for our purposes a PA is an AHCP.

30 University of Delaware DPT Curriculum. https://cpb-us-w2.wpmucdn.com/sites.udel.edu/dist/2/3447/files/2014/10/DPT-CURR-chart-sample-1.pdf., Accessed January 17, 2021.

31 Guide to Physical Therapist Practice. http://guidetoptpractice.apta.org/content/1/SEC31.body Accessed January 17, 2021. See also, Chapter 3: What Types of Interventions Do Physical Therapists Provide? http://guidetoptpractice.apta.org/site/misc/guide_chapter_3_interventions.pdf. Accessed January 17, 2021.

32 ASHA Scope of Practice in Speech-Language Pathology. https://www.asha.org/siteassets/publications/sp2016-00343.pdf. Accessed May 20, 2021.

33 Brody H, Miller FG. The internal morality of medicine: explication and application to managed care. *J Med Philosophy*. 1998;23:384–410.

American courts charged with reviewing the constitutional legitimacy of governmental acts employ means-goal fit tests as part of *substantive due process* analysis. Under a substantive due process analysis, governmental acts affecting fundamental rights are struck down as unconstitutional unless *necessary* to achieve a *compelling* government purpose (strict scrutiny standard); governmental acts affecting nonfundamental rights are upheld as constitutional as long as they are *reasonably related* to any *legitimate* government purpose (rational basis test).[34] In the context of means-goal fit testing, a sliding scale exists: The more intrusive the act under consideration, the tighter the fit must be.

1.4. Employing the Internal Morality of Medicine Analysis

I have previously suggested an approach to considering whether a particular act is consistent with the internal morality of medicine.[35,36] Such an approach would involve consideration of the following three questions: (1) Is a legitimate medical goal being pursued? (2) Are the means being employed legitimate medical means? (3) Are the goals and the means appropriately related? Accordingly, health professionals act in conformity with the internal morality of medicine when they employ legitimate and appropriate medical means in the pursuit of a legitimate medical goal. In contrast, when the goal being pursued or the means being employed are not legitimate, or when the means and the goal are not appropriately related, the act is violative of the internal morality of medicine.[37] Acts violating the internal morality of medicine can be subclassified depending on which of the previous three questions elicits a negative response.

1.4.1. Goal Illegitimacy

Where the goal of the act, though achievable, is not a legitimate medical goal, the act is a violation of the internal morality of medicine because of goal illegitimacy.[38]

Consider a case in which a young woman with a breast size of 34C requests breast augmentation (to postprocedure size 56FF) so that she can further her career as an exotic dancer. Is breast augmentation in this woman consistent with the internal morality of medicine?

We submit that it is not. Recall that the goals of medicine as enumerated previously included (1) the prevention of disease and injury and the promotion and maintenance of health; (2) the relief of pain and suffering caused by maladies; (3) the care and cure of those with a malady, and the care of those who cannot be cured; (4) the avoidance of premature death and the pursuit of a peaceful death; (5) diagnosing disease or injury; and (6) reassuring the worried well. Surgical breast augmentation in this woman advances none of these legitimate medical goals (i.e., it is goal illegitimate) and is therefore arguably a violation of the internal morality of medicine.[39]

34 Substantive due process. Legal Information Institute. https://www.law.cornell.edu/wex/substantive_due_process. Accessed March 29, 2019.

35 Paola F, Nixon L, Walker R. Beyond medical futility: a proposed taxonomy of ultra vires acts in medicine. *Internal and Emergency Medicine*. 2006;1(4):267–272.

36 Paola F. Professionalism and the internal morality of medicine. In: Paola F, Nixon LL, Walker RW. *Medical Ethics and Humanities*. Sudbury, MA: Jones and Bartlett; 2010: 121–144.

37 Elsewhere, acts that violate the internal morality of medicine have been called *medically ultra vires*. See Paola FA, Nixon LL, Walker RM. Beyond medical futility: a proposed taxonomy of ultra vires acts in medicine. *Internal and Emergency Medicine*. 2006;1(4):267–272.

38 Elsewhere, acts that violate the internal morality of medicine because of goal illegitimacy have been referred to as *medically ultra fines*. See Paola FA, Nixon LL, Walker RM. Beyond medical futility: a proposed taxonomy of ultra vires acts in medicine. *Internal and Emergency Medicine*. 2006;1(4):267–272.

39 Paola F, Nixon L, Walker R. Beyond medical futility: a proposed taxonomy of ultra vires acts in medicine. *Internal and Emergency Medicine*. 2006;1(4):267–272.

1.4.2. Means Illegitimacy

Where the means being employed are not legitimate medical means, the act may be said to be a violation of the internal morality of medicine because of means illegitimacy.[40]

Consider a case in which a retired brigadier general with excruciating pain secondary to incurable metastatic cancer asks his health professional to shoot him to end his pain because, in the words of his hero George S. Patton, "There's only one proper way for a professional soldier to die: the last bullet of the last battle of the last war."[41] Would complying with this patient's wishes be consistent with the internal morality of medicine?

Again, I submit that it would not be consistent with the internal morality of medicine. The act under consideration does further goal two (the relief of pain and suffering caused by a malady—metastatic cancer in this case) and arguably goal four (the pursuit of a peaceful death), and so is goal legitimate. However, the means under consideration are clearly nonmedical, involving as they do no special medical knowledge or skill; thus, the act in question is arguably a violation of the internal morality of medicine because of means illegitimacy.[42]

You might well ask, what if the retired general had requested a lethal injection instead of a bullet? Would that circumvent the internal morality of medicine problem? No, because lethal injection is not a *legitimate* medical means. In such cases of what is called *voluntary active euthanasia* (see Chapter 9), the *final*[43] goals—the relief of pain/suffering and the pursuit of a peaceful death—are being achieved by means of the prohibited *instrumental*[44] goal of euthanasia. Whether viewed as a prohibited instrumental goal or as an illegitimate medical means or both, the internal morality of medicine problem remains.

Practicing outside the scope of one's practice is a form of means illegitimacy. Thus,

> The referring practitioner ordered that a patient receive a two-person assist during transfers because of her size. The PTA ignored the recommendation and attempted to lift the patient by himself. The PTA dropped the patient, resulting in the patient suffering a fracture to her femur.[45]

1.4.3. Means-Goal Disjunction

Where the means and the goal are not appropriately related—in other words, where the means-goal fit is not sufficiently tight—the act may be said to be a violation of the internal morality of medicine because of means-ends disjunction.[46]

Consider the case of a patient with a thin (less than 0.76 mm) melanoma on his left leg. The medically indicated treatment is a local excision, with virtually a 100% cure rate. The patient, however, requests that his surgeon amputate his entire limb "just to be on the safe side." Would such an

---

40 Elsewhere, acts that violate the internal morality of medicine because of means illegitimacy have been referred to as *medically ultra modos*. See Paola FA, Nixon LL, Walker RM. Beyond medical futility: a proposed taxonomy of ultra vires acts in medicine. *Internal and Emergency Medicine*. 2006;1(4):267–272.

41 Patton (Twentieth Century Fox, 1970). https://www.imdb.com/title/tt0066206/characters/nm0001715.

42 Paola F, Nixon L, Walker R. Beyond medical futility: a proposed taxonomy of ultra vires acts in medicine. *Internal and Emergency Medicine*. 2006;1(4):267–272.

43 "Suppose I wake one morning wanting to go for a two-mile run. Perhaps I have this goal as an end in itself; I want to run two miles just for the sake of being out there running. In this case, the goal of running two miles is a final end. Or perhaps I want to run for the sake of some other goal. I run because I want to be healthy. In this case, running two miles is an instrumental end, instrumental to the further end of being healthy." See, Schmidtz D. Choosing ends. *Ethics*. 1994;104:226–251.

44 See footnote 30.

45 CNA Physical Therapy Professional Liability Exposure: 2016 Claim Report Update. https://www.hpso.com/Documents/pdfs/CNA_PT_CS_020116_CF_PROD_ASIZE_ONLINE_040417_SEC.pdf, at p. 9.

46 Elsewhere, acts that violate the internal morality of medicine because of means-ends disjunction have been referred to as *medically ultra nexus*. See Paola FA, Nixon LL, Walker RM. Beyond medical futility: a proposed taxonomy of ultra vires acts in medicine. *Internal and Emergency Medicine*. 2006;1(4):267–272.

amputation be consistent with the internal morality of medicine?

Once again, I submit that it would not be. While the goals being pursued (cure of disease and prevention of premature death) and the means employed (amputation) here are legitimate, in this case the relation between them is too loose. The standard of care demands the less extensive surgery (the local excision) because the performance of the more extensive surgery (amputation) will neither increase the likelihood of cure nor decrease the likelihood of premature death. Amputation of the limb would be a violation of the internal morality of medicine because of means-goal disjunction.

1.5. Medical Futility[47]

What is medical futility, and why are we talking about it in a chapter on the internal morality of medicine?

1.5.1. The Nature of Medical Futility

The concept of medical futility dates to antiquity. "In the Hippocratic writing entitled *The Art*, the physician is advised to . . . 'refuse to treat those who are overmastered by their diseases, recognizing that in such cases medicine is powerless.'"[48]

Something "useless" or "producing no result" is said to be futile.[49] Something is *medically futile* if it has "no realistic chance of achieving the goals of medicine,"[50] which we discussed previously.

As a practical matter, medical futility matters because health professionals are generally not obligated to provide medically futile treatments.[51,52,53,54] Jecker and Schneiderman have made the even stronger argument that health professionals are prohibited from providing medically futile treatment.[55] As such, medical futility arguably delimits the sphere of proper unilateral decision making by health professionals.

It is important that this concept of unilateral decision-making not be misinterpreted or overstated. In most instances the selection of actual clinical goals requires the input and consent of the patient (or his/her surrogate); and when one must choose between two legitimate but mutually exclusive medical goals (e.g., palliative care versus attempted cure with aggressive chemotherapy), we generally allow patients to decide. However, when acceding to a patient's request would violate the internal morality of medicine, the health professional is justified in refusing.

Medical futility may be classified into three subtypes: *physiologic, qualitative* and *quantitative*.

1.5.1.1. Physiologic Futility. An act is *physiologically futile* if it is futile in achieving its physiologic goal and so offers no physiologic benefit to the patient. Such acts are sometimes characterized as *medically futile because ineffective*. The use of CPR on a patient in whom rigor mortis has set in or on a patient decapitated in a motor vehicle accident would be physiologically futile because it cannot achieve its intended goal—the restoration of cardiopulmonary function. This is the least controversial subtype of medical futility because it is essentially devoid of any value judgment.

---

47 Again, we employ the term medical futility as opposed to healthcare futility because it is the former term that is found in the literature.

48 Jonsen AR, Siegler M, Winslade WJ. *Clinical ethics*. 6th ed. New York: McGraw-Hill, 2006:28.

49 Oxford American Dictionary (Heald Colleges Edition, 1980).

50 Schneiderman LJ, Jecker NS, Jonsen AR. Medical futility: response to critiques. *Ann Int Med*. 1996;125:669–674.

51 Brett AS, McCullough LB. When patients request specific interventions: defining the limits of the physician's obligation. *N Engl J Med*. 1986;315:1347–1351.

52 Blackhall LJ. Must we always use CPR? *N Engl J Med*. 1987;317:1281–1285.

53 Paris JJ, Crone RK, Reardon F. Physician's refusal of requested treatment. The case of Baby L. *N Engl J Med*. 1990;322:1012–1015.

54 McCormick RA. To save or let die. The dilemma of modern medicine. *JAMA*. 1974;229:172–176.

55 Jecker NS, Schneiderman LJ. Medical futility: the duty not to treat. *Camb Q Healthc Ethics*. 1993;2:151–159.

1.5.1.2. Qualitative Futility. An act is *qualitatively futile* if it has physiologic effects that are adjudged to be nonbeneficial to the patient as a person. Such acts are sometimes characterized as *medically futile because nonbeneficial*. The use of artificial feeding and hydration (ANH) in patients in permanent vegetative state (PVS) (e.g., Terry Schiavo case; see Chapter 9) is arguably qualitatively futile. Because such patients lack consciousness and consciousness is a trait thought by many to be central to the concept of personhood,[56] ANH arguably does not benefit PVS patients as persons despite the fact that it is physiologically effective in meeting their nutritional and fluid requirements. As you might imagine, this is a more controversial type of medical futility, since it incorporates a value judgment—that human life without consciousness is not the proper object of medicine.

1.5.1.3. Quantitative Futility. An act is *quantitatively futile* if it is very unlikely to produce either a desired physiologic effect or personal benefit. Such acts are sometimes described as being *medically futile because improbable*. The question that follows naturally is, How improbable must an effect be to render an act quantitatively medically futile? Schneiderman et al. proposed that "when physicians conclude (either through personal experience, experiences shared with colleagues, or consideration of reported empiric data) that in the last 100 cases, [sic] a medical treatment has been useless, they should regard that treatment as futile."[57] Any such cutoff is arbitrary and hence controversial.

1.5.2. Medical Futility and the Internal Morality of Medicine

Recall that it has been argued that providing medically futile treatment is a violation of the internal morality of medicine.[58] If it is, as I submit it is, how is it a violation? Consider again a patient in whom CPR is begun after rigor mortis has already set in. CPR is clearly a legitimate medical means.[59] Further, the goal of CPR is the avoidance of premature death. But while that is a legitimate medical goal, neither it nor any other medical goal is achievable in this case. What makes resuscitation in this case an arguable violation of the internal morality of medicine is neither goal illegitimacy nor means illegitimacy, but rather a complete lack of any nexus between the goal and the means. Thus, medical futility represents an extreme form of means-goal disjunction, one where the discontinuity between goals and means is complete.

CASE 2.A

Jahi McMath was a 13-year-old African American girl pronounced dead by brain death criteria[60] in Oakland, California, on December 12, 2013, following a postsurgical cardiac arrest. Because she was on a ventilator, her breathing and heartbeat continued even after death.

> The family . . . claimed that their child was not dead because she had a continually beating heart and was moving in response to touch. They demanded that the hospital continue to provide medical care . . . in

56 Warren MA. On the moral and legal status of abortion. *Th Monist*. 1973;57(1):43–61.

57 Schneiderman LJ, Jecker NS, Jonsen AR. Medical futility: its meaning and ethical implications. *Ann Int Med*. 1990;112:949–954.

58 Jecker NS, Schneiderman LJ. Medical futility: the duty not to treat. *Camb Q Healthc Ethics*. 1993;2:151–159.

59 CPR and First Aid. https://cpr.heart.org/AHAECC/CPRAndECC/AboutCPRECC/WhatIsCPR/UCM_499896_What-is-CPR.jsp. Accessed on March 31, 2019.

60 The diagnosis was made by a staff neurologist and a staff pediatric intensivist and later confirmed by an outside pediatric neuro-oncologist. See, Burkle CM, Sharp RR, Wijdicks EF. Why brain death is considered death and why there should be no confusion. *Neurology*. 2014;83(16):1464–1469.

hopes that she might recover. The family also maintained that the hospital's failure to provide the requested medical care to Jahi was disrespectful of her and her family's religious values. Due to the underlying conflict . . . the case was brought before the Alameda California Superior County Court in December 2013. Judge Evilio Grillo issued a temporary restraining order (TRO) stopping the hospital from disconnecting her ventilator. He also appointed an independent physician . . . to reevaluate Jahi . . . [who] confirmed the girl's status as brain dead . . . . With this additional independent confirmation, Judge Grillo ordered that the hospital could remove ventilator support but not until December 30 (18 days after the hospital's original diagnosis of death) in order to allow the family time to seek out other institutions for care. Hours before the December 30 deadline, Judge Grillo issued another restraining order . . . giving the family until January 7, 2014, to make arrangements for her transfer. . . . [T]he hospital refused to allow either their surgical staff or outside medical staff to perform a tracheostomy and feeding tube placement necessary for her transfer to a long-term care facility . . . . On January 3, 2014, the coroner issued a death certificate stating that Jahi died on December 12, the day that doctors originally declared her dead. On January 6, Jahi's parents removed her body from the hospital with assistance from an ambulance service.[61]

The body was subsequently moved to a long-term care facility in New Jersey, where state law prohibits a declaration of death where the declarant "has reason to believe...that such a declaration would violate the personal religious beliefs of the individual."[62] There she was subjected to two surgical procedures—a tracheostomy and a g-tube placement, which enabled long-term mechanical ventilation and long-term artificial feeding/hydration, respectively. It was subsequently reported that Jahi McMath "died" on June 22, 2018. By report, she had experienced internal bleeding due to kidney and liver failure, so her doctors removed her from life support, allowing her to "die."

Analyze this case from an internal morality of medicine perspective.

Analysis: ________________________________

____

____

____

____

____

____

____

____

____

2. Professionalism

2.1. Professionalism Defined

A *profession* is "a vocation or occupation requiring special, usually advanced, education, knowledge and skill."[63] Traditionally the professions included medicine, law, and divinity. Some definitions of *professionalism* include aspects of one's character or spirit[64] and refer to

61 Burkle CM, Sharp RR, Wijdicks EF. Why brain death is considered death and why there should be no confusion. *Neurology.* 2014;83(16):1464–1469.

62 Braindeath.org Legal Resources. New Jersey Statute. http://www.braindeath.org/law/newjersey.htm Accessed July 25, 2019.

63 Black's Law Dictionary, p. 841 (6th ed. 1991, abridged).

64 Dictionary.com, "professionalism", https://www.dictionary.com/browse/professionalism.

"those qualities and modes of conduct proper to professions."[65,66] The link to character suggests that one way to conceptualize professionalism is as the virtue-based analog of the duties corresponding to the internal morality of medicine—virtue ethics focuses on the character of the agent, and medical professionalism focuses on the character of medical professionals. Health professionals should aspire to make themselves into the kind of persons who will be good health professionals.[67]

2.2. Parsonian Model of Professionalism

Latham has written about the Parsonian model of professionalism that, while perhaps failing "as a factual description of medical[68] professionalism in America . . . [has] much to recommend it as a normative description of what American medical professionalism ought to look like."[69] According to this model, elements of medical professionalism include (1) the expert authority of the medical professional; (2) the medical professional's role as a mediator between individual patients and society; (3) the medical professional's motivations; and (4) the medical professional's acts of profession, which include acts related to professional self-regulation.

2.2.1. The Authority of the Health Professional

Authority is "essentially the probability that one's commands [will] be obeyed."[70] I am an authority if my commands are obeyed without either coercion or persuasion.[71] Types of authority include:

> . . . *legal authority*, in which people obey your commands because they recognize the legal legitimacy of your having issued them; *traditional authority*, in which people obey your commands because they have always done so; and *charismatic authority*, in which people obey your commands because something in your personality emotionally compels their obedience. [footnote omitted] Parsons . . . felt . . . [there was] a fourth . . . variety of legitimate authority. This was *expert authority:* people obey your commands because they believe you know something they don't know.[72]

It is this expert authority—grounded in the expertise of health professionals—that Parsons associated with professionalism.

65 Pellegrino ED. Professionalism, profession and the virtues of the good physician. *Mount Sinai Journal of Medicine*. 2002;69(6):378–384, at 378.

66 The American Board of Medical Specialties has defined medical professionalism as "a belief system in which group members ("professionals") declare ("profess") to each other and the public the shared competency standards and ethical values they promise to uphold in their work and what the public and individual patients can and should expect from medical professionals." See, ABMS Definition of Medical Professionalism (Long Form). https://www.abms.org/media/84742/abms-definition-of-medical-professionalism.pdf. Accessed July 17, 2019.

67 "The good [AHCP] will be one who exhibits those character traits which [sic] most effectively achieve and indeed are indispensable for attainment of the ends of medicine. . . [including] . . . fidelity to trust . . . benevolence . . . intellectual honesty . . . courage . . . compassion . . . [and] truthfulness . . . ." See, Pellegrino ED. Professionalism, profession and the virtues of the good physician. *Mount Sinai Journal of Medicine*. 2002;69(6):378–384.

68 Again, we employ the term "medical professionalism" here out of deference to the literature. Section 2.2 is applicable to all health professionals.

69 Latham SR. Medical professionalism: a Parsonian view. *Mount Sinai Journal of Medicine*. 2002;69(6):363–369, at 365.

70 Latham SR. Medical Professionalism: a Parsonian view. *Mount Sinai Journal of Medicine*. 2002;69(6):363–369, at 365.

71 Arendt H. What is authority? In: Arendt H. *Between Past and Future*. New York: Penguin Books: 1968. Pp. 93, 106, 122–123.

72 Latham SR. Medical professionalism: a Parsonian view. *Mount Sinai Journal of Medicine*. 2002;69(6):363–369, at 364.

CASE 2.B[73]

In November 2004, Kentucky Governor Ernie Fletcher, a former family physician, signed the death warrant for 51-year-old convicted killer Thomas Clyde Bowling. In doing so, did he violate the internal morality of medicine? If so, which prong(s) of the trident was/were violated?

Analysis: ______________________________

____

____

____

____

____

____

____

____

____

2.2.2. Health Professionals as Mediators

Usually the patient's goals and society's goals are in harmony. The patient is sick and wants to get well; society, too, wants him/her to get well—perhaps because of public health considerations, or perhaps because we want him/her to return to work.

Sometimes, however, the goals of the patient and society are discordant. It is in such cases that health professionals act as mediators between individuals and society. Sometimes health professionals use their expert authority to curb their patient's deviance, "to align their [patient's] interests and actions with broad social norms."[74] An example would be the physician or PA who properly refuses to write a sick note for a well patient looking for an excuse to avoid work. "In [such a] case, the 'deviant' . . . is 'mainstreamed' through the intercession of the professional. On the other hand, professional authority is sometimes used to create safety zones for individuals against the demands of social norms."[75] An example would be the physician or PA whoproperly writes a note excusing a sick patient from work.

CASE 2.C[76]

A 68-year-old prisoner on death row for shooting a police officer in 1985 suffered a series of strokes and was diagnosed as suffering from vascular dementia. The prisoner petitioned for a stay of execution on the ground that he was mentally incompetent. The U.S. Supreme Court held that the Eighth Amendment's prohibition of cruel and unusual punishment prevents the state from executing a prisoner whose mental illness is such that he cannot understand the State's rationale for his execution.

Assume that the State of Alabama wants the prisoner medicated, against wishes expressed by the prisoner prior to losing decisional capacity, with donepezil and memantine[77] in the hope that he can be restored to competency and executed. May PAs medicate the prisoner?

73 Death penalty, medical ethics collide in Kentucky. http://archive.boston.com/news/nation/articles/2004/11/19/death_penalty_medical_ethics_collide_in_kentucky/. Accessed April 9, 2019.

74 Latham SR. Medical professionalism: a Parsonian view. *Mount Sinai Journal of Medicine*. 2002;69(6):363–369, at 364.

75 Latham SR. Medical professionalism: a Parsonian view. *Mount Sinai Journal of Medicine*. 2002;69(6):363–369, at 364.

76 Madison v. Alabama, 586 U.S.__ (2019). https://www.supremecourt.gov/opinions/18pdf/17-7505_2d9g.pdf. Accessed April 4, 2019.

77 Wright CB. Treatment and prevention of vascular dementia. UpToDate. https://www-uptodate-com.ezproxylocal.library.nova.edu/contents/treatment-and-prevention-of-vascular-dementia?search=vascular%20dementia%20treatment&sectionRank=1&usage_type=default&anchor=H9&source=machineLearning&selectedTitle=1~57&display_rank=1#H17. Accessed April 4, 2019.

Analysis: ______________________________

____

____

____

____

____

____

____

____

____

2.2.3. The Health Professional's Motivations

The third element of the Parsonian model of professionalism involves the motivations of professionals.

> Professionals . . . must not be too strongly motivated by the desire for power, lest they attempt to achieve it by promoting social norms at the expense of individual liberty. On the other hand, they must not be too strongly motivated by profit, lest they allow their authority to be bought out by wealthy private [patients] seeking exemption from social norms. Instead . . . the professional project is successful only because professionals are motivated primarily by the desire for status and reputation—both among their peers and in society at large—rather than by the desire for money or power.[78]

This element is of particular importance when it comes to selecting among applicants to health professional training programs and when it comes to designing healthcare systems and incentivizing/disincentivizing certain behaviors.

CASE 2.D

In *Sloan v. South Carolina Board of Physical Therapy Examiners*,[79] the South Carolina legislature enacted a statute authorizing the South Carolina Board of Physical Therapy Examiners to

> refuse to renew the license of a licensed person . . . [or to] suspend, revoke, or otherwise restrict the license of a licensed person who: (1) requests, receives, participates or engages directly or indirectly in the dividing, transferring, assigning, rebating, or refunding of fees received for professional services or profits by means of a credit or other valuable consideration, including, but not limited to, wages, an unearned commission, discount, or gratuity with a person who referred a patient, or with a relative or business associate of the referring person; . . . .

The Supreme Court of South Carolina was asked to decide whether this provision "prohibit[ed] a physical therapist from working as an employee of a physician when the physician refers patients to the physical therapist for services?" The Court held that the provision did in fact prohibit such arrangements, known as physician-owned physical therapy service (POPTS). Why might a legislature concerned about professionalism have enacted such a provision?

Analysis: ______________________________

____

____

____

78 Latham SR. Medical professionalism: a Parsonian view. *Mount Sinai Journal of Medicine*. 2002;69(6):363–369, at 364.

79 Sloan v. South Carolina Board of Physical Therapy Examiners, 370 S.C. 452.

CASE 2.E

Consider the following case.

> ... Anthony Neade ... had a family history of heart disease, suffered from hypertension and a high cholesterol count, smoked heavily and was overweight. In 1990, at age 37, Mr. Neade began to [experience] ... chest pain extending into his arm and shortness of breath. Mr. Neade's primary care physician, Steven Portes, MD, hospitalized Mr. Neade from August 10 through August 13, 1990. During this hospitalization, Mr. Neade received several tests, including a thallium stress test and an electrocardiogram (EKG). Dr. Thomas Engel (not a party to this appeal) found the results of the tests to be normal and diagnosed Mr. Neade with hiatal hernia and/or esophagitis. Mr. Neade was thereafter discharged. After his hospitalization, Mr. Neade visited Dr. Portes on August 17, August 28, and September 24, 1990, at [Dr. Portes'] Primary Care Family Center, complaining of continued chest pain radiating to his neck and arm. Relying on the results of the thallium stress test and EKG ... Dr. Portes informed Mr. Neade that his chest pain was not cardiac related. In October 1990, Mr. Neade returned ... complaining of stabbing chest pain. ... [Dr. Portes' part-time associate Dr. Huang examined Mr. Neade and] recommended that Mr. Neade undergo an angiogram—a test ... more specific for diagnosing coronary artery disease than a thallium stress test. ... Despite Dr. Huang's recommendation, Dr. Portes did not authorize an angiogram for Mr. Neade. Mr. Neade again returned to Primary Care in June 1991, complaining of chest pain. Dr. Portes asked Dr. Schlager, another [part-time associate] ... to examine Mr. Neade. ... Dr. Schlager also recommended that Mr. Neade undergo an angiogram, but Dr. Portes ... did not authorize the angiogram .... Subsequently, on September 16, 1991, Mr. Neade suffered a massive myocardial infarction [and] ... [n]ine days later, Mr. Neade died. [His estate sued.]
>
> Dr. Portes was the president of Primary Care and ... negotiated contracts with various organizations on behalf of himself and the clinic. Chicago HMO, of which Mr. Neade was a member, was one of the organizations with which Dr. Portes had contracted for the provision of services. According to plaintiff's complaint, Dr. Portes personally negotiated with Chicago HMO in 1990 and 1991 and agreed that Dr. Portes and his group would receive from Chicago HMO ... $75,000 annually. The $75,000 was to be used by Dr. Portes ... to cover costs for patient referrals and outside medical tests prescribed for Chicago HMO members. This fund was termed the "Medical Incentive Fund."
>
> Pursuant to the contract ... any portion of the Medical Incentive Fund that was not used for referrals or outside tests would be divided at the end of each year between Primary Care's full time physicians and Chicago HMO, with the physicians receiving 60% of the remaining money and Chicago HMO receiving 40%. If the Medical Incentive Fund was exhausted prior to the end of the year, Dr. Portes and his group would be required to fund any additional consultant fees and outside tests. Plaintiff and Mr. Neade were not informed of this arrangement between Dr. Portes, Primary Care, and Chicago HMO.[80]

What problems are presented by the arrangement between Dr. Portes and Chicago HMO from a professionalism standpoint?

80 Neade v. Portes, Available at https://caselaw.findlaw.com/il-supreme-court/1469353.html.

Analysis: ______________________________

____

____

____

____

____

____

____

____

____

When professionals are motivated by political power or wealth instead of by professional status and reputation, professional *self-regulation* (see 2.2.4 Acts of profession, next) becomes an opportunity for self-advancement.

> [Professionals'] interests . . . in status and reputation rather than in political power and wealth . . . affords a crucial counterbalance to the professionals' right of self-regulation: for while the right of *self-regulation* implies that professionals could not be induced by regulators into favoring the public interest over that of their private [patients], the non-pecuniary character of professionals' . . . interests helps guarantee that they could not be induced to favor private, moneyed interests over the interests of the public. . . . Parsons was adamant that professional *self-regulation* can work . . . even if physicians are . . . self-interested. What is required is only that their self-interest be non-pecuniary in character.[81] (italics added)

2.2.4. Acts of Profession

The fourth element of the Parsonian model of professionalism involves acts of profession. According to Pellegrino, in the medical context such acts of profession occur in two ways.

> One is the public profession—the solemn proclamation on graduation from medical school when the "Oath" is taken. This is the moment when the newly graduated physician enters the profession, not when she receives her degree. The degree . . . says nothing of the commitment to the way the acquired knowledge and skill are to be used. When the Oath is proclaimed . . . the graduate has then made his "profession." . . . The second way the profession is "declared" is in the daily encounter with patients. Every time a physician sees a patient and asks, "What can I do for you, what is wrong, what is the problem?" he or she is professing . . . two things: one is competence . . . and the other is to use that competence in the best interests of the patient. This "profession" or commitment, by its very declaration, invites trust. The doctor voluntarily promises that he can be trusted and incurs the moral obligations of that promise.[82]

The acts described in the previous excerpt are individual acts, but acts of profession can also be collective, such as when codes of ethics are

81 Latham SR. Medical professionalism: a Parsonian view. *Mount Sinai Journal of Medicine*. 2002;69(6):363–369, at 367.

82 Pellegrino ED. Professionalism, profession and the virtues of the good physician. *Mount Sinai Journal of Medicine*. 2002;69(6):378–384, at 378.

promulgated by professional organizations,[83] or when acts of professional *self-regulation* (e.g., peer-review) take place.

CASE 2.F

Consider the following recent news item:

Doctor says "sham peer review" used to destroy his career after pointing out VA problems[84]

By HEATH DRUZIN | STARS AND STRIPES
Published: December 15, 2014

SALEM, Va.—For 24 years, Navy Cmdr. Jeff Hawker served his country, leaving active duty to continue treating his military brethren as a Department of Veterans Affairs doctor. After he started working at the Salem VA Medical Center, though, he said it took just a few months for officials at the medical center to oust him and to destroy his career after he reported dangerous medical practices. . . .

Hawker said he was the victim of a so-called "sham peer review," a problem many say is widespread in the VA and little reported because the victims fear bringing attention to their negative reviews.

Hawker said vindictive local VA officials have effectively ended his career after he voiced serious concerns about patient safety at a busy Virginia hospital, including a doctor performing procedures Hawker said he wasn't trained to do and life-threatening medical errors. Worse, Hawker said, veterans there are still at serious risk months after he reported the problems. . . .

Hawker, who has been unemployed since January, filed a whistleblower protection complaint with the Office of Special Counsel claiming wrongful termination and asking for reinstatement as a VA physician. He said he will wait for that process to play out before deciding whether to file a lawsuit. . . .

In April 2013, Hawker started work at the Salem Veterans Affairs Medical Center. . . .

Hawker . . . said he . . . noticed unsafe practices in the hospital, one of the most egregious being a mismanagement of a patient who appeared to be having a stroke. When the patient began exhibiting signs of a stroke, a senior doctor did nothing, putting the patient's life at risk, Hawker said. The patient lived, but Hawker was disturbed and said he began lodging his concerns with colleagues and superiors. . . .

[Hawker] was fired Jan. 3, 2014. . . .

According to documents reviewed by *Stars and Stripes*, Hawker did lodge concerns before being fired. A letter from the office of Rep. Randy Forbes, R-Va., confirming receipt of Hawker's concerns is dated Nov. 12, 2013, nearly two months before he was removed from federal service. Four reports he sent to the Virginia Board of Medicine are dated Nov. 26, 2013. . . . After Hawker started reporting unsafe practices . . . he got a letter announcing that the hospital would be reducing his salary due to "deficiencies" in his abilities. That letter came just two months after a contradictory letter granting his medical "privileges" after he successfully completed the customary trial period.

That letter, signed by Hawker's boss, Salem VAMC image service chief Rathnakara Sherigar, states that following

83 See, for example, AAPA, Guidelines for ethical conduct for the PA profession. https://www.aapa.org/wp-content/uploads/2017/02/16-EthicalConduct.pdf. Accessed January 17, 2021. See also, Code of ethics for the physical therapist, https://www.apta.org/apta-and-you/leadership-and-governance/policies/code-of-ethics-for-the-physical-therapist. Accessed January 17, 2021. See also, American Association for Respiratory Care statement of ethics and professional conduct. https://www.aarc.org/wp-content/uploads/2017/03/statement-of-ethics.pdf. Accessed January 17, 2021. See also, AOTA 2020 occupational therapy code of ethics. https://www.aota.org/-/media/Corporate/Files/Practice/Ethics/AOTA-2020-Code-of-Ethics.pdf. Accessed January 25, 2021.

84 https://www.stripes.com/news/veterans/doctor-says-sham-peer-review-used-to-destroy-his-career-after-pointing-out-va-problems-1.319484.

"real-time observation" and review of his work from April to July 2013, Hawker was cleared to treat patients unsupervised. Two months later, he received another letter signed by Sherigar, citing his "limited competencies" . . . .

Things soon worsened for Hawker. He was told his work was being reviewed and he was brought in front of a Medical Executive Board that included some of the people he had mentioned in his concerns. They determined he had made errors in patient care and that he was not qualified for his job.

Before the hospital moved to fire him, he was shown a proficiency report signed by Sherigar that gave him an "unsatisfactory" rating for his work during the same time period as Sherigar's earlier review that found him competent to perform his duties.

Hawker said he had never been shown either proficiency report until Oct. 17, 2013, three months after the end of the review period listed on the initial report. He suspects the reports were made retroactively to boost the board's case to fire him. . . .

James Martin, a doctor and national representative for the American Federation of Government Employees, said he is working on multiple cases of sham peer reviews in which VA doctors have been forced out by unethical administrators.

"I've got all kinds of stories," he said.

According to Martin—who's not personally involved in Hawker's case—it's fairly easy for administrators to oust doctors because the entire process is done in house. Doctors who report wrongdoing or malpractice are often judged by the very same people they have criticized. . . .

Analyze the VA's handling of the case of Dr. Hawker from a professionalism standpoint.

Analysis: ______________________________

____

____

____

____

____

____

____

____

Following are reproduced three of the oaths most commonly taken at the time of medical school graduation.[85]

The Hippocratic Oath

I swear by Apollo the physician, and Asclepius, and Hygieia and Panacea and all the gods and goddesses as my witnesses, that, according to my ability and judgement, I will keep this Oath and this contract:

To hold him who taught me this art equally dear to me as my parents, to be a partner in life with him, and to fulfill his needs when required; to look upon his offspring as equals to my own siblings, and to teach them this art, if they shall wish to learn it, without fee or contract; and that by the set rules, lectures, and every other mode of instruction, I will impart a knowledge of the art to my own

85 By report, "[m]ost [medical] schools stick with one of three main versions of the oath, often for the sake of tradition—Hippocrates's, [Louis] Lasagna's [modified version of the Oath], and the Declaration of Geneva." See: So long, Hippocrates. Medical students choose their own oaths. https://www.statnews.com/2016/09/21/hippocratic-oath-medical-students-doctors/. Accessed April 8, 2019.

sons, and those of my teachers, and to students bound by this contract and having sworn this Oath to the law of medicine, but to no others.

I will use those dietary regimens which will benefit my patients according to my greatest ability and judgement, and I will do no harm or injustice to them.

I will not give a lethal drug to anyone if I am asked, nor will I advise such a plan; and similarly I will not give a woman a pessary to cause an abortion.

In purity and according to divine law will I carry out my life and my art.

I will not use the knife, even upon those suffering from stones, but I will leave this to those who are trained in this craft.

Into whatever homes I go, I will enter them for the benefit of the sick, avoiding any voluntary act of impropriety or corruption, including the seduction of women or men, whether they are free men or slaves.

Whatever I see or hear in the lives of my patients, whether in connection with my professional practice or not, which ought not to be spoken of outside, I will keep secret, as considering all such things to be private.

So long as I maintain this Oath faithfully and without corruption, may it be granted to me to partake of life fully and the practice of my art, gaining the respect of all men for all time. However, should I transgress this Oath and violate it, may the opposite be my fate.[86]

The Hippocratic Oath: Modern Version (Louis Lasagna, 1964)

I swear to fulfill, to the best of my ability and judgment, this covenant:

I will respect the hard-won scientific gains of those physicians in whose steps I walk, and gladly share such knowledge as is mine with those who are to follow.

I will apply, for the benefit of the sick, all measures [that] are required, avoiding those twin traps of overtreatment and therapeutic nihilism.

I will remember that there is art to medicine as well as science, and that warmth, sympathy, and understanding may outweigh the surgeon's knife or the chemist's drug.

I will not be ashamed to say "I know not," nor will I fail to call in my colleagues when the skills of another are needed for a patient's recovery.

I will respect the privacy of my patients, for their problems are not disclosed to me that the world may know. Most especially must I tread with care in matters of life and death. If it is given me to save a life, all thanks. But it may also be within my power to take a life; this awesome responsibility must be faced with great humbleness and awareness of my own frailty. Above all, I must not play at God.

I will remember that I do not treat a fever chart, a cancerous growth, but a sick human being, whose illness may affect the person's family and economic stability. My responsibility includes these related problems, if I am to care adequately for the sick.

I will prevent disease whenever I can, for prevention is preferable to cure.

I will remember that I remain a member of society, with special obligations to all my fellow human beings, those sound of mind and body as well as the infirm.

If I do not violate this oath, may I enjoy life and art, respected while I live and remembered with affection thereafter. May I always act so as to preserve the finest traditions of my calling and may I long

86 The Hippocratic Oath. Translated by Michael North, National Library of Medicine, 2002. https://www.nlm.nih.gov/hmd/greek/greek_oath.html. Accessed April 9, 2019.

experience the joy of healing those who seek my help.[87]

The Physician's Pledge (WMA)

AS A MEMBER OF THE MEDICAL PROFESSION:

I SOLEMNLY PLEDGE to dedicate my life to the service of humanity;

THE HEALTH AND WELL-BEING OF MY PATIENT will be my first consideration;

I WILL RESPECT the autonomy and dignity of my patient;

I WILL MAINTAIN the utmost respect for human life;

I WILL NOT PERMIT considerations of age, disease or disability, creed, ethnic origin, gender, nationality, political affiliation, race, sexual orientation, social standing or any other factor to intervene between my duty and my patient;

I WILL RESPECT the secrets that are confided in me, even after the patient has died;

I WILL PRACTISE my profession with conscience and dignity and in accordance with good medical practice;

I WILL FOSTER the honour and noble traditions of the medical profession;

I WILL GIVE to my teachers, colleagues, and students the respect and gratitude that is their due;

I WILL SHARE my medical knowledge for the benefit of the patient and the advancement of healthcare;

I WILL ATTEND TO my own health, well-being, and abilities in order to provide care of the highest standard;

I WILL NOT USE my medical knowledge to violate human rights and civil liberties, even under threat;

I MAKE THESE PROMISES solemnly, freely, and upon my honour.[88]

Following is reproduced the Model Pledge of the Academy of Physical Therapy Education.

As a physical therapist dedicated to providing the highest quality care and services, I solemnly pledge I will:

- Respect the rights and dignity of all individuals who seek my services or with whom I work.
- Act in a compassionate and trustworthy manner in all aspects of my services.
- Exercise sound professional judgment while abiding by legal and ethical requirements.
- Demonstrate integrity during interactions with colleagues, other health care providers, students, faculty, researchers, the public, and payers for the enhancement of patient care and the advancement of the profession.
- Enhance my practice through life-long acquisition and application of knowledge, skills, and professional behavior.
- Participate in efforts to meet physical therapy and health care needs of local, national, and global communities.

Thus, with this oath, I accept the duties and responsibilities that embody the physical therapy profession.

Revised and Adopted February 2011
APTA Education Section[89]

Following is reproduced an oath representative of the respiratory therapy (RT) profession:

- I solemnly pledge to dedicate my life to the care of the sick, the promotion of health and the service of humanity.
- I will practice respiratory therapy with conscience and in truth. The health and dignity

87 The Hippocratic Oath: Modern Version. https://www.pbs.org/wgbh/nova/doctors/oath_modern.html. Accessed April 9, 2019.

88 WMA Declaration of Geneva. https://www.wma.net/policies-post/wma-declaration-of-geneva/. Accessed April 9, 2019.

89 Academy of Physical Therapy Model Pledge. https://aptaeducation.org/pdfs/Model%20Pledge.pdf Accessed May 21, 2021.

of my patients will be my first concern. I will hold in confidence any patient relation information. I will not permit considerations of gender, race, religion, sexual orientation, ethnicity, or social standing to influence my duty to care for those in need of my service.

- I will respect the moral rights of my patients to fully participate in the medical decisions that affect them. I will assist my patients to make choices that coincide with their own values and beliefs.
- I will strive to improve my competency constantly. I will recognize my limitations and work within my scope of practice and competency level at all times. I will work within appropriate guidelines and legal framework governing the practice of respiratory therapy.
- I will promote health as well as treat disease.
- I will hold in regard my colleagues in other professions, those who teach and those who broaden our knowledge through research. I will encourage good team dynamics and encourage mutual critical evaluation of our work.
- I will seek constantly to grow in knowledge, understanding and skill and will work with my colleagues to promote and advance all that is worthy in the profession.
- I make this pledge freely and upon my honour.[90]

CASE 2.G

Consider the following case:

> In Nova Scotia in 2019, family physician Dr. Paul Young pushed back against companies that require detailed sick notes to excuse absences from work. Dr. Young indicated that some companies, such as absence-management corporations and insurance companies, require information that he feels violate patient privacy. Examples of such requirements include a 2-page form or 3 months of a patient's chart, which can specifically identify the illness, condition, or medical diagnosis the patient is experiencing. Young stated, "The employers should not need to know a medical diagnosis," said Young. "All they need to know is that there's a medical reason for [the absence] . . . . It's inappropriate . . . . The patient's privacy should trump." One absence-management company that required such documentation was Morneau Shepell. According to Dr. Young, when he refused to send the information due to patient privacy confidentiality, Morneau Shepell responded that without such documentation, a worker may not be paid.
>
> The vice president of health and productivity solutions, Kristin Coady, at Morneau Shepell responded to CBC News that personal employee information is kept confidential, further indicating that Morneau Shepell does not reveal the full contents of a physician form to an employer, also referencing separate information transfer and display processes. In addition, this was also cited as standard industry practice that facilitates the work of case managers, who can inform clients "on whether an absence meets the definition of disability in an employer's short-term disability policy or accommodation policy."[91]

Which elements of medical professionalism are implicated?

90 The Respiratory Therapy Student Oath—October 30, 2014. The Michener Institute of Education at UHN. https://michener.ca/2014-stethoscope-ceremony/. Accessed May 31, 2021.

91 CBC news. Why a Nova Scotia doctor is fighting back against sick notes. https://www.cbc.ca/news/canada/nova-scotia/ns-doctor-fights-sick-notes-1.5118809. Accessed June 6, 2019.

Analysis: ______________________________

____

____

____

____

____

____

____

____

____

WRAP-UP

Chapter Summary

The goals and means of medicine constitute an *internal morality of medicine,* and the professional integrity of health professionals is constituted by allegiance to this internal morality. Where the goal (or end) of an act, though achievable, is not a legitimate medical goal, the act violates the internal morality of medicine because of *goal illegitimacy*. Where the means employed are not legitimate medical means, the act violates the internal morality of medicine because of *means illegitimacy*. Where the means and the ends are not appropriately related—in other words, where the means-end fit is not sufficiently tight—the act violates the internal morality of medicine because of *means-ends disjunction*.

Medical futility represents an extreme form of means-ends disjunction, one where the disconnectedness between goals and means is complete. Something is medically futile if it has no realistic chance of achieving any legitimate medical goal. Subtypes of medical futility include physiologic futility, qualitative futility (medically futile because nonbeneficial) or quantitative futility (probabilistically futile). Health professionals are generally under no obligation to provide medically futile treatments.

Just as virtue ethics focuses on the character of moral agents as opposed to the rightness or wrongness of particular acts, medical *professionalism* focuses on the character of medical professionals. The Parsonian model of professionalism is characterized by the following elements: (1) the expert authority of the professional, (2) the professional as a mediator between individuals and society, (3) professional motivations, and (4) acts of profession, which include self-regulation.

Review Questions

1. What does the term *under color of medical authority* mean?
2. List six goals of medicine.
3. What are the three ways in which an act may violate the *internal morality of medicine*?
4. How is *medical futility* related to the *internal morality of medicine*?
5. What are the three subtypes of medical futility?
6. Explain the relationship between *professionalism* and the *internal morality of medicine*.
7. Explain the relationship between *professionalism* and the virtues.
8. According to Parsons, what elements should characterize a profession?

Case Analyses

Case 2.A Analysis

The California portion of the McMath case illustrates the concept of *goal illegitimacy*. The goals of medicine (see previous discussion) all presume the existence of a living patient. Alas, Jahi McMath was declared dead by brain death criteria on December 12, 2013. Once it was determined that she was dead, no legitimate medical goals remained. Because California law requires that hospitals "adopt a policy for providing family or next of kin with a reasonably brief period of accommodation,"[92] the California hospital arguably properly petitioned the court for permission to end accommodative efforts and properly refused to allow the performance of any surgical procedures on a dead patient. (While our focus here is on matters medical, one could argue that the involvement of the California courts in restraining Children's Hospital from discontinuing mechanical ventilation, no matter how well intentioned, was an unjustified violation of the rule "do not break the law.")[93]

Because New Jersey law provides for a religious exception to the determination of death by neurologic criteria, Jahi's family could argue that legitimate medical goals (specifically, the care of those with a malady and the avoidance of premature death) were still attainable. However, one could argue that artificial ventilation and artificial hydration and nutrition of Jahi was *qualitatively medically futile* because it could not benefit Jahi as a person. Further, with regard to her family's stated goal (that she might recover), one could argue that continued life support was *physiologically medically futile,* since that goal could not be achieved.

Case 2.B Analysis

We submit that the described act is unambiguously nonmedical. The authority involved in this case was Fletcher's legal authority, not his expert authority as a physician. The signing of the death warrant did not take place within the context of a doctor-patient relationship. Fletcher employed no medical means in signing the death warrant, nor did he pursue any medical ends. In short, Fletcher was acting as the chief executive of a state, not as a physician. Consequently, Fletcher's act, while controversial, cannot be said to violate the internal morality of medicine. Indeed, the Kentucky Board of Medical Licensure ruled that there was no merit to the complaint that Gov. Fletcher had violated any tenets of medical ethics when he signed the death warrant.[94] In contrast, consider another case in which the Georgia Board of Medicine ruled that a Dr. H. V. Sanjeeva Rao did not violate the state's medical practice act when he inserted a catheter into a prisoner to start a lethal injection. Dr. Rao employed medical means in placing the intravenous catheter, thus triggering the internal morality of medicine inquiry, but was arguably engaged in the pursuit of no legitimate medical goals. Further, the American Medical Association has declared, "A physician . . . should not be a participant in a legally authorized execution."[95] We believe, therefore, that Dr. Rao's act was arguably a violation of the internal morality of medicine.

Case 2.C Analysis

The ethical issue is whether medicating the prisoner involuntarily is an appropriate exercise

92 California Health and Safety Code 1254.4(a). http://coalitionccc.org/_pdf/public-policy/policy-ab_2565.pdf. Accessed January 15, 2014.

93 Paola FA. The case of Jahi McMath: Professionalism and knowing one's limitations. *The Journal of Physician Assistant Education.* 2014;25(1):59–61.

94 Robeznieks A. Ethics charges related to executions dropped. *AMA News.* 2005 Jan 31:21.

95 See COUNCIL ON JUDICIAL AND ETHICAL AFFAIRS, AM. MED. ASS'N., CODE OF MEDICAL ETHICS § 2.06 (2008). http://www.ama-assn.org/ama/pub/physician-resources/medical-ethics/code-medical-ethics/opinion206.shtml [hereinafter CODE OF MEDICAL ETHICS].

of the PA's role as mediator between the individual (here, the prisoner-patient) and society. Recalling that professionalism and the internal morality of medicine are two sides of the same coin, we begin by asking whether there is a legitimate medical goal to be attained by treating the prisoner. There is— "the care of those with a malady," and possibly "the relief of pain and suffering caused by maladies"—if the prisoner is suffering mentally. Next, is the involuntary treatment of this prisoner a legitimate medical means? Arguably not, since treatment of a patient against his wishes is a prima facie violation of the rule "do not deprive of freedom" (or of the principle of respect for autonomy). One might try to argue that this is a justified paternalism, but that argument is clearly a loser. The PA knows that if his treatment is successful, the prisoner's mental illness will improve, and he will promptly be executed. Under the circumstances, a powerful argument can be made against involuntarily medicating this patient.

Case 2.D Analysis

The Legislature was likely concerned about the third element of the Parsonian model of professionalism—the motivations of professionals. Recall that where the profit motive is excessive, concern exists that professionals might allow their authority to be bought out. In fact, the South Carolina Supreme Court wrote in its opinion:

> Although we lack the benefit of any legislative history explaining the Legislature's specific motivation for enacting this statute, it is no great stretch to conclude the statute was passed for the same reasons which prompted enactment of the state Provider Self-Referral Act and the federal Stark laws—to protect consumers as well as government-sponsored health care programs such as Medicare and Medicaid from actual and potential conflicts of interest which are likely to lead to overuse of medical services by physicians who, for their own financial gain rather than their patients' medical needs, refer patients to entities in which the physicians hold a financial interest.[96]

The Legislature was likely also concerned about the effect of the profit motive on the physical therapists, since "[t]herapists who work in POPT clinics may . . . feel pressured to over-utilize therapy services to promote profits, rather than patient wellbeing."[97]

Case 2.E Analysis

Recall that the third element of the Parsonian model of professionalism concerns the motivations of medical professionals. Medical professionals "must not be too strongly motivated by profit"[98]; but how strongly one is motivated by profit depends both on that person's innate greed (or lack thereof) and on the economic milieu in which he/she practices. In this case, the financial arrangement between Dr. Portes and Chicago HMO created powerful economic incentives for Dr. Portes to avoid referring member patients to consultants or for outside testing. The incentives came in the form of both a carrot and a stick. On the carrot side, Dr. Portes would, assuming he were the sole full-time physician at Primary Care Family Center, receive 60% of any portion of the $75,000 (potentially $45,000) Medical Incentive Fund (MIF) not used for referrals or outside tests. On the stick side, if the $75,000 MIF was exhausted prior to the end of the year, Dr. Portes would be required to pay the costs of any additional consultations or medical testing. While all

96 Sloan v. South Carolina Board of Physical Therapy Examiners, 370 S.C. 452.

97 Working in a physician-owned physical therapy clinic: Arguments for and against. myPTsolutions. https://myptsolutions.com/working-physician-owned-physical-therapy-clinic-arguments/. Accessed May 21, 2021.

98 Latham SR. Medical professionalism: a Parsonian view. *Mount Sinai Journal of Medicine*. 2002;69(6):363–369, at 364.

payment systems (fee-for-service, salaried positions, and HMO arrangements as here) can create perverse economic incentives—some to overtreat, some to undertreat—what is remarkable about the arrangement here is the strength of the incentive created. Simply stated, financial arrangements such as the MIF described here pose a threat to medical professionalism.

Case 2.F Analysis

"Peer review is the process whereby doctors evaluate the quality of their colleagues' work in order to ensure that prevailing standards of care are being met."[99] Peer review is a collective act of profession in which the medical community, acting through agents, proclaims publicly that an individual practitioner is or is not competent, or has or has not used that competence in the best interest of patients. Sham peer review or malicious peer review (MPR)—malice masquerading as justice—occurs when a physician is sanctioned in bad-faith for some improper motive. Examples of such motives include personality conflicts, the desire to eliminate competitors, and the desire to be rid of a whistleblower.

Dr. Hawker appears to have been the victim of MPR at the hands of a Veterans Administration motivated to rid itself of whistleblowers. Recall Parsons' position that the professionalism concept, which includes professional self-regulation (a collective act of profession), can be successful only if professionals are motivated primarily by the desire for status and reputation—both among their peers and in society at large—rather than by the desire for money or power. Here the motivations of Dr. Hawker's superiors were corrupt, and this led to a corruption of the act of profession that is peer review.

In terms of the professionalism project, MPR is a no-win situation. To the extent that observers accept as just the outcome of the peer review, Dr. Hawker's career and professional reputation have been wrongfully damaged. To the extent observers know or suspect that the peer review process was unjust, their faith in the medical profession's ability to self-regulate—and with it their faith in medical professionalism—is undermined. Further, it should be noted that MPR need not even actually take place in order to subvert medical professionalism; simply the possibility of MPR is enough: "The wide perception among doctors that whistleblowers may be punished with sham peer review has . . . an in terrorem effect, discouraging doctors from challenging hospital administrators on issues of health care quality. Ironically, fear of sham peer review . . . leads doctors to avoid criticizing the work of colleagues when they believe such criticism may be unwelcome to hospital administrators . . . ."[100]

Case 2.G Analysis

The elements of medical professionalism that are implicated include the *expert authority* of the medical professional; the medical professional's *role as a mediator* between individual patients and society; and the medical professional's *acts of profession*. The requirement that physicians fill out a two-page form and include up to 3 months of the patient's chart so that case managers can advise Morneau Shepell's clients regarding whether the absence is covered under disability policies is a direct challenge to the (expert) authority of physicians in Nova Scotia. To paraphrase Dr. Young, all they should need to know is that a physician has determined that there's a medical reason for the absence. As mentioned earlier in the text, the writing of sick notes generally illustrates the medical professional's *role as a mediator* between the individual

99 Vyas D, Hozain AE. Clinical peer review in the United States: History, legal development and subsequent abuse. *World J Gastroenterol.* 2014 Jun 7;20(21):6357–6363.

100 Benson MD, Benson JB, Stein MS. Hospital quality improvement: Are peer review immunity, privilege, and confidentiality in the public interest? 11 *Nw. J. L. & Soc. Pol'y* 1.

and society, as professional authority is used to create a safety zone for sick individuals against the demands of society. In the real-world example of Dr. Young, we see a thoughtful and principled attempt to fulfill his role responsibilities without forsaking his public and private *acts of profession*, which include the duty of confidentiality.[101]

101 As you shall see in Chapter 4, the duty of confidentiality is intrinsic to medical practice; is protected by law; and is contained in numerous oaths and codes of medical ethics. See, e.g., the Canadian Medical Association Code of Ethics. https://policybase.cma.ca/documents/policypdf/PD04-06.pdf. Accessed June 6, 2019.

CHAPTER 3

Case-Based Reasoning in Ethics

LEARNING OBJECTIVES

1. Define *case*.
2. Explain how *cases* relate to *individual moral judgments*.
3. List sources of rules/norms in the I-R-A-C mnemonic.
4. Explain the role of morality in resolving controversial cases.
5. Define *precedent* and *stare decisis*.
6. Explain how *case analysis* is related to the making of *individual moral judgments*.
7. Employ *analogy* and *distinction* in *case analysis*.
8. Recognize and distinguish *specific* and *general beneficence*.
9. Recognize and distinguish *obligatory beneficence* and *ideal beneficence*.
10. Define *constructive knowledge*.
11. Define the term *ratio decidendi*.

To the American lawyer there would be nothing strange about putting our emphasis on specific acts, for these correspond in his professional vocabulary to specific cases and controversies. He has made it a habit to concentrate on the techniques and processes that culminate in a decision, and a decision is the resolution of some highly specific collision of demands. A decision is not only a resolution; it is a victory and a promise of peace after a real conflict. American judges will not decide cases unless they represent genuine controversies. They refuse to give advisory opinions governing possible future circumstances that may or may not ever develop. So far as the moral experience is comparable to the judicial process, the American lawyer would applaud our concentrating on what is unique, immediate, and apprehensible in each specific moral crisis.[1]

Recall the metaphorical ethics pyramid, introduced in Chapter 1, with ethical theory at its apex. Moving down the pyramid, ethics becomes increasingly concrete—at the level of *moral principles*, then the *moral rules*, and finally, *individual moral judgments* at the base of the pyramid.

1 Cahn E. *The Moral Decision: Right and Wrong in the Light of American Law*. Bloomington: Indiana University Press; 1955:11.

Individual moral judgments represent ethics at its most material. Health professionals should find that comforting; after all, practicing health professionals spend their working days making specific clinical decisions regarding the care of specific patients. To paraphrase William Osler, one does not practice medicine in the abstract,[2] divorced from its application to specific patients.

You will recall that individual moral judgments take place either retrospectively, the moral decision already having been made—so-called *moral justification*—or prospectively, with the moral decision yet to come—so-called *moral decision-making*.[3]

Individual moral judgments are generally made in *cases*. A case is "an aggregate of facts which furnishes occasion for the exercise of . . . [judgment]."[4] Cases serve as the setting for individual moral judgments—hence the title of this chapter. Herein we consider the place of individual moral judgments in ethics. Specifically, we consider both the process of making those individual moral judgments and the effect or significance of such judgments.

1. Making Individual Moral Judgments: Case Analysis

In making an individual moral judgment in a case, we begin with a careful consideration of the facts. Then, we apply the mnemonic I-R-A-C: spot the Issue(s); identify the applicable Rule(s)/norms; Apply the rule(s) to the facts of the case; and draw a Conclusion.

1.1. Spot the Issue(s)

Consider the following:

> **A "Robot" Doctor Told a Patient He Was Dying. It Might Not Be the Last Time.**
> March 13, 2019
> (Vox)—The rapid influx of advanced technology is changing the practice of medicine—at times for the better, but sometimes for the worse. Nowhere is this more apparent than a story where a physician told a fatally ill man in a Fremont, California, hospital that he was dying via video chat on a screen attached to a robot. The news should serve as a wake-up call to the medical establishment on the limits of technology.[5]

What ethical issue(s) is/are raised by this report? Well, what is concerning or unusual in the report is the fact that bad news was conveyed to a patient impersonally—not face-to-face, but via video chat on a screen attached to a robot. What ethical issue(s) does that raise? Think back to Chapter 1 and the so-called substance of morality (see the section, 2. The Substance of Morality). Normally, telling someone he is going to die can be expected to cause pain and suffering; but doing so is an inescapable part of medical practice, and if done in an appropriately professional manner does not violate the rule "do not cause pain/suffering." So the ethical issue here is whether it was done in an appropriately professional manner. Stated otherwise, does telling a patient he is dying via video chat on a screen attached to a robot violate the rule "do not neglect your duty"? An alternative

---

2 Osler actually said, "The good physician treats the disease; the great physician treats the patient who has the disease. . . . He who studies medicine without books sails an uncharted sea, but he who studies medicine without patients does not go to sea at all." See: William Osler, https://www.brainyquote.com/quotes/william_osler_386616. Accessed March 19, 2019.

3 Hauser MD, Young L, Cushman F. Reviving Rawls's linguistic analogy: operative principles and the causal structure of moral actions. In: W. Sinnott-Armstrong, Ed. *Moral Psychology, Vol. 2. The Cognitive Science of Morality: Intuition and Diversity*. Cambridge, MA: MIT Press; 2008:107–143.

4 The Law Dictionary. https://thelawdictionary.org/case/. Accessed March 25, 2019.

5 Bioethics.com. http://www.bioethics.com/archives/45895. Accessed March 21, 2019.

formulation of the same issue would be to ask whether the physician had behaved cruelly (or callously) toward this patient in conveying the news as he did.[6]

Try your hand at the following.

CASE 3.A

Spot the ethical issue(s) raised by the following bill:

> In March 2019, the Kentucky legislature passed a bill banning abortions desired on the basis of the fetus's race, gender, or disability. In a vote of 32-4, the Senate passed the bill, which will be sent to the governor, Republican Matt Bevin. Given Governor Bevin's anti-abortion stance, further legal action from abortion-rights activists is expected.[7]

Analysis: ______________________________

____

____

____

____

____

____

____

____

____

1.2. Identify the Applicable Rule(s)/Norm(s)

The next step involves identifying the applicable Rule(s)/norm(s).[8] The norm being applied might be a *moral rule*, or it might be a *moral ideal* or a *moral principle* (see Chapter 1). Alternatively, norms might be located within the *internal morality of medicine* (see Chapter 2); and, as we shall see next, sometimes norms are derived from an analysis of similar cases decided previously.

Let's consider the previous case of the robot doctor. We decided that the ethical question was, "Does telling a patient he is dying via video chat on a screen attached to a robot violate the rule 'do not neglect your duty'?" So is the applicable rule simply "do not neglect your duty"? The answer is no. Why? Well, whatever norm we identify as applicable must help us address the issue. Does the rule "do not neglect your duty" help us decide whether the doctor involved neglected his duty? Clearly not. So, what norms would help? Neglect of duty questions should make you think of the *internal morality of medicine*, and specifically of the standard of care[9] as discussed in Chapter 2. I would argue that the applicable norm would be a formulation of the standard of care:

> The physician [it was a physician in this case] is under an obligation to exercise the same degree of knowledge, skill, diligence, and care that the ordinary, competent practitioner would exercise under the same or similar circumstances. The physician is under the further obligation to use his best judgment in exercising his skill and applying his knowledge.[10]

---

6 We saw a similar situation in chapter one. Recall case 1.F, in which Fountain Valley Regional Hospital's respiratory therapists asked hospital CEO McFarland to meet to discuss the crisis created by the COVID-19 pandemic. They initially received no response, and after a second request were told by McFarland's delegate (Human Resources Officer Mark Fisher), "There is a lot going on and I am please asking you to be patient," Fisher wrote, explaining leaders were too busy working in patient care to address the issues. "Please outline your concerns in writing and then I will work with the leaders who can address."

7 Bioethics.com. http://www.bioethics.com/archives/45903. Accessed March 21, 2019.

8 I have written "Identify the applicable Rule(s)/norm(s)" instead of "Identify the applicable norm(s)" to preserve the IRAC mnemonic.

9 The standard of care is both a legal and a moral concept.

10 *Pike v Honsiger*, 155 N.Y. 201 (1898).

CASE 3.B

Reconsider the facts of Case 3.A. What is/are the applicable rule(s)/norm(s)?

> In March 2019, the Kentucky legislature passed a bill banning abortions desired on the basis of the fetus's race, gender, or disability. In a vote of 32-4, the Senate passed the bill, which will be sent to the governor, Republican Matt Bevin. Given Governor Bevin's anti-abortion stance, further legal action from abortion-rights activists is expected.[11]

Analysis: ______________________________

____

____

____

____

____

____

____

____

____

1.3. Apply the Applicable Norm(s) to the Facts of the Case

The next step involves applying the applicable norm to the facts of the case under consideration.

Consider again the case of the robot doctor. The ethical issue was, "Does telling a patient he is dying via video chat on a screen attached to a robot violate the rule 'do not neglect your duty'?" The norm we decided to apply above was the formulation of the standard of care taken from the *Pike v. Honsiger* case:

> The physician is under an obligation to exercise the same degree of knowledge, skill, diligence, and care that the ordinary, competent practitioner would exercise under the same or similar circumstances.[12]

Did the physician behave as an ordinary, competent practitioner would have behaved under like circumstances? Arguably no. In general, bad news should be given face-to-face.[13] The physical presence of the practitioner communicates to the patient that the practitioner cares and allows for the use of touch where appropriate.[14] While there might be extenuating circumstances justifying or even necessitating the giving of bad news in other than a face-to-face manner, no such circumstances were described in the previous robot doctor excerpt.

---

11 Bioethics.com. http://www.bioethics.com/archives/45903. Accessed March 21, 2019.

12 *Pike v. Honsiger*, 155 N.Y. 201 (1898).

13 Nalley C. Patient communication: The do's & don'ts of delivering a cancer diagnosis. *Oncology Times*. 2019;41(S6):13–14. https://journals.lww.com/oncology-times/Fulltext/2019/03201/Patient_Communication__The_Do_s___Don_ts_of.10.aspx. Accessed May 1, 2019.

14 Vandekieft GK. Breaking bad news. *Am Fam Physician*. 2001;64(12):1975–1979. https://www.aafp.org/afp/2001/1215/p1975.html. Accessed May 1, 2019.

1.4. Draw a Conclusion

CASE 3.C

Reconsider the facts of Case 3.A. Apply the applicable rule(s)/norm(s) to the facts of the case and draw a conclusion.

> In March 2019, the Kentucky legislature passed a bill banning abortions desired on the basis of the fetus's race, gender, or disability. In a vote of 32-4, the Senate passed the bill, which will be sent to the governor, Republican Matt Bevin. Given Governor Bevin's anti-abortion stance, further legal action from abortion-rights activists is expected.[15]

Analysis: ______________________________

____

____

____

____

____

____

____

____

____

2. The Effect of Individual Moral Judgments

Bernard Gert wrote that morality does not provide unique solutions to most controversial cases.[16] Rather, it helps us distinguish between solutions that are morally acceptable and those that are not.[17] Reasonable decision-makers (either individual or group decision-makers) often disagree about how to resolve a case. Justice, however, requires that any decision-maker be consistent over time and resolve similar cases similarly. Consider a baseball analogy. Two reasonable umpires might disagree about whether a pitch on the outside part of the plate is a strike or not; but if umpire one called that pitch a strike in the top of the first inning, we expect (and fairness requires) him to call a similarly located pitch a strike in the bottom of the ninth inning.

That being the case, it should be clear that one reason an individual moral judgment matters is that it serves as *precedent* of sorts. Precedent refers to an earlier case or cases close in fact or moral principles to the case under consideration. Precedent is a source of norms that we can use in analyzing a case (recall the R in IRAC). In Anglo-American law, the doctrine that courts should adhere to their own precedent is known as *stare decisis*, which is Latin for "to adhere to decided cases." The doctrine of *stare decisis* promotes security and certainty (since people know what they can expect from the court based on precedent) and justice. These same considerations apply in moral decision making.

Keep in mind, though, that *stare decisis* is not an absolute. Decision-makers can depart from precedent when justice demands it—as, for example, when it is apparent that an earlier case was wrongly decided.

3. Analysis of Precedent: Analogy and Distinction[18]

Here I mean to discuss the process of looking at previously decided similar cases (*precedent*) to facilitate moral decision-making and moral justification. In the legal context, this is referred to as *common law*

15 Bioethics.com. http://www.bioethics.com/archives/45903. Accessed March 21, 2019.

16 Gert B, Culver CM, Clouser KD. *Bioethics: A Return to Fundamentals.* New York: Oxford University Press, 1997:21–24.

17 Gert B, Culver CM, Clouser KD. *Bioethics: A Return to Fundamentals.* New York: Oxford University Press, 1997:21–24.

18 Dernbach JC, Singleton RV. *A Practical Guide to Legal Writing and Legal Method.* Littleton, Colorado: Fred B Rothman & Co.; 1981:47.

analysis. Because our focus here is on morality rather than law, we will use the term *analysis of precedent*.

Any analysis of precedent should begin with a thorough understanding of each one of the previously decided similar cases—including the relevant facts, as well as the reasons and policy considerations implicated. (For the sake of simplicity, the illustrative hypothetical cases employed next are rather spartan and do not lend themselves to such in-depth understanding.)

Consider the following short series of hypothetical legal cases, which we will use to illustrate the process of analyzing precedent.

Case 1: Dr. X learns that his promiscuous single patient, John Doe, is HIV+. Dr. X cautions Doe re: transmissibility of HIV but does not inquire further into his (Doe's) sex life. Doe has sex with and infects his girlfriend, Jane Q-Public. Q-Public sues Dr. X, arguing that he should have warned her. The court holds (decides) that there was no duty to warn under the circumstances.

Case 2: Dr. Y learns that his married patient, Joe Doakes, is HIV+. He fails to warn Doakes' wife, who is also his patient. She contracts the disease and sues Dr. Y. The court holds that Dr. Y's failure to warn was wrongful under the circumstances.

Case 3: Dr. Z learns that his patient and best friend, Smith, is HIV+. He fails to warn Smith's wife, who is Dr. Z's wife's best friend, though not Dr. Z's patient. Mrs. Smith contracts HIV and sues Dr. Z, arguing that he had a duty to warn her. The court holds that Dr. Z's failure to warn . . . .

Well, how did the court rule? If you were charged with deciding (prospectively) case 3, how should you rule? Alternatively, if you were charged with deciding the appeal of a decision already made with regard to case 3, how should you rule? How would you go about using the decisions reached in cases 1 and 2 to reach a decision or to justify (or not) one already made?

The answer is that you would compare and contrast the previously decided similar cases with the case under consideration.

> The primary methods of . . . analysis are analogy and distinction. Every case involving the application of a . . . rule involves two basic questions: (1) How are the decided cases similar to . . . [the case at hand?] (2) How are the decided cases different from . . . [the case at hand?][19]

In comparing and contrasting the previously decided similar cases with the case under consideration, you will consider the facts of the cases, but also the reasons/policy considerations that underlay the decisions in the earlier cases. In effect, in analysis of precedent you are trying to glean from the previously decided cases the rule or norm that should be applied in the case at hand.

So, let's try it here using the cases above.

Analysis of precedent: There are two possible outcomes in case 3—either Dr. Z owed a duty to warn, or he did not. Let's call the first outcome the duty position, and the second the no-duty position.

- **How do the decided cases support each position?**
  The verdict in case 1 supports the no-duty position in case 3 to the extent that the two cases are analogous and the duty position to the extent they are distinguishable. The verdict in case 2 supports the duty position in case 3 to the extent that the two cases are analogous and the no-duty position to the extent they are distinguishable.
- **How are cases 1 and 3 analogous?**
  In both cases the person arguing that she was owed a duty (the plaintiff) was a third party,

19 Dernbach JC, Singleton RV. *A Practical Guide to Legal Writing and Legal Method*. Littleton, Colorado: Fred B Rothman & Co.; 1981:47.

not a patient of the doctor in question. That would seem to be important since we know that, while morality requires that health professionals act in the best medical interests of their patients (i.e., *obligatory specific beneficence*), morality generally only encourages (as opposed to requiring) us to help others with whom we are not in a special relationship (*ideal general beneficence*).

- **How are cases 1 and 3 distinguishable?**
  However, case 1 is distinguishable in that the involved health professional appears not to have had actual knowledge of the plaintiff (although arguably such knowledge might be imputed to him—constructive knowledge—as something he arguably should have known), whereas in case 3 the health professional knows the plaintiff—she being both his best friend's wife and his wife's best friend.

  Another possible way of distinguishing case 3 from case 1 is to ask, "Why was case 1 decided as it was?" Asked otherwise, what was the *ratio decidendi*—the reason underlying the decision? Sometimes decision-makers tell you why they decided as they did; sometimes finding the underlying reason(s) requires reading between the lines. In case 1, the court might have decided as it did because it believed that, regarding non-patient Jane Q-Public, only (ideal) *general beneficence*, as opposed to (obligatory) *specific beneficence*, was implicated. Alternatively, the court might have believed that an obligatory duty of *general beneficence* (see Chapter 2, footnote 42) was implicated, but that one or more of the necessary conditions was lacking. Still another possibility is that the court believed that any duty to warn was trumped by the duty of confidentiality Dr. X owed his patient John Doe. Finally, the court might have decided that Dr. X owed no duty to Jane Q-Public because he wasn't aware of her existence. To the extent that a strong argument can be made that this was the court's reasoning, case 3 is distinguishable.
- **How are cases 2 and 3 analogous?**
  In both cases the plaintiff was the wife of the infectious patient. Does this matter? Maybe. It would matter if the court believes that a duty to warn exists when the third party in question is herself in a special relationship (in this case, husband-wife) with the patient with whom the physician is in a special relationship (physician-patient). Alternatively, it would matter if the court believes that any duty to warn requires that the third party be individually identifiable. I suppose a court might believe that it is fairer to expect a health professional to know that his/her patient is married than to know that the patient is involved in a non-marital sexual relationship, although admittedly patients are routinely asked about their sexual history when a medical history is taken.
- **How are cases 2 and 3 distinguishable?**
  On the other hand, case 2 is plainly and powerfully distinguishable in that the plaintiff in that case was herself a patient of the physician and so was owed a fiduciary duty directly and not derivatively.
- **Evaluate the strength of each position**
  Based on the previous considerations, one could argue that the previously decided similar cases more strongly support the no-duty position in case 3. It's relatively easy to distill a rule/norm from those cases to justify this decision. The rule/norm would read something to the effect, "Physicians owe a duty of warning regarding HIV infection only to their own patients." In contrast, trying to formulate a rule/norm to justify the duty position in case 3 would require a greater intellectual stretch and would result in a less intuitive norm/rule, one such as, "Physicians owe a duty of warning regarding HIV infection to the wives but not the girlfriends of their patients."

CASE 3.D

Consider the following series of cases.

Case 1: An 80-year-old male patient with end-stage COPD has become ventilator dependent and has failed numerous attempts at extubation. He asks his physician assistant (PA) and respiratory therapist (RT) to discontinue mechanical ventilation, communicating to them in writing, "I know it means I will die. While I do not want to die, nor do I want to live this way, tethered to a machine. Besides, my beloved wife, who I lost five years ago, is waiting for me in heaven." The hospital ethics committee (HEC) is consulted and opines that discontinuing mechanical ventilation under the circumstances would constitute voluntary passive euthanasia (VPE)[20] and would be morally permissible.

Case 2: An otherwise healthy 30-year-old female patient on IV antibiotics and mechanical ventilation for aspiration pneumonia following a failed suicide attempt by opioid overdose on the heels of a divorce requests that her PA discontinue mechanical ventilation and IV antibiotics. The HEC is consulted and opines that to discontinue medical treatment under the circumstances would be to facilitate the completion of the patient's suicide attempt and would be impermissible.

Case 3: A 55-year-old male patient suffers high cervical spinal cord injury (SCI) after a motor vehicle accident (MVA) in which his wife was killed. He is rendered quadriplegic and permanently ventilator dependent. One week after the MVA, he requests that he be removed from the ventilator and allowed to die. The HEC is consulted.

What should the committee recommend? Perform an analysis of precedent and explain how case 3 should be decided. Give supporting reasons.

Analysis: ______________________________

____

____

____

____

____

____

____

____

____

4. The Realm-Individual Process-Situation (RIPS) Model

Certain health professionals—physical therapists particularly—will have experience with the so-called RIPS model of ethical decision-making.[21] The RIPS model may be thought of as a way of organizing one's approach to ethical decision-making. It is not so much an alternative to the case analysis described previously so much as a structured way of thinking comprehensively about a particular case.

Under the RIPS model, four steps are involved. Step 1 involves recognizing and defining the ethical issues, and it is this step that gives the model its name. In step 1, one ascribes the issue or issues involved into one or more of the following ethical realms (R): *individual*, *organizational/institutional*, or *societal*. Next, the decision-maker asks about what the ethical situation demands of him/her—the so-called individual process (IP) inquiry. Possible responses at this point include that I recognize the ethical situation (*moral sensitivity*); that I make a decision about right or wrong (*moral judgment*); that I put moral values above other values (*moral motivation*); or that I implement my decision (*moral courage*). Finally, one classifies

20 Voluntary passive euthanasia (VPE) refers to the withdrawal or withholding of life-sustaining treatment (LST) in accordance with the wishes of a competent patient or duly appointed surrogate. See chapter.

21 Swisher L, Arslanian L, Davis C. The Realm-Individual Process-Situation (RIPS) model of ethical decision making. *HPA Resour.* 2005;5(3):1, 3–8.

the ethical situation as an *ethical issue/problem*,[22] a *dilemma*,[23] *distress*,[24] *temptation*,[25] or *silence*.[26]

Step 2 involves "reflecting upon and interpreting the information gathered in step one," as well as considering the following questions:

- Who are the major stakeholders?
- What are the possible consequences (intended and unintended)?
- What are the relevant laws, duties, obligations, and ethical principles?
- What professional resources (Code of Ethics, Guide for Professional Conduct, Core Values) speak to this situation?
- Are any of the five tests for right versus wrong situation positive?[27]

The "five tests for right versus wrong" serve as a sort of common sense check to decrease the likelihood that one will in effect "miss the forest for the trees." Those tests include the following:

- Legal test—Is something illegal? (Be aware of your Practice Act and the Rules and Regulations that interpret the Act). If so, it is probably not a true dilemma but a "hard choice."
- Stench test—Does it "feel" wrong? Such as a "gut" reaction?
- Front-page test—How would you like this on the front-page of your local newspaper?
- Mom test—If I were my mother (or parent/guardian), would I do this?[28]

The fifth test was already mentioned previously and consists of asking whether the act in question runs afoul of some professional norm.

In step 3, one decides what to do. Where the right course of action is clear (i.e., a so-called case of "right versus wrong"), this step may require little analysis. Where the correct or best course of action is not immediately apparent, deciding what to do will generally involve applying some ethical norm (theory, principle, or rule) to the situation.

Step 4 involves implementation of one's decision, followed by evaluation of the outcomes of that implementation and reassessment in light of those outcomes.

Students are encouraged to revisit the cases discussed in the text so far and to try their hands at employing the RIPS decision-making model.

---

22 "Important values are present or may be challenged." See Swisher L, Arslanian L, Davis C. The Realm-Individual Process-Situation (RIPS) model of ethical decision making. *HPA Resour.* 2005;5(3):1, 3–8, at p. 5.

23 "Two alternative courses of action may be taken, both of which fulfill an important duty, and it is not possible to fulfill both obligations." See Swisher L, Arslanian L, Davis C. The Realm-Individual Process-Situation (RIPS) model of ethical decision making. *HPA Resour.* 2005;5(3):1, 3–8, at p. 5.

24 "You know the right course of action but are not authorized or empowered to perform it. Note that ethical distress may present as a later 'complication' of any of the ethical situations. Ethical distress is often identified during the implementation phase of decision-making." See Swisher L, Arslanian L, Davis C. The Realm-Individual Process-Situation (RIPS) model of ethical decision making. *HPA Resour.* 2005;5(3):1, 3–8, at p. 5.

25 "Involves a choice between a 'right' and a 'wrong,' and in which you may stand to benefit from doing the wrong thing." See Swisher L, Arslanian L, Davis C. The Realm-Individual Process-Situation (RIPS) model of ethical decision making. *HPA Resour.* 2005;5(3):1, 3–8, at p. 5.

26 "Ethical values are challenged, but no one is speaking about this challenge to values. This may actually be the course taken by an individual who is experiencing moral distress." See Swisher L, Arslanian L, Davis C. The Realm-Individual Process-Situation (RIPS) model of ethical decision making. *HPA Resour.* 2005;5(3):1, 3–8, at p. 5.

27 Swisher L, Arslanian L, Davis C. The Realm-Individual Process-Situation (RIPS) model of ethical decision making. *HPA Resour.* 2005;5(3):1, 3–8, at p. 5.

28 Swisher L, Arslanian L, Davis C. The Realm-Individual Process-Situation (RIPS) model of ethical decision making. *HPA Resour.* 2005;5(3):1, 3–8, at p. 5.

5. What About Narrative?

Recent years have seen the emergence of a field called *narrative medicine*,[29] with *narrative ethics*[30,31] as a subdivision of sorts. Narrative ethics emphasizes the role of story or narrative in ethics and bears certain similarities to virtue (see Chapter 1). While a discussion of narrative ethics is beyond the scope of this chapter, the following points are worth making here.

First, remember that when it comes time to gather the facts about a particular case as the first step in analyzing the ethics of a situation, there is no substitute—in terms of detail, nuance, concerns, and accuracy—for the accounts of the primary stakeholders.

Second, stories are capable of teaching lessons in a very powerful way. They illustrate ethical theories, principles, and rules in action, as applied to real-life situations far from the ivory tower. Consider that it is largely through stories that we teach our children moral lessons.[32]

Third, stories elicit the emotional aspects of cases. Consider the following:

> One limitation of the RIPS model is that [while] it offers a rational, linear approach to resolving an ethical problem . . . many elements of ethical situations are not solely rational. For example, there are emotional and relational elements of ethical situations that are not easily factored into decision-making frameworks. . . . Moreover, some would argue that ethics is always, in some way, a "narrative" process. Ethical situations are by their very nature about someone's story, and some would argue that the very details that are most critical to the story are easily lost in decision-making frameworks such as the RIPS model.[33]

WRAP-UP

Chapter Summary

In clinical medicine, *individual moral judgments* are generally made in *cases*. In reaching an individual moral judgment concerning the facts of a single case (so-called case analysis), one employs the I-R-A-C mnemonic—identify the Issue(s); identify the appropriate Rule(s)/norm(s); Apply the rule(s) to the facts of the case; and draw a Conclusion. Individual moral judgments constitute precedent of sorts, where precedent refers to an earlier case or cases close in facts or moral principles to a case under consideration. The doctrine of stare decisis holds that decision-makers should adhere to their own precedent. When faced with a case that is similar to previously decided cases, one should analyze those previously decided similar cases (analysis of precedent) employing the methods of analogy and distinction.

29 Charon R. *Narrative Medicine: Honoring the Stories of Illness*. Oxford University Press; 2006.

30 Narrative ethics: The role of stories in bioethics. https://www.thehastingscenter.org/publications-resources/special-reports-2/narrative-ethics-the-role-of-stories-in-bioethics/. Accessed June 2, 2021.

31 Lagay F. The ethical force of stories: narrative ethics and beyond. *AMA Journal of Ethics*; August 2014. https://journalofethics.ama-assn.org/article/ethical-force-stories-narrative-ethics-and-beyond/2014-08. Accessed June 2, 2021.

32 See, e.g., Bennett WJ. *The Book of Virtues*. Simon & Schuster; 1993. See also Bennett WJ. *The Moral Compass*. Simon & Schuster; 1995.

33 Swisher L, Arslanian L, Davis C. The Realm-Individual Process-Situation (RIPS) model of ethical decision making. *HPA Resour.* 2005;5(3):1, 3–8, at p. 7.

Review Questions

1. Under what circumstances are *individual moral judgments* made?
2. What is a *case*?
3. List the four steps involved in analyzing an individual case.
4. Regarding the I-R-A-C mnemonic, list some sources of rules/norms.
5. Define *precedent* and explain why it matters.
6. Define *stare decisis*. Is the doctrine absolute?
7. What is meant by *analysis of precedent*, and by what methods is it achieved?

Case Analyses

Case 3.A Analysis

One could point to a number of issues here, including whether the moral rules prohibit abortion (either as a violation of the rule prohibiting killing, or of the rule prohibiting the causing of pain/suffering) or whether abortion is a violation of the internal morality of medicine (see Chapter 2); however, we were prompted to spot the issues raised by the bill, which "would ban abortion for women seeking to end their pregnancies because of the gender, race or disability of the fetus." What should attract your attention here is the fact that the freedom/liberty of future pregnant women is arguably being limited, but only under certain circumstances. Recalling the substance of morality discussed in Chapter 1, the ban would seem to implicate the rule "do not deprive of freedom," since it would prohibit abortions that were allowed before the ban. The fact that the new prohibition would apply only to women seeking abortion "because of the gender, race or disability of the fetus" should lead you to the *principle of justice*, which requires that we treat equals equally and unequals unequally but in proportion to their relevant inequalities. So there are two ethical issues. The first is, does the ban violate the rule "do not deprive of freedom"? (An alternative formulation of the same issue would be, does the ban violate the principle of respect for autonomy?) The second issue is, does the ban violate the principle of justice?

Case 3.B Analysis

You will recall we decided that there were two ethical issues:

- Does the ban violate the rule "do not deprive of freedom" (or the principle of respect for autonomy)?
- Does the ban violate the principle of justice?

These issues are related; if the ban does not violate the principle of justice, then any deprivation of freedom that it brings about is justifiable.[34] So let's focus on the second issue. Does the ban violate the justice principle? Recall that the *principle of formal justice* requires that we treat equals equally and unequals unequally but in proportion to their *relevant* inequalities; therefore, the ban is unjust unless women who seek abortion "because of the gender, race or disability of the fetus" can be said to be the "unequals" of women who seek abortion for any other motive, or indeed for no expressed motive at all. Stated otherwise, the ban is unjust unless a gender, race or disability-based motive is somehow relevant to the *legal* permissibility of the abortion. Is it? You might recall from Chapter 1 that

34 Consider that my freedom does NOT include the right to kill my neighbor; that would violate the moral rule, "Do not kill." Likewise, one of the other moral rules is "Do not break the law." If the law is not immoral, then my freedom CANNOT include the right to break it.

the relationship between intentions/motives and *moral* permissibility was discussed in the context of the rule of the double effect (RDE). You might also recall (see *Washington v. Glucksberg* and *Quill v. Vacco*) that the law distinguishes between the administration of a large, foreseeably fatal, dose of opiates intended to relieve the pain of a suffering, terminally ill patient (legally permissible) and the administration of a large, foreseeably fatal, dose of opiates intended to hasten the death of a suffering, terminally ill patient (legally impermissible).[35] Under these cases (here comes the rule!), having legally improper motives for acting—motives that violate a legitimate state interest[36]—may render legally impermissible an action that would otherwise have been legally permissible.

Case 3.C Analysis

Here we apply our chosen rule/norm to the facts of the case and draw a conclusion.

Does the ban violate the principle of justice? Arguably not. As we saw in *Washington v. Glucksberg* and *Quill v. Vacco*, state laws upheld by the U.S. Supreme Court distinguish between death-producing acts done with the intent of relieving suffering (legally permissible) and death-producing acts done with the intent of hastening death (legally impermissible).[37] Therefore, having legally improper motives for acting—motives that violate a legitimate state interest—may render legally impermissible an action that would otherwise have been legally permissible.

In the case of the ban at issue, while abortion in itself is legally permissible, abortions motivated by the "gender, race or disability of the fetus" arguably violate governmental interests in civil rights as expressed, for example, in state[38] and federal[39] civil rights laws.[40] (These interests, in contrast, are not implicated in abortions done for other motives, or for no expressed motive at all.) Because gender, race or disability-based motives violate a legitimate governmental interest in civil rights, they are legally improper. Since abortions done "because of the gender, race or disability of the fetus" violate governmental civil rights interests, legal prohibitions of such abortions are arguably not unjust.

Because the abortion topic is so contentious, and in order to demonstrate that reasonable

---

35 For example, others have written that regarding "racism as a basis for action . . . [it] makes sense . . . for law . . . to say that it is impermissible to make decisions over a wide range of matters that are normally open to the public—going into stores, buying houses, applying for jobs—on the basis of race." See, PEA Soup. Intentions and permissibility. April 26, 2012. https://peasoup.typepad.com/peasoup/2012/04/intentions-and-permissibility.html. Accessed July 31, 2019.

36 In the case of laws prohibiting physician assisted suicide, the state has interests in preservation of life, prevention of suicide, and maintaining the ethical integrity of the medical profession.

37 There are other lines of cases supporting the proposition that having improper motives for acting (or not acting) may render legally impermissible something that might otherwise have been permissible. For example, "While physicians or hospitals may, for most patients, refuse to treat for 'good' reasons (such as inability to pay) or even for no particular reason, they may not deny care for the wrong reasons. For example, the federal civil rights acts make it unlawful . . . to discriminate on the basis of a patient's race, sex, religion, disability, or other enumerated characteristics." See: Hall MA, Bobinski MA, Orentlicher D. The treatment relationship: formation and termination. In: *Health Care Law and Ethics*. 6th ed.; 2003:128.

38 https://statelaws.findlaw.com/civil-rights-laws.html.

39 https://civilrights.findlaw.com/enforcing-your-civil-rights/civil-rights-laws.html.

40 In enacting the Florida Civil Rights Act of 1992, the Florida legislature wrote, "The general purposes of the Florida Civil Rights Act of 1992 are to secure for all individuals within the state freedom from discrimination because of race, color, religion, sex, pregnancy, national origin, age, handicap, or marital status and thereby to protect their interest in personal dignity, to make available to the state their full productive capacities, to secure the state against domestic strife and unrest, to preserve the public safety, health, and general welfare, and to promote the interests, rights, and privileges of individuals within the state." Florida Statutes, Title XLIV, Chapter 760.01 (2). http://www.leg.state.fl.us/statutes/index.cfm?App_mode=Display_Statute&URL=0700-0799/0760/Sections/0760.01.html. Accessed July 31, 2019.

persons can reasonably disagree on some (not all) moral questions, allow me to offer an argument in support of the position that the legal prohibition of abortion motivated by "gender, race or disability of the fetus" is arguably unjust. The argument would go as follows. According to the U.S. Supreme Court, prior to the point of viability the fetus is not a legal person. Therefore, an abortion, even if motivated by the "gender, race or disability" of the fetus does not violate the legitimate governmental interest in civil rights and so cannot rightly be prohibited.

Case 3.D Analysis

Two recommendations are possible in case 3—withdraw mechanical ventilation in accordance with the patient's wishes or continue mechanical ventilation. Case 1 supports the withdrawal decision in case 3 to the extent the two cases are analogous; case 2 supports the decision to continue treatment in case 3 to the extent the two cases are analogous.

Cases 1 and 3 are analogous in that both involve patients who are permanently ventilator dependent, and in neither case is the ventilator dependence the result of a suicidal act. They are distinguishable, however, in several ways. First and perhaps most importantly, the patient in case 3 is in the acute stage of spinal cord injury (SCI) and is in the throes of dealing with this and with the recent loss of his wife. This should raise concerns as to whether the patient's request to discontinue mechanical ventilation is truly autonomous, or whether it is the product of grief/shock. Second, the facts of case 3 raise concerns about whether the intended goal of the SCI patient is to end his own life (by means of withdrawing mechanical ventilation), as opposed to the situation in case 1, where the patient's stated goal was to be free of the ventilator, with death as an unwanted but foreseen consequence (remember the RDE). Third, the patient in case 3 is 25 years younger, though his life expectancy might not differ significantly from that of patient 1.[41]

Cases 2 and 3 are analogous in that both involve younger patients, as opposed to the prototypical end-of-life scenario described in case 1. Further, the facts of case 3 raise concerns that the patient, like the patient in case 2, intends to hasten his own death, as we discussed previously.

Based on these considerations, one could argue that the previously decided similar cases more strongly support the decision not to withdraw mechanical ventilation at this time.

41 Spinal cord injury patients face many serious health problems besides paralysis. https://www.sciencedaily.com/releases/2017/02/170216103931.htm. Accessed April 26, 2019.

CHAPTER 4

U.S. Law

LEARNING OBJECTIVES

1. Compare and contrast *federalist*, *unitary*, and *confederalist* forms of government.
2. List the branches of government, and explain the powers of each.
3. Explain *federal question jurisdiction* and *diversity jurisdiction*.
4. Explain what *judicial review* means in the United States.
5. Recognize and be able to apply the *rational basis* and *strict scrutiny* standards of *substantive due process*.
6. Define *police power*, and explain who possesses it and from whence it derives.
7. Explain how healthcare providers are regulated in the United States.
8. Explain and apply the *Supremacy Clause*.
9. Discuss the organization/hierarchy of state and federal courts.
10. Compare and contrast *common law* and *civil law*.
11. Define *justiciability* and explain why it matters.

William Roper: *So, now you give the Devil the benefit of law!*

Sir Thomas More: *Yes! What would you do? Cut a great road through the law to get after the Devil?*

William Roper: *Yes, I'd cut down every law in England to do that!*

Sir Thomas More: *Oh? And when the last law was down, and the Devil turned 'round on you, where would you hide, Roper, the laws all being flat? This country is planted thick with laws, from coast to coast, Man's laws, not God's! And if you cut them down, and you're just the man to do it, do you really think you could stand upright in the winds that would blow then? Yes, I'd give the Devil benefit of law, for my own safety's sake!*[1]

1 Bolt, Robert, A Man for all Seasons, © 1960. Reprinted by permission of Pearson Education Limited.

© Agsandrew/Shutterstock

1. The U.S. System of Government

The U.S. Constitution established an American system of government that is a *federalist* system, in which governmental power is divided and shared between the states and the central ("national" or "federal") government. Alternatives to federalism include *unitary* systems, "in which the central government holds most or all of the governing power" (think Great Britain at the time of the American Revolution, or the modern-day communist state on mainland China[2]), and *confederal* political systems "with a weak or loose organization of states, under which the central government is granted limited authority by the constituent states"[3] (think the United States under the Articles of Confederation, the Confederate States of America during the American Civil War, and the modern-day European Union). "Thus, federalism created a structure in which the national government could work on behalf of the country as a whole but the states remained free to exercise choices suitable to each state."[4]

1.1. The Federal Government

As we all know, the federal government comprises three branches: the legislative branch (Congress), the executive branch (including the president of the United States and the executive agencies), and the judicial branch (including the U.S. Supreme Court and lower federal courts).

Under the U.S. Constitution, the powers of the federal government are limited to those specifically enumerated in the Constitution.

1.1.1. The Legislative Branch

The legislative powers of the federal government are vested in Congress, which consists of the Senate and the House of Representatives. The powers of Congress are enumerated in Article I, Section 8 of the Constitution, and include, for example, the power to tax and spend "for the general welfare of the United States,"[5] and the power to regulate interstate commerce. Congress exercises its enumerated legislative powers by enacting laws or *statutes* "necessary and proper for carrying into Execution" those powers.[6]

It should be mentioned here that Congress has delegated some of its legislative power to the executive branch. We shall discuss this next.

1.1.2. The Executive Branch

The executive powers of the federal government are vested in the president, and his powers are enumerated in Sections 2 and 3 of Article II.

Additionally, the executive branch includes the members of the president's cabinet and the *federal executive departments* that they head.[7] The executive branch also includes *independent agencies* that are not represented in the cabinet, including the Social Security Administration and the U.S. Postal Service.

As we mentioned previously, Congress has delegated some of its power to the federal executive

---

2 China's Legislative System. http://english.www.gov.cn/archive/china_abc/2014/08/23/content_281474982987230.htm. Accessed January 18, 2021.

3 Federalism in the United States. https://www.coursehero.com/sg/american-government/federalism-and-its-alternatives/. Accessed January 18, 2021.

4 Federalism in the United States. https://www.coursehero.com/sg/american-government/federalism-and-its-alternatives/. Accessed January 18, 2021.

5 The Constitution of the United States: A Transcription. https://www.archives.gov/founding-docs/constitution-transcript. Accessed January 21, 2021.

6 The Constitution of the United States: A Transcription. https://www.archives.gov/founding-docs/constitution-transcript. Accessed January 18, 2021.

7 These are the Departments of Agriculture; Commerce; Defense; Education; Energy; Health and Human Services; Homeland Security; Housing and Urban Development; Justice; Labor; State; Interior; Treasury; Transportation; and Veterans Affairs. See, Branches of the U.S. Government. https://www.usa.gov/branches-of-government. Accessed January 21, 2021.

departments or to independent agencies. Why? The reason is that "in our increasingly complex society, replete with ever changing and more technical problems, Congress simply cannot do its job absent an ability to delegate power under broad general directives."[8] Major federal government regulatory agencies relevant to health professionals include the Food and Drug Administration (FDA, part of the Department of Health and Human Services) and the Occupational Safety and Health Administration (OSHA, part of the Department of Labor).[9]

> The administrative law takes a number of forms—rules, regulations, procedures, orders, and decisions. Administrative agencies act both *quasi-judicially* and *quasi-legislatively*. The administrative agencies act like a legislature when developing or promulgating rules and regulations. They act like a court when conducting hearings and issuing rulings and decisions.
>
> Federal agencies, when issuing rules, have to follow the steps laid out in the Administrative Procedure Act of 1946. The Administrative Procedure Act was passed in order to ensure public participation in the rulemaking process, and also to ensure that agencies followed a consistent set of procedures for issuing rules. Proposed rules and final rules are initially published in the Federal Register; after the publication of the final rule, the rules that are currently in force are organized by subject and published annually in the Code of Federal Regulations.[10]

1.1.3. The Judicial Branch

The judicial powers of the federal government are vested in the U.S. Supreme Court, and in lower federal courts, and are spelled out in Article III, Section 2.

The Constitution gives federal courts the power to decide "cases." As such, federal courts do not have the power to give advisory opinions, or nonbinding interpretations of the law. Furthermore, for a federal court to decide a case—stated otherwise, to have jurisdiction over the subject matter of a case—that case must involve some federal question (an issue implicating the U.S. Constitution, a federal statute, or federal rule/regulation—so-called *federal question jurisdiction*) or must involve parties that are citizens of different states (*diversity jurisdiction*).

The concept of *judicial review* is worth discussing here. Judicial review refers to:

> One court's review of another court's proceedings and judgments . . . typically, a higher court review of a lower court. . . . [It can also refer to] a review of an administrative body's factual or legal findings. The reviewing court can . . . uphold or reverse any order reviewed.[11]

In the United States, since the landmark case of *Marbury v. Madison*,[12] the power of judicial review has also included the power to decide the constitutionality of laws, including acts of Congress. All laws declared unconstitutional by the U.S. Supreme Court are null and void barring a constitutional amendment. This is different from the situation in England, for example, where the law does not permit judicial review of laws passed by Parliament.

8 *Mistretta v. United States,* 488 U.S. 361, 372 (1989). See also *Sunshine Anthracite Coal Co. v. Adkins,* 310 U.S. 381, 398 (1940) ("Delegation by Congress has long been recognized as necessary in order that the exertion of legislative power does not become a futility").

9 Federal Administrative Law: A Brief Overview. https://www.llsdc.org/federal-administrative-law-a-brief-overview. Accessed January 21, 2021.

10 How Laws Are Made: The Administrative Agencies. https://libguides.law.uga.edu/c.php?g=667086&p=4692072#:~:text=Agencies%20only%20have%20the%20authority,%2Djudicially%20and%20quasi%2Dlegislatively. Accessed January 21, 2021.

11 What Is Judicial Review? https://thelawdictionary.org/judicial-review/. Accessed January 21, 2021.

12 *Marbury v. Madison,* 5 U.S. 137 (1803)

CASE 4.A

Consider the following:

Facts of the case

In 1970, Jane Roe (a fictional name used in court documents to protect the plaintiff's identity) filed a lawsuit against Henry Wade, the district attorney of Dallas County, Texas, where she resided, challenging a Texas law making abortion illegal except by a doctor's orders to save a woman's life. In her lawsuit, Roe alleged that the state laws were unconstitutionally vague and abridged her right of personal privacy, protected by the First, Fourth, Fifth, Ninth, and Fourteenth Amendments.[13]

This case was decided by the U.S Supreme Court in favor of the plaintiff Roe. (1) Was this question properly before a federal court? In other words, did the Court have subject matter jurisdiction?

Analysis: ______________________________

____

____

____

____

____

____

____

____

____

The Court decided 7-2 that:

The Due Process Clause of the Fourteenth Amendment protects against state action the right to privacy, and a woman's right to choose to have an abortion falls within that right to privacy. A state law that broadly prohibits abortion without respect to the stage of pregnancy or other interests violates that right. Although the state has legitimate interests in protecting the health of pregnant women and the "potentiality of human life," the relative weight of each of these interests varies over the course of pregnancy, and the law must account for this variability.

In the first trimester of pregnancy, the state may not regulate the abortion decision; only the pregnant woman and her attending physician can make that decision. In the second trimester, the state may impose regulations on abortion that are reasonably related to maternal health. In the third trimester, once the fetus reaches the point of "viability," a state may regulate abortions or prohibit them entirely, so long as the laws contain exceptions for cases when abortion is necessary to save the life or health of the mother.[14]

(2) What was the effect of the Court's decision as it relates to the Texas statute?

Analysis: ______________________________

____

____

____

____

____

____

____

____

____

13 Oyez: *Roe v. Wade*. https://www.oyez.org/cases/1971/70-18. Accessed January 21, 2021.

14 Oyez: *Roe v. Wade*. https://www.oyez.org/cases/1971/70-18. Accessed January 21, 2021. Roe was overruled in June 2022 by *Dobbs v. Jackson Women's Health Organization*, available at https://www.supremecourt.gov/opinions/21pdf/19-1392_6j37.pdf, but that that does not change the relevance of Roe to the discussion in this chapter.

One important check on legislative power is the Due Process Clause.[15] Besides requiring that government employ a fair procedure before depriving persons of life, liberty, or property ("procedural due process"), it has also been interpreted as having a substantive component—that is to say, certain laws depriving persons of life, liberty, or property are beyond governmental authority no matter how fair the procedure employed in their enactment.

> In deciding whether a certain . . . law violates the Due Process Clause substantively, the Court first determines whether the liberty of which the person is being deprived is fundamental. If so, then the . . . law causing that deprivation will be struck down as unconstitutional unless the [government] can demonstrate that the law achieves a compelling government purpose (the "strict scrutiny" standard). If instead the Court determines that the liberty is not fundamental, the . . . law will be upheld unless the person whose liberty is being infringed can prove that the . . . law is not rationally related to any conceivable legitimate government purpose (the "rational basis" standard).[16]

So, for example, in *Roe v. Wade* discussed in Case 4.A, The U.S. Supreme Court decided that the liberty of which plaintiff Roe was being deprived was fundamental. As a result, the Court strictly scrutinized and struck down as unconstitutional the Texas statute in question.

1.2. The State Governments

Like the federal government, the state governments are divided into three branches—legislative (the state legislatures), executive (including the governors and state executive agencies), and judicial (the state court system).

Unlike the federal government, the state governments enjoy broad *police powers*: the inherent right of a government (here a state) to protect its territory and its population from threats to the public health, safety, morals, and general welfare.[17] That police power devolved upon the American states upon their adoption of the Declaration of Independence in 1776, and the police power of the states is expressly provided for in the Constitution by Amendment X, which provides, "The powers not delegated to the United States by the Constitution, nor prohibited by it to the States, are reserved to the States respectively, or to the people."[18]

CASE 4.B

Does the Constitution give either the president or the Congress of the United States the power to implement a blanket—"wear a mask at all times in public"—nationwide mask mandate in response to the COVID-19 pandemic?[19] (See Articles I and II of the U.S. Constitution.)

Analysis: ______________________________

____

____

15 The Due Process Clause of the Fifth Amendment restricts the power of the federal government. The Due Process Clause of the Fourteenth Amendment restricts the powers of the states.

16 Paola FA. How dead is the federal constitutional right to assisted suicide? *Am J Med.* 1998;104:565–568.

17 The police power. https://biotech.law.lsu.edu/map/ThePolicePower.html. Accessed January 20, 2021.

18 Constitute. https://www.constituteproject.org/constitution/United_States_of_America_1992. Accessed January 20, 2021.

19 Could the President or Congress Enact a Nationwide Mask Mandate? https://crsreports.congress.gov/product/pdf/LSB/LSB10530. Accessed January 21, 2021.

1.2.1. Professional Regulation

The regulation of the practice of the health professions falls largely to the states under their police power. I shall use the state of Florida as an example.

In Florida, the health professions are regulated by the Medical Quality Assurance (MQA) Division[20] of the Florida Department of Health (FDOH), an executive branch state agency led by the Florida Surgeon General.[21] Specifically, MQA's Bureau of Health Care Practitioner Regulation "regulates over 40 healthcare professions through coordination with 22 boards and six councils."[22] Some of these boards/councils include the advisory council of medical physicists; the board of athletic training; the board of clinical laboratory personnel; the board of medicine (responsible for regulating physician assistants as well as physicians); the board of occupational therapy practice; the board of physical therapy practice; the board of respiratory care; the bureau of emergency medical services; and speech-language pathology and audiology.[23]

> State governments regulate the vast majority of the health professions. This regulation is accomplished through *health profession practice acts*, which recognize and enforce a health profession's scope of practice. The recognition and enforcement of the scope of practice of a health profession establishes and maintains boundaries that practitioners in other health professions may not cross. A state practice act enables a health profession to defend its state-recognized area of expertise from takeover by other health care practitioners. Such regulation is necessary and proper due to overlapping scopes of practice, which include services and treatment.[24] (italics added)

1.2.2. Health Profession Practice Acts

The states differ in their approaches to the regulation of the health professions.

> Many states have enacted separate practice acts for health care professions such as athletic trainers (AT), chiropractic (CHIRO), occupational therapy (OT), and physical therapy (PT). . . . In other states, a health care profession may not have its own practice act, but the profession is regulated through another statute,

20 Florida Department of Health Statement of Agency Organization and Operation. http://www.floridahealth.gov/about/_documents1/doh-statement-of-agency-organization.pdf. Accessed January 21, 2021.

21 Florida Health: About Us. http://www.floridahealth.gov/about/index.html. Accessed January 21, 2021.

22 Florida Department of Health Statement of Agency Organization and Operation. http://www.floridahealth.gov/about/_documents1/doh-statement-of-agency-organization.pdf at p. 6. Accessed January 21, 2021.

23 Department of Health Discipline and Administrative Actions. https://mqa-internet.doh.state.fl.us/MQASearchServices/EnforcementActionsPractitioner. Accessed January 21, 2021.

24 Hilliard JW, Johnson ME. State practice acts of licensed health professions: scope of practice. *DePaul Journal of Health Care Law*. 2004; 8(237). https://advance-lexis-com.ezproxylocal.library.nova.edu/api/document?collection=analytical-materials&id=urn:contentItem:4GJM-66R0-00CV-J0B0-00000-00&context=1516831.

usually the state's medical practice act. In Illinois, for example, while AT, OT, and PT each has its own practice act, CHIRO is subsumed and regulated by the state's medical practice act.[25]

In Florida, the professions are regulated in Title XXXII of the Florida Statutes as illustrated in **Table 4.1.**[26]

In Chapter 8, we shall have more to say about the regulation by Florida of selected health

Table 4.1 **Regulation of the Health Professions in Florida**

TITLE XXXII	REGULATION OF PROFESSIONS AND OCCUPATIONS (Ch.454-493)
Chapter 456	HEALTH PROFESSIONS AND OCCUPATIONS: GENERAL PROVISIONS
Chapter 457	ACUPUNCTURE
Chapter 458	MEDICAL PRACTICE
Chapter 459	OSTEOPATHIC MEDICINE
Chapter 460	CHIROPRACTIC MEDICINE
Chapter 461	PODIATRIC MEDICINE
Chapter 462	NATUROPATHY
Chapter 463	OPTOMETRY
Chapter 464	NURSING
Chapter 465	PHARMACY
Chapter 466	DENTISTRY, DENTAL HYGIENE, AND DENTAL LABORATORIES
Chapter 467	MIDWIFERY
Chapter 468	MISCELLANEOUS PROFESSIONS AND OCCUPATIONS
Part I:	SPEECH-LANGUAGE PATHOLOGY AND AUDIOLOGY (ss. 468.1105-468.1315)
Part II:	NURSING HOME ADMINISTRATION (ss. 468.1635-468.1756)
Part III:	OCCUPATIONAL THERAPY (ss. 468.201-468.225)
Part IV:	RADIOLOGICAL PERSONNEL CERTIFICATION (ss. 468.3001-468.315)
Part V:	RESPIRATORY THERAPY (ss. 468.35-468.369)
Part X:	DIETETICS AND NUTRITION PRACTICE (ss. 468.501-468.518)
Part XIII:	ATHLETIC TRAINERS (ss. 468.70-468.723)
Part XIV:	ORTHOTICS, PROSTHETICS, AND PEDORTHICS (ss. 468.80-468.813)
Chapter 474	VETERINARY MEDICAL PRACTICE

(continues)

25 Hilliard JW, Johnson ME. State practice acts of licensed health professions: scope of practice. *DePaul Journal of Health Care Law.* 2004;8(237):248. https://advance-lexis-com.ezproxylocal.library.nova.edu/api/document?collection=analytical-materials&id=urn:contentItem:4GJM-66R0-00CV-J0B0-00000-00&context=1516831.

26 The 2020 Florida Statutes. http://www.leg.state.fl.us/Statutes/index.cfm?App_mode=Display_Index&Title_Request=XXXII#TitleXXXII. Accessed January 24, 2021.

Table 4.1 Regulation of the Health Professions in Florida *(continued)*

Chapter 480	MASSAGE PRACTICE
Chapter 483	HEALTH TESTING SERVICES
Part I:	CLINICAL LABORATORY PERSONNEL (ss. 483.800-483.828)
Part II:	MEDICAL PHYSICISTS (s. 483.901)
Chapter 484	DISPENSING OF OPTICAL DEVICES AND HEARING AIDS
Part I:	PREPARING AND DISPENSING OF EYEGLASSES AND OTHER OPTICAL DEVICES (ss. 484.001-484.018)
Part II:	FITTING AND DISPENSING OF HEARING AIDS (ss. 484.0401-484.059)
Chapter 485	HYPNOSIS
Chapter 486	PHYSICAL THERAPY PRACTICE
Chapter 490	PSYCHOLOGICAL SERVICES
Chapter 491	CLINICAL, COUNSELING, AND PSYCHOTHERAPY SERVICES

The 2020 Florida Statutes. http://www.leg.state.fl.us/Statutes/index.cfm?App_mode=Display_Index&Title_Request=XXXII#TitleXXXII. Accessed January 24, 2021.

professionals. A discussion of the approaches of all 50 states is beyond the scope of this text. Students of the various allied health professions will need to become familiar with the approach of the state in which they intend to practice.

1.2.3. An Illustrative Case

Let's look in some detail at a recent case decided by the Court of Appeal of Florida, Third District. For our purposes here, this is an interesting case, involving as it does a "turf war" between groups of health professionals (physical therapists and massage therapists) and raising questions about the scope of practice and reimbursement issues.

The case arose out of auto accidents triggering personal injury protection (PIP) insurance coverage under the insureds' General Insurance Company's (GEICO) automobile insurance policies.[27]

> [The insured were referred to] Beacon Healthcare Center, Inc. (Beacon) . . . the clinic that provided the rehabilitation therapies to the GEICO insureds. During [their] initial consultations at Beacon, the treating physician (and Beacon's medical director), Dr. Michael Formisano, prescribed physical therapy using what are known as therapy "modalities," that include use of hot/cold packs, electric stimulation, ultrasound, myofascial release (manual therapy), and traction, among others. These therapies were provided to the insureds by massage therapists who held massage therapy licenses, but did not hold licenses in physical therapy. The massage therapists were not directly supervised on site by either a licensed physical therapist or by a medical physician when they performed the treatments. The massage therapists used the prescribed therapy modalities that Dr. Formisano recommended.
>
> Beacon Healthcare subsequently billed GEICO for "physical therapy"

27 *Geico Gen. Ins. Co. v. Beacon Healthcare Ctr. Inc.*, 298 So. 3d 1235, 2020 Fla. App. LEXIS 2284, 45 Fla. L. Weekly D 437, 2020 WL 912938 (Court of Appeal of Florida, Third District, February 26, 2020, Opinion Filed). https://advance-lexis-com.ezproxylocal.library.nova.edu/api/document?collection=cases&id=urn:contentItem:5Y97-YP61-JCJ5-20YW-00000-00&context=1516831.

treatments, and erroneously indicated on one part of the billing form . . . that Dr. Formisano provided the treatments, rather than the massage therapists. The billing statements also indicated that the massage therapists performed "physical therapy" under the direct supervision of Dr. Formisano. . . . GEICO had notice of these errors in the billing and denied the claims entirely, rather than the specific line item claims. GEICO then sued Beacon in federal court for submitting claims for charges for physical therapy services that were unlawfully rendered by unsupervised massage therapists . . .

While that case was pending, Beacon filed suit against GEICO for a declaratory judgment that . . . the therapy modalities were lawfully rendered as services "incidental" to the licensed practice of massage and thus the therapists did not need to be licensed as physical therapists . . . . The trial court certified two questions to [the Court of Appeal, Third District of Florida] . . . .

[1] MAY A HEALTH CARE CLINIC LICENSED UNDER PART X CHAPTER 400 RECEIVE PIP REIMBURSEMENTS FOR PHYSICAL THERAPY SERVICES ENUMERATED IN § 486.021(11) RENDERED BY A LICENSED MASSAGE THERAPIST EMPLOYED BY THE CLINIC THAT IS NOT "MASSAGE" AS DEFINED BY § 480.033(3), FLA. STAT.?

[2] MAY A PERSON WHO IS LICENSED AS A MASSAGE THERAPIST, BUT NOT LICENSED AS A PHYSICAL THERAPIST, LAWFULLY RENDER PHYSICAL THERAPY MODALITIES ENUMERATED IN § 486.021(11) WHERE SUCH THERAPY IS PART OF OR INCIDENTAL TO THE LAWFUL PRACTICE OF MASSAGE THERAPY?

Let's analyze this case in plain English. There are two practical issues at stake. First, is Beacon entitled to payment from GEICO for the services rendered by their massage therapists? Second, and perhaps more importantly (because legal sanctions might be forthcoming depending on the answer to this question), did Beacon and the health professionals involved violate the Florida Physical Therapy Practice Act's prohibition of the practice of physical therapy by anyone without a physical therapy license?

How does the court go about answering the first question? Well, it turns out that in Florida there is a law/statute that is controlling: the Florida Motor Vehicle No-Fault (or PIP) Statute.[28] The court notes, "The PIP Statute was amended, effective January 1, 2013, to exclude massage from the types of health care services that are eligible for PIP reimbursement. The statute also prohibits massage therapists from receiving PIP reimbursement."[29] So, the answer to question one regarding reimbursement is "no."[30]

What about the second question? How does the court approach the question about the lawfulness or not of the use of PT modalities by licensed massage therapists? As you might imagine, it begins by looking at the relevant health professions practice acts. Title XXXII, Chapter 486 (the Florida Physical Therapy Practice Act) includes the following provision:

28 § 627.736. Required personal injury protection benefits; exclusions; priority; claims., Fla. Stat. § 627.736 (Current through all 2020 general legislation). https://advance-lexis-com.ezproxylocal.library.nova.edu/api/document?collection=statutes-legislation&id=urn:contentItem:5YFS-91R3-CH1B-T3RT-00000-00&context=1516831.

29 *Geico Gen. Ins. Co. v. Beacon Healthcare Ctr. Inc.*, 298 So. 3d 1235, 2020 Fla. App. LEXIS 2284, 45 Fla. L. Weekly D 437, 2020 WL 912938 (Court of Appeal of Florida, Third District, February 26, 2020, Opinion Filed). https://advance-lexis-com.ezproxylocal.library.nova.edu/api/document?collection=cases&id=urn:contentItem:5Y97-YP61-JCJ5-20YW-00000-00&context=1516831.

30 GEICO is known for its ad, "Fifteen minutes could save you fifteen percent or more." See, e.g., https://geicocarinsurance.fandom.com/wiki/15_minutes_could_save_you_15_percent_or_more_on_car_insurance. Accessed January 24, 2021. It's not clear how much time GEICO spent contesting the charges or how much they saved.

> 486.028 License to practice physical therapy required.—No person shall practice, or hold herself or himself out as being able to practice, physical therapy in this state unless she or he is licensed in accordance with the provisions of this chapter; *however, nothing in this chapter shall prohibit any person licensed in this state under any other law from engaging in the practice for which she or he is licensed.*[31] (italics added)

The second, italicized portion of 486.028 is important, suggesting that there is some overlap between the practice of physical therapy and some of the other licensed health professions; and indeed in a subsequent provision of Chapter 486, this point is made more explicitly:

> § 486.161. Exemptions.
>
> (1) No provision of this chapter shall be construed to prohibit any person licensed in this state from using any physical agent as a part of, or incidental to, the lawful practice of her or his profession under the statutes applicable to the profession of chiropractic physician, podiatric physician, doctor of medicine, *massage therapist*, nurse, osteopathic physician or surgeon, occupational therapist, or naturopath.[32]

So, the answer to question two regarding whether a licensed massage therapist may lawfully render physical therapy modalities when incidental to the practice of massage therapy is "yes."

CASE 4.C

Consider the following case:

> Appellant physical therapist challenged an order of the Civil District Court for the Parish of Orleans (Louisiana),[33] which upheld a decision of the Louisiana State Board of Medical Examiners placing the physical therapist on probation for violating the Physical Therapy Practice Act, La. Rev. Stat. Ann. § 37:2401-2418, after being reprimanded for undertaking and purporting to diagnose and prescribe treatment for an injury.
>
> On January 6, 1986, Douglas Smith, a [high school] student . . . injured his right ankle at basketball practice. After putting ice on the ankle, the athletic coach, Robin Becker, brought Smith to Lavergne's office to have Lavergne look at the injury. Lavergne [a PT] volunteered his services to the local high schools to screen injuries incurred during athletic events. Lavergne examined the ankle, performed a heel strike test and concluded the ankle was not likely broken. Lavergne told Smith to keep the ice on the ankle, try to put weight on it and if pain persisted, he should see his family physician or return to Lavergne's office and Lavergne would refer him to a physician.
>
> A complaint was filed with the Louisiana State Board of Medical Examiners against Lavergne and a formal administrative hearing was held on November 18, 1986. The board ruled against Lavergne, reprimanded him for . . . "engaging in the practice of

---

31 Online Sunshine. http://www.leg.state.fl.us/Statutes/index.cfm?App_mode=Display_Statute&Search_String=&URL=0400-0499/0486/Sections/0486.028.html. Accessed January 24, 2021.

32 § 486.161. Exemptions., Fla. Stat. § 486.161 (Current through all 2020 general legislation.). https://advance-lexis-com.ezproxylocal.library.nova.edu/api/document?collection=statutes-legislation&id=urn:contentItem:5C24-MGV1-6SKW-D50M-00000-00&context=1516831.

33 The judicial branch of the government of the state of Louisiana includes the Louisiana Supreme Court (the state's highest court), five courts of appeal, and 43 district courts. https://www.louisiana.gov/government/judicial-branch/. Accessed January 28, 2021.

physical therapy in excess of the scope of physical therapy practice as defined by the Physical Therapy Practice Act of Louisiana, La. R.S. 37:2401-2418 . . . by undertaking and purporting to diagnose and prescribe appropriate treatment for an acute athletic injury" [and placed him on probation for two years].[34]

Answer the following two questions: (1) Why do you think the Louisiana State Board of Medical Examiners was involved in this case? (2) Why is this case now before in Louisiana state court?

Analysis: ______________________________

____

____

____

____

____

____

____

____

____

2. Federal-State Interactions: The Supremacy Clause

Article VI, Paragraph 2 of the U.S. Constitution is referred to as the Supremacy Clause. It reads as follows:

> This Constitution, and the Laws of the United States which shall be made in Pursuance thereof; and all Treaties made, or which shall be made, under the Authority of the United States, shall be the supreme Law of the Land; and the Judges in every State shall be bound thereby, any Thing in the Constitution or Laws of any State to the Contrary notwithstanding.

The effect of this clause is that the U.S. Constitution and federal laws (statutes, rules/regulations, etc.) take legal precedence over state laws and state constitutions.

3. The American Legal System

3.1. Federalism and Hierarchy

The American legal system, like American government, reflects the principle of federalism or decentralization, with dual court systems—federal and state.

The federal courts are organized into three levels: the U.S. District Courts, of which there are 94, are trial courts; the U.S. Courts of Appeals (the "Circuit" courts, of which there are 13) are appellate courts; the U.S. Supreme Court is the court of last resort.

In general, the state court systems are similarly structured.

3.2. Common Law as Distinguished from Civil Law

The American legal system is a *common law* system, as distinguished from a *civil law* system.

> The American system is a "common law" system, which relies heavily on court precedent in formal adjudications. In our common law system, even when a statute is at issue, judicial determinations in earlier court cases are extremely critical to the court's resolution of the matter before it. Civil law systems rely less

34 *Lavergne v. Louisiana State Bd. of Medical Examiners*, 539 So. 2d 656, 1989 La. App. LEXIS 110 (Court of Appeal of Louisiana, Fourth Circuit January 30, 1989, Decided). https://advance-lexis-com.ezproxylocal.library.nova.edu/api/document?collection=cases&id=urn:contentItem:3S3K-46Y0-008T-X08M-00000-00&context=1516831.

> on court precedent and more on codes, which explicitly provide rules of decision for many specific disputes. When a judge needs to go beyond the letter of a code in disposing of a dispute, the judge's resolution will not become binding or perhaps even relevant in subsequent determinations involving other parties.[35]

Besides the United States, common law systems are found throughout the Anglosphere.[36] Civil law systems predominate elsewhere, including in France and Spain. While 10 American states initially settled by France, Spain, or Mexico had civil law legal systems at the time of American acquisition, only Louisiana retained civil law, the remaining nine adopting common law.[37]

At this point the reader is referred to Chapter 3 for a discussion of common law concepts including *precedent*, *stare decisis*, analogy and distinction as they relate to case analysis, and *ratio decidendi*.

3.3. Justiciability

Justiciability refers to the types of cases that a court can decide. To say that a case is nonjusticiable is to say that the court cannot hear it. I have already mentioned that under the Constitution, federal courts may not render *advisory opinions*—"a court's nonbinding interpretation of a legal question"[38]—because they do not meet the definition of a case or controversy. Besides the prohibition against advisory opinions, four other hurdles must be overcome for a case to be justiciable: *standing*, *ripeness*, *political question*, and *mootness*.

> *Standing* addresses whether the plaintiff is the proper party to assert a claim in federal court. *Ripeness* considers whether a party has brought an action too early for adjudication. The *political question* doctrine makes nonjusticiable controversies that involve an issue constitutionally committed to the political branches of government. . . . *Mootness* may occur when a controversy initially existing at the time the lawsuit was filed is no longer "live" due to a change in the law or in the status of the parties involved, or due to an act of one of the parties that dissolves the dispute. When a federal court deems a case to be moot, the court no longer has the power to entertain the legal claims and must dismiss the complaint. [Internal footnotes omitted.][39]

The courts have recognized a number of exceptions to the mootness doctrine, two of which are discussed here.

3.3.1. Capable of Repetition Yet Evading Review

The first exception to mootness is the doctrine *capable of repetition yet evading review*. Perhaps the best-known example of this exception was in *Roe v. Wade*. Consider the following excerpt.

---

35 Basic Concepts of American Jurisprudence. https://www.lexisnexis.com/en-us/lawschool/pre-law/intro-to-american-legal-system.page#:~:text=The%20American%20system%20is%20a,court%20precedent%20in%20formal%20adjudications.&text=Civil%20law%20systems%20rely%20less,decision%20for%20many%20specific%20disputes. Accessed January 21, 2021.

36 It's Time to Revive the Anglosphere. https://www.wsj.com/articles/its-time-to-revive-the-anglosphere-11596859260. Accessed January 21, 2021.

37 Berkowitz D, Clay K. American civil law origins: implications for state constitutions. *American Law and Economics Review*. 2005;7(1):62–84. https://doi.org/10.1093/aler/ahi007.

38 Justiciability. https://www.law.cornell.edu/wex/justiciability#:~:text=Overview,that%20a%20court%20can%20adjudicate.&text=Typically%20to%20be%20justiciable%2C%20the,of%20the%20political%20question%20doctrine. Accessed January 21, 2021.

39 Mootness: An Explanation of the Justiciability Doctrine. https://www.everycrsreport.com/reports/RS22599.html. Accessed January 21, 2021.

Roe v. Wade, 410 U.S. 113 (1973)

Decided January 22, 1973

MR. JUSTICE BLACKMUN delivered the opinion of the Court.

. . . Jane Roe, a single woman who was residing in Dallas County, Texas, instituted this federal action in March 1970 against the District Attorney of the county. She sought a declaratory judgment that the Texas criminal abortion statutes were unconstitutional on their face, and an injunction restraining the defendant from enforcing the statutes. . . .

We are next confronted with issues of justiciability . . . . For purposes of her case, we accept as true, and as established, . . . her pregnant state, as of the inception of her suit in March 1970 and as late as May 21 of that year when she filed an alias affidavit with the District Court . . .

Viewing Roe's case as of the time of its filing . . . there can be little dispute that it then presented a case or controversy . . . . The appellee [District Attorney Wade] notes, however, that . . . Roe's case must now be moot because she and all other members of her class are no longer subject to any 1970 pregnancy.

The usual rule in federal cases is that an actual controversy must exist at stages of appellate or certiorari review, and not simply at the date the action is initiated. But when, as here, pregnancy is a significant fact in the litigation, the normal 266-day human gestation period is so short that the pregnancy will come to term before the usual appellate process is complete. If that termination makes a case moot, pregnancy litigation seldom will survive much beyond the trial stage, and appellate review will be effectively denied. Our law should not be that rigid. Pregnancy often comes more than once to the same woman, and in the general population, if man is to survive, it will always be with us. Pregnancy provides a classic justification for a conclusion of nonmootness. It truly could be "capable of repetition, yet evading review."

We, therefore, agree with the District Court that Jane Roe . . . presented a justiciable controversy, and that the termination of her 1970 pregnancy has not rendered her case moot . . . .[40]

3.3.2. Voluntary Cessation

A second exception to the mootness doctrine is the *voluntary cessation* exception.

> If a defendant voluntarily terminates the allegedly unlawful conduct after the lawsuit has been filed but retains the power to resume the practice at any time, a federal court may deem the case nonmoot. The "heavy burden" of persuading the court that a case has been mooted by the defendant's voluntary actions lies with the party asserting mootness, and [that party must prove that it is] . . . "absolutely clear that the allegedly wrongful behavior [can] not reasonably be expected to recur."[41]

---

40 *Roe v. Wade,* 410 U.S. 113 (1973).

41 Mootness: An Explanation of the Justiciability Doctrine. https://www.everycrsreport.com/reports/RS22599.html. Accessed January 23, 2021.

WRAP-UP

Chapter Summary

The American system of government is a *federalist* system, as opposed to *unitary* and *confederalist* systems existing elsewhere in space-time. While the powers of the U.S. Congress are limited to those enumerated in the Constitution, the state legislatures enjoy broad police power, which enables them to legislate in furtherance of public health, safety, morals and general welfare. Both the federal and the state governments are divided into three branches—the *executive*, the *legislative*, and the *judicial*, and the powers of each branch are specified in the applicable constitution. In the United States, as decided by the U.S. Supreme Court in *Marbury v. Madison*, the federal courts' power of *judicial review* includes the power to determine the constitutionality of acts of the political branches of government. The regulation of healthcare professionals falls largely to the states under their police power, exercised through *healthcare professional practice acts*.

Review Questions

1. What do the terms *federalist*, *unitary*, and *confederalist* mean as they relate to systems of government? How is power divided between the federal government and the states in the United States?
2. What are the three branches of government in the American system?
3. How does a case end up in federal, as opposed to state, court?
4. Define *judicial review*, and explain how American judicial review differs, for example, from English judicial review?
5. How does a court decide whether an act of the political branches of government is or is not unconstitutional? What tests does it apply?
6. How does *police power* relate to the regulation of the healthcare professions?
7. How does *common law* differ from *civil law*?
8. How are *justiciability* and *mootness* related to each other?

Case Analyses

Case 4.A Analysis

(1) Yes, the federal courts had subject matter jurisdiction over the case/controversy because it involved a federal question (*federal question jurisdiction*). The federal question was whether the Texas statute prohibiting all except lifesaving abortions violated a pregnant woman's constitutional rights protected by the First, Fourth, Fifth, Ninth, and Fourteenth Amendments. (2) The Court's decision that the Texas statute violated the Fourteenth Amendment means that the statute is unconstitutional and hence null and void.

Case 4.B Analysis

Regarding the president, maybe but probably not.[42] Recall that the powers of the federal government are limited to those enumerated in the Constitution, and a perusal of Article II reveals no relevant presidential power. Presidential powers also include those delegated to the executive branch by Congress.

> One such . . . [delegation] could be section 361 of the Public Health Service Act (PHSA). That provision . . . grants the Secretary of Health and Human Services—delegated in part to the CDC—the authority to make and enforce regulations necessary "to prevent the introduction, transmission, or spread of communicable diseases from foreign countries into the States or possessions, or from one State or possession into any other State or possession." [As you might have guessed, section 361 of the PHSA is grounded in Congress' Commerce Clause power.] A broad construction of this authority may permit the CDC to issue regulations mandating the use of masks in circumstances that would prevent the foreign or interstate transmission of COVID-19.

The problem is that a blanket nationwide mask mandate would by definition not be limited to circumstances threatening the foreign or interstate transmission of COVID-19, and so would probably exceed congressional authority. Regarding Congress' authority to enact a blanket national mask mandate, the answer is also maybe but probably not.[43] Congressional powers are limited to those enumerated in Article I, and those powers do include the Commerce power (the power "To regulate Commerce with foreign Nations, and among the several States, and with the Indian Tribes").[44] Under this power, Congress could theoretically act "to prevent the introduction, transmission, or spread of communicable diseases from foreign countries into the States . . . or from one State . . . into any other State . . . ."[45] But again, a blanket mandate would probably exceed congressional Commerce power.

On the other hand, the federal government does enjoy *police power* over the "District of Columbia and other areas over which Congress has exclusive authority,"[46] and this explains the executive order issued by President Joseph Biden on January 20, 2021, mandating the wearing of face masks *on federal property*.[47,48]

---

42 Subramaniam T. Fact check: Can the president enact a nationwide mask mandate? CNN Politics. Updated November 1, 2020. https://www.cnn.com/2020/11/01/politics/mask-mandate-fact-check/index.html. Accessed January 20, 2021.

43 The weight of opinion seems to be against congressional authority to mandate the use of masks on a national level. "A national mandate is not possible because public health powers belong to the states, not the federal government," said Lawrence Gostin, director of Georgetown University's O'Neill Institute for National and Global Health Law. "The federal government couldn't implement its own mask mandates, nor could it force the states to do it." (See Hauck G. Biden wants mask mandates nationwide, but he can't actually enforce them. Here's what he could do instead. USA Today, November 11, 2020. https://www.usatoday.com/story/news/nation/2020/11/11/joe-biden-national-face-mask-mandate-covid/6233249002/. Accessed January 20, 2021.)

44 Article I. Section 8.

45 Subramaniam T. Fact check: Can the president enact a nationwide mask mandate? CNN Politics. Updated November 1, 2020. https://www.cnn.com/2020/11/01/politics/mask-mandate-fact-check/index.html. Accessed January 20, 2021.

46 Justia US Law: Federal Police Power. https://law.justia.com/constitution/us/amendment-10/03-federal-police-power.html#:~:text=The%20powers%20not%20delegated%20to,respectively%2C%20or%20to%20the%20people.&text=Federal%20Police%20Power. Accessed January 20, 2021.

47 Leary A. Biden's first-day orders will include mask mandate, blocking Keystone pipeline. *Wall Street Journal*. January 20, 2021. https://www.wsj.com/articles/bidens-first-day-orders-will-include-mask-mandate-blocking-keystone-pipeline-11611136804. Accessed January 20, 2021.

48 Executive Order on Protecting the Federal Workforce and Requiring Mask-Wearing. https://www.whitehouse.gov/briefing-room/presidential-actions/2021/01/20/executive-order-protecting-the-federal-workforce-and-requiring-mask-wearing/. Accessed January 21, 2021.

Case 4.C Analysis

(1) The involvement of the Louisiana Board of Medical Examiners (LSBME) in this case must mean that at the time of the events described (1986), physical therapists (PTs) were licensed and regulated by the LSBME. In fact, it turns out that the Louisiana legislature passed the first Physical Therapy Practice Act in 1966, under which PTs were licensed and regulated by the LSBME, and it wasn't until 1987 that the Legislature created the Louisiana Physical Therapy Board (LPTB) to license and regulate PTs in Louisiana. The Physical Therapy Rules and Regulations were written by the board members and were adopted on December 20, 1987.[49] (2) The case is before a Louisiana state court because regulation of the health professions is within the police power of the Louisiana legislature. The legislature delegated this power to the Louisiana executive branch (the Department of Health and Hospitals, formerly the Department of Health and Human Resources), of which the LSBME was part. As an administrative agency, licensing boards such as the LSBME exercised both quasi-legislative (promulgation of rules and regulations) and quasi-judicial powers (deciding cases).[50] As such, the board had the statutory authority to interpret the Louisiana Physical Therapy Practice Act, under which PTs were licensed and regulated, and to sanction violators of the act. The Louisiana court system became involved because of the concept of judicial review, which includes not only a higher court's review of a lower court's proceedings and judgments, but also (as here) a court's review of an administrative agency's decisions.[51]

49 Louisiana Physical Therapy Board. History. https://www.laptboard.org/index.cfm/page/4. Accessed January 28, 2021.
50 See section 1.1.2 The Executive Branch, in this chapter.
51 See section 1.1.3 The Judicial Branch, in this chapter.

SECTION 2

The Provider-Patient Relationship

Building upon the foundation we have laid down in Chapters 1 through 4, the next three chapters of this book explore some of the ethical and legal aspects of the relationship between the health professional and the patient.

In Chapter 5, we discuss the ethical and legal aspects of the health professional's duty of *confidentiality.*

In Chapter 6, we discuss the potential threat posed to the therapeutic relationship by *conflicts of interest* (COIs) and appropriate means of addressing them.

In Chapter 7, we discuss the ethical and legal aspects of *informed consent*.

CHAPTER 5

Confidentiality

LEARNING OBJECTIVES

1. Define *confidentiality*.
2. Explain the moral basis of the *duty of confidentiality*.
3. List the types of *privacy* and explain how *privacy* relates to *confidentiality*.
4. Understand and distinguish the various policy rationales underlying the doctrine.
5. Be familiar with protections afforded to *confidentiality* by the common law and statutory law, including HIPAA.
6. Be familiar with the cases exploring the limits of confidentiality and the reasoning of the courts therein.
7. Understand the limits of *confidentiality* and be able to recognize situations in which a *duty to warn* or otherwise protect third parties might exist.

More. . . . *On the King's divorce which he'll now grant himself, the marriage he'll then make—have you heard me make a statement?*

Alice. *No—and if I'm to lose my rank and fall to housekeeping I want to know the reason; so make a statement now.*

More. *No—[Alice exhibits indignation.] Alice, it's a point of law! Accept it from me, Alice, that in silence is my safety under the law, but my silence must be absolute, it must extend to you.*

Alice. *In short you don't trust us!*

More. *A man would need to be half-witted not to trust you—but—[Impatiently.] Look—[He advances on her.] I'm the Lord Chief Justice, I'm Cromwell, I'm the King's Head Jailer—and I take your hand [He does so.] and I clamp it on the Bible, on the Blessed Cross [clamps her hand on his closed fist] and I say: "Woman, has your husband made a statement on these matters?" Now—on peril of your soul remember—what's your answer?*

Alice. *No.*

More. *And so it must remain . . . .*[1]

1 Bolt R. A man for all seasons. In: *Laurel British Drama: The Twentieth Century.* New York, NY: Dell Publishing; 1965:410.

1. Confidentiality: Its Sources

As we discussed in Chapter 1, the doctrine of confidentiality is an example of a *particular moral rule* that is derived from interplay between the general moral rules and a particular cultural institution or practice.

> In medicine, the need for the physician to obtain information from the patient, in addition to the fact that people generally do not want information about themselves to be revealed, in conjunction with the general moral not to cause pain generates the medical ethical rule "do not breach confidentiality."[2]

Breaching confidentiality therefore violates the moral rule "do not neglect your duty." Further, a health professional who has taken an oath containing a confidentiality provision violates the moral rule "do not break your promise" when he or she unjustifiably reveals a confidence. Additionally, because as we shall see next, confidentiality enjoys legal protection, unjustifiably revealing a confidence would also violate the moral rule "do not break the law."

1.1. Confidentiality and Acts of Profession

The doctrine of confidentiality in medicine dates back at least to the Hippocratic Oath, which reads in part, "What I may see or hear in the course of the treatment or even outside of the treatment in regard to the life of men, which on no account one must spread abroad, I will keep to myself . . . ."[3]

More modern statements of ethics echo the fundamentality of confidentiality. Thus, the fourth (IV.) of the *Principles of Medical Ethics* of the American Medical Association holds, "A physician shall . . . safeguard patient confidences within the constraints of the law."[4]

The *Guidelines for Ethical Conduct for the Physician Assistant Profession* of the American Academy of Physician Assistants includes a statement on confidentiality, which reads in part:

> Physician assistants should maintain confidentiality. By maintaining confidentiality, PAs respect patient privacy and help to prevent discrimination based on medical conditions. If patients are confident that their privacy is protected, they are more likely to seek medical care and more likely to discuss their problems candidly. . . . Any communication about a patient conducted in a manner that violates confidentiality is unethical. Computerized record keeping and electronic data transmission present unique challenges that can make the maintenance of patient confidentiality difficult. PAs should advocate for policies and procedures that secure the confidentiality of patient information.[5]

The *Code of Ethics for the Physical Therapist* provides, in Principle 2E, "Physical therapists shall protect confidential patient and client information and may disclose confidential information to appropriate authorities only when allowed or as required by law."[6]

---

2 Gert B, Culver CM, Danner Clouser KD. *Bioethics: A Return to Fundamentals*. New York, NY: Oxford University Press; 1997:62.

3 The Hippocratic Oath. http://en.wikipedia.org/wiki/Hippocratic_Oath. Accessed June 6, 2019.

4 Principles of medical ethics. American Medical Association. https://www.ama-assn.org/about/publications-newsletters/ama-principles-medical-ethics. Accessed June 6, 2019.

5 The guidelines for ethical conduct for the physician assistant profession. American Academy of Physician Assistants. https://www.aapa.org/wp-content/uploads/2017/02/16-EthicalConduct.pdf. Accessed June 6, 2019.

6 Code of Ethics for the Physical Therapist. https://www.apta.org/siteassets/pdfs/policies/codeofethicshods06-20-28-25.pdf. Accessed January 25, 2021.

The *American Association of Respiratory Care (AARC) Statement of Ethics and Professional Conduct* states in part, "Divulge no protected information regarding any patient or family unless disclosure is required for the responsible performance of duty as authorized by the patient and/or family, or required by law."[7]

> The *AOTA 2020 Occupational Therapy Code of Ethics* includes the following provision:
> Principle 3. Autonomy
> Occupational therapy personnel shall respect the right of the person to self-determination, privacy, confidentiality, and consent.
> The Principle of Autonomy expresses the concept that occupational therapy personnel have a duty to treat the client or service recipient according to their desires, within the bounds of accepted standards of care, and to protect their confidential information.[8]

1.2. Legal Protection of Confidentiality

As stated previously, the medical ethical rule "do not breach confidentiality" is derived from an application of the general moral rules to the practice of medicine. The promise not to disclose inappropriately is implied, whether or not the oath one took contained such an explicit promise. The duty of confidentiality is considered so important that it is afforded legal protection as well, and health professionals who breach their duty of confidentiality may face legal sanctions.

Legal protection of confidentiality includes both common law protections and statutory protections. In general, the common law "is a body of law that develops and derives through judicial decisions, as distinguished from legislative enactments." Conversely, statutory law is "that body of law created by acts of the legislature." (See Chapter 4.)

> Most states provide a private cause of action against licensed health care providers who impermissibly disclose [to third parties] confidential information obtained in the course of the treatment relationship. . . . Depending on the jurisdiction, the claim may be phrased as a breach of contract, as an act of malpractice, as a breach of fiduciary duty, as an act of fraud/misrepresentation, or as a breach of a specific civil statute permitting the award of damages. . . . In addition, licensed health care providers who breach the confidentiality of their patients run the risk of professional disciplinary action.[9]

Under the laws of many states, breach of patient confidentiality by healthcare professionals is considered unprofessional conduct and warrants disciplinary action, up to and including license revocation.

It is also important for practicing health professionals to be aware that there exist certain disease-specific state statutes imposing specific confidentiality requirements. We shall consider, as an example, the special case of HIV later. Additionally, federal law imposes confidentiality requirements on records of patients in federally funded drug and alcohol treatment programs.

---

7 AARC Statement of Ethics and Professional Conduct. https://www.aarc.org/wp-content/uploads/2017/03/statement--ethics.pdf. Accessed January 25, 2021.

8 AOTA 2020 Occupational Therapy Code of Ethics. https://www.aota.org/-/media/Corporate/Files/Practice/Ethics/AOTA-2020-Code-of-Ethics.pdf. Accessed January 25, 2021.

9 Hall MA, Bobinski MA, Orentlicher D. *Health Care Law and Ethics*. 7th ed. Austin, TX: Aspen Publishers, 2007:179.

2. Rationales Underlying the Doctrine of Confidentiality

The existence of the doctrine of confidentiality suggests that it serves a purpose or purposes. What are they?

First, knowing that their healthcare providers owe them a moral and legal duty of confidentiality encourages patients "to seek medical care when they might otherwise avoid doing so out of shame . . . ."[10] If I had an STD, I might be less likely to seek medical attention if I knew that my healthcare provider was free to share information about the state of my genitalia with the public at large. This benefits the sick, the well (who will, after all, someday be sick), and society as a whole in the form of improved public health.

A second rationale underlying the doctrine of confidentiality is that it furthers the *principle of respect for autonomy,* in this case patients' autonomy over their personal medical information.[11] Patients decide to whom (if anyone) they wish to disclose personal medical information.

Third, the sharing of secrets with select others fosters relational intimacy.[12] In the excerpt with which we opened this chapter (taken from Robert Bolt's play *A Man for All Seasons*) Thomas More's wife, Alice, is angered by his refusal to tell her his position on the divorce of King Henry VIII. Looking at this exchange now, what you should find odd is that More's character had no expectation of privacy in a situation (the marital relationship) that we Americans regard as almost quintessentially private. There was no expectation that medieval English law would protect such communications from forced disclosure on the witness stand. One can appreciate the price paid by those who live in a world without privacy and confidentiality—a price measured in the currency of lost intimacy.

3. Confidentiality and Privacy

Corresponding to the health professional's duty of confidentiality is the patient's *right of privacy*. Gert et al. have written, "An individual . . . has privacy in a situation with regard to others if and only if in that situation the individual . . . is normatively protected from *intrusion*, *interference* and *information access* by others."[13] (Italics added.) In other words, the *right of privacy* is in fact a bundle of rights that includes but is not limited to a right to control the access that others have to one's personal information. *Confidentiality* is related to this *information access* aspect of privacy.

> People hold information in confidence because the rules of a private situation require them not to reveal that situation. Confidentiality thus refers to a duty within a private situation. Some party—a doctor, nurse, or physician assistant [or other health professional]—has the . . . responsibility not to divulge information

---

10 Hall MA, Ellman IM, Strouse DS. *Health Care Law and Ethics in a Nutshell*. 2nd ed. St. Paul, MN: West Group; 1999:118.

11 Hall MA, Ellman IM, Strouse DS. *Health Care Law and Ethics in a Nutshell*. 2nd ed. St. Paul, MN: West Group; 1999:118

12 Bok S. *Secrets: On the Ethics of Concealment and Revelation*. New York, NY: Vintage Books; 1983:119–124.

13 Gert B, Culver CM, Clouser KD. *Bioethics: A Return to Fundamentals*. New York, NY: Oxford University Press; 1997:183. The *non-intrusion* aspect of privacy refers to an individual's right to be free of intrusions—by the government or by other persons—into his/her private life. WebcamGate was an example of this kind of privacy invasion. In that case, a school district in southeastern Pennsylvania issued to all 2,620 students in the district MacBooks equipped with Webcams that could be turned on remotely by school officials. (See, Webcamgate Is an Expensive Lesson in Security, Privacy. https://www.pcworld.com/article/192194/webcamgate_is_an_expensive_lesson_in_security_privacy.html. Accessed May 5, 2019.) The *non-interference* aspect of privacy refers to an individual's freedom to act in personal matters without external interference. Examples of such personal matters include decisions regarding the use of contraceptives (see, e.g., *Griswold v. Connecticut*, 381 U.S. 479 (1965).

> to inappropriate parties. Privacy is *invaded;* but confidentiality is *violated*—that is, the duty of confidentiality is violated . . . .[14] (Internal footnotes omitted.)

Confidential communications are "statement[s] made under circumstances showing that the speaker intended [the] statement[s] only for [the] ears of [the] person addressed," and examples of such communications can include "those between spouses, physician-patient, attorney-client, confessor-penitent, etc."[15] The law protects confidential communications from forced disclosure on the witness stand at the option of the witness spouse, patient, client or penitent.

CASE 5.A

Consider the following case:

> Sharp Grossmont Hospital installed cameras in the three operating rooms of its Women's Health Center in July 2012, claiming it was done to try to catch a doctor suspected of stealing drugs. The cameras were meant only to record the individuals near the anesthesia cart, but patients and medical personnel can also be seen in the videos . . . .
>
> The procedures recorded include C-sections, hysterectomies and birth complications. The cameras were motion activated and installed inside computer monitors. More than 6,966 video clips were [allegedly] recorded over the 11-month period . . . .[16]
>
> In addition to filming patients without their consent . . . Sharp [allegedly] saved the video clips on computers available to many people, some without password protection.

Explain if and in what way(s) privacy was invaded.

Analysis: ______________________________

____

____

____

____

____

____

____

____

____

CASE 5.B

A video posted on YouTube in April 2008 showed a raucous Philippine operating room full of doctors and nurses laughing and cheering during an operation to remove a canister of perfume from the rectum a 39-year-old male patient.

> The unauthorized nearly 3-minute video of a noisy operating room shows doctors and nurses laughing, giggling and cheering. At one point, a hand appears with a cell phone camera taking a close-up picture of the surgery. As a doctor gingerly pulls out the 6-inch long canister from the male patient's rectum, someone shouts, "Baby out!" amid loud cheers. The doctor then removes the canister cap and sprays the contents toward the crowd of nurses and doctors viewing the procedure. . . . [M]ore than 10 people were involved—including

---

14 Gert B, Culver CM, Clouser KD. *Bioethics: A Return to Fundamentals*. New York, NY: Oxford University Press; 1997:126.

15 *Black's Law Dictionary*. Abridged 6th ed. St. Paul, MN: West Publishing, 1991:830.

16 Sharp HealthCare sued for recording 1,800 surgeries without patient consent. Modern Healthcare. https://www.modernhealthcare.com/providers/sharp-healthcare-sued-recording-1800-surgeries-without-patient-consent. Accessed May 5, 2019.

staff and medical and nursing students from a nearby operating room.[17]

The video was apparently shot by one of the student nurses.[18] Whose conduct was blameworthy? Why? What should the consequences have been for those involved?

Analysis: ______________________________

____

____

____

____

____

____

____

____

____

4. Federal Privacy Regulations (HIPAA)

The Health Insurance Portability and Accountability Act of 1996[19] (aka HIPAA) delegated to the Secretary of Health and Human Services the power to regulate certain aspects of medical privacy.[20] The federal privacy regulations were released in December 2000[21] and revised in 2002[22] and 2013.[23]

> In general, the federal privacy regulations impose an obligation to maintain the confidentiality of individually identifiable health information on certain "covered entities," which include health plans, health care clearinghouses, and health care providers who transmit health information in electronic form during certain transactions. These entities must (1) adopt internal procedures to protect the privacy of protected health information; (2) train employees regarding privacy procedures; (3) designate a privacy officer; (4) secure patient records that contain protected information; and (5) ensure that agreements with other entities (called "business associates") include terms requiring the protection of privacy. . . . A violation of the regulations may result in a significant civil penalty or criminal liability or both. The regulations do not provide a private cause of action or remedy.[24] (Internal citations omitted.)

Briefly, entities to which HIPAA applies may not disclose protected health information unless either permitted or required by the HIPAA Privacy Rule[25] or authorized in writing by the individual who is the subject of the information.

---

17 Philippine surgeons goof off on YouTube. CBS News. https://www.cbsnews.com/news/philippine-surgeons-goof-off-on-youtube/. Accessed June 3, 2019.

18 DoH suspends 2 docs, nurse in rectal surgery scandal. Inquirer.net. http://newsinfo.inquirer.net/breakingnews/regions/view/20080514-136496/DoH-suspends-2-docs-nurse-in-rectal-surgery-scandal. Accessed May 22, 2008.

19 Pub. L. 104-191.

20 This is an example of a delegation of Congress' legislative power to the executive branch of the federal government. See Chapter 4.

21 65 Fed. Reg. 82, 462-82, 829 (Dec 28, 2000).

22 67 Fed. Reg. 53, 182 (Aug 14, 2002).

23 Modifications to the HIPAA Privacy, Security, Enforcement, and Breach Notification Rules Under the Health Information Technology for Economic and Clinical Health Act and the Genetic Information Nondiscrimination Act; Other Modifications to the HIPAA Rules. https://www.federalregister.gov/documents/2013/01/25/2013-01073/modifications-to-the-hipaa-privacy-security-enforcement-and-breach-notification-rules-under-the. Accessed June 6, 2019.

24 Hall MA, Bobinski MA, Orentlicher D. *Health Care Law and Ethics*. 7th ed. Austin, TX: Aspen Publishers, 2007: 181.

25 Summary of the HIPAA Privacy Rule. U.S. Department of Health and Human Services. https://www.hhs.gov/sites/default/files/privacysummary.pdf. Accessed June 6, 2019.

CASE 5.C

Consider the following case.

> [A] pediatric ICU/ER nurse worked at Texas Children's Hospital and posted a series of comments on [a Facebook page called Proud Parents of Unvaccinated Children] about a rare case of measles at the hospital. The nurse was an anti-vaxxer and posted about the experience of seeing a boy at the hospital suffering from the disease—a disease that could have been prevented through vaccination. Her comments explained how the disease was much worse than she expected it to be, having not encountered anyone with the measles in the past. She explained that it was a "rough" experience seeing the boy suffering from the disease. She also explained in her posts, "I think it's easy for us non-vaxxers to make assumptions, but most of us have never and will never see one of these diseases," and "By no means have I changed my vax stance, and I never will. But this poor kid was bad off and as a parent, I could see vaccinating out of fear."[26]

The patient was never identified by name, but the posting nurse was identified, along with the hospital where she worked. Are there any HIPAA concerns? What consequences might ensue?

Analysis: ______________________________

____

____

____

____

____

____

____

____

____

5. Confidentiality Exceptions: The Duty to Warn or Otherwise Protect Third Parties

You will recall from Chapter 1 that not all *prima facie* violations of the moral rules are wrongful—that under certain circumstances, such violations are justified. Likewise, the duty of confidentiality is not absolute. Under certain circumstances, a health professional's duty of confidentiality to the patient must yield to a countervailing *duty to warn* or *duty to protect third parties*. As is the case with the legal duty of confidentiality, the legal duty to warn or to protect third parties sometimes derives from the common law and sometimes derives from statute.

5.1. Statutory Exceptions to Confidentiality

One of the oldest exceptions to the duty of confidentiality is the required duty of healthcare professionals (HCPs) to report certain communicable diseases—such as AIDS/HIV—to state public health authorities. The policy rationale underlying this exception is the protection of identifiable third parties at risk (e.g., sexual contacts of the infected patient). The same policy rationale

26 Texas nurse fired for social media HIPAA violation. HIPAA Journal. https://www.hipaajournal.com/texas-nurse-fired-for-social-media-hipaa-violation/. Accessed May 6, 2019.

underlies statutory duties to report child and elder abuse and the uncontrolled epilepsy of licensed drivers.[27]

In contrast, the policy rationale underlying another class of exceptions—for example, statutes mandating that HCPs report knife and gunshot wounds—is different. "Here the policy is generally to catch and punish wrongdoers, rather than to protect third parties against continuing or future harms."[28] While you will recall that one rationale underlying confidentiality is to encourage persons to seek treatment, it is generally thought that because of the violent and often serious nature of such knife and gunshot wounds, even victims guilty of crimes are highly unlikely to avoid seeking emergency medical treatment.[29]

5.2. Common Law Limits of Confidentiality

Lines of cases establish a legal duty on the part of an HCP to protect third parties where the HCP's patient poses a significant danger to others. Traditionally, case law supports the finding of such a duty in patients suffering from contagious disease, in violent psychiatric patients, and in patients with medically related driving impairments. Under the common law, health professionals may be liable for harm to third parties where three conditions are met: (1) there exists a "known or reasonably foreseeable hazard that arises in some way from the [health professional's] patient";[30] (2) there are *foreseeable*[31] (not necessarily *individually identifiable*[32]) third parties placed at risk by the hazard; and (3) the health professional behaves unreasonably under the circumstances.[33]

The following cases will illustrate how some courts have gone about weighing a patient's privacy interests against the health/safety interests of third parties. As you will see, the meaning of "hazard arising in some way from the [health professional's] patient" has been interpreted liberally by some courts as of late, enlarging the scope of the health professional's duty to third parties.

5.2.1. Tarasoff v. Regents of U. of Cal. *(1976)*[34]

In 1969, Prosenjit Poddar told his University of California psychologist, Dr. Lawrence Moore, that he intended to kill Tatiana Tarasoff. Dr. Moore attempted to commit Poddar for treatment, but the campus police released him because he appeared rational. Dr. Moore's superior then directed that no further efforts be made to detain Poddar. Tatiana Tarasoff was never warned of the threats against her. Shortly thereafter, Poddar killed Tatiana Tarasoff.

A criminal prosecution resulted,[35] but Tatiana's family also brought a liability action against the psychologists involved for failure to warn. The legal issue was whether the university owed Tatiana Tarasoff an affirmative *duty to*

---

27 Hall MA, Ellman IM, Strouse DS. *Health Care Law and Ethics in a Nutshell*. 2nd ed. St. Paul, MN: West Group, 1999:122.

28 Hall MA, Ellman IM, Strouse DS. *Health Care Law and Ethics in a Nutshell*. 2nd ed. St. Paul, MN: West Group, 1999:123.

29 Hall MA, Ellman IM, Strouse DS. *Health Care Law and Ethics in a Nutshell*. 2nd ed. St. Paul, MN: West Group, 1999:123.

30 Hall MA, Ellman IM, Strouse DS. *Health Care Law and Ethics in a Nutshell*. 2nd ed. St. Paul, MN: West Group, 1999: 124.

31 *Foreseeable* means "that which is objectively reasonable to expect, not merely what might conceivably occur." See *Black's Law Dictionary*. Abridged 6th ed. St. Paul, MN: West Publishing; 1991:449. If a PA fails to report the uncontrolled epilepsy of one of her patients and that patient suffers a seizure while driving and kills a third party, that third party victim was *foreseeable*, though not individually identifiable.

32 Third parties are *individually identifiable* if it would be reasonable to believe that an individual could be identified. In the *Tarasoff* case, Tatiana Tarasoff was an *individually identifiable* third party.

33 Hall MA, Ellman IM, Strouse DS. *Health Care Law and Ethics in a Nutshell*. 2nd ed. St. Paul, MN: West Group; 1999:124.

34 *Tarasoff v. Regents of U. of Cal.*, 17 Cal. 3d (1976).

35 *People v. Poddar*, 518 P.2d 342 (1974).

warn. As you will recall from Chapter 1, the HCP-patient relationship is one of those intimate/special relationships that imposes affirmative duties on HCPs to act in the best medical interests of their patients. In the *Tarasoff* case, however, there was no HCP-patient relationship between Tarasoff and any of the psychologists. Nevertheless, the court held that the absence of such a relationship did not foreclose liability. The court wrote:

> Although under the common law, as a general rule, one person owed no duty to control the conduct of another, nor to warn those endangered by such conduct, the courts have noted exceptions to this rule. . . . [The] courts have imposed a duty of care . . .[in] . . . cases in which *the defendant stands in some special relationship to* either *the person whose conduct needs to be controlled* or in a relationship to the foreseeable victim of that conduct . . . . [This exception applies] to the facts of this case.[36] (Internal footnotes omitted; italics added.)

In other words, the court found that the special relationship existing between Poddar and his psychologists was enough to create an affirmative duty on the psychologists' part to warn Poddar's foreseeable victim. *Tarasoff* stands for the principle that, once a therapist determines (or in the exercise of reasonable professional judgment should determine) that a patient poses a serious danger of violence to others, that therapist must exercise reasonable care to protect the foreseeable victim of that danger.[37]

5.2.2. Bradshaw v. Daniel *(1993)*[38]

As mentioned previously, a health professional may have a legal duty to protect third parties where his or her patient poses a significant danger to others due to contagiousness. In *Bradshaw*, patient Elmer Johns was admitted to the hospital in July 1986 with symptoms of Rocky Mountain Spotted Fever (RMSF). Defendant Dr. Daniel treated him appropriately, but Johns' condition deteriorated, and he died. "Although Dr. Daniel communicated with Elmer Johns' wife, Genevieve . . . , he never advised her of the risks of exposure to Rocky Mountain Spotted Fever, or that the disease could have been the cause of Johns' death."[39]

A week after Elmer's death, Genevieve was admitted with similar symptoms and treated for RMSF. She, too, died, within three days. Dr. Daniel was not Genevieve's physician.

Her family filed suit, alleging that Dr. Daniel had been negligent in failing to warn her of the risk of exposure.

Dr. Daniel argued that he owed Genevieve no legal duty because she was not his patient, and that while there was precedent for holding physicians liable for injuries to nonpatients caused by contagious diseases, RMSF is not contagious. Unlike the situation in *Tarasoff*, therefore, in *Bradshaw v. Daniel* the patient was not the source of the danger to the plaintiff. Nevertheless, the court held for the plaintiff.

> [It] is undisputed that there was a physician-patient relationship between Dr. Daniel and Elmer Johns. . . . [I]t is also undisputed that Elmer Johns' wife, who was residing with him, was at risk of contracting the disease . . . even though the disease is not contagious . . . . [F]amily members of patients suffering from Rocky Mountain Spotted Fever are at risk of contracting the disease due to a phenomenon called clustering, which is related to the activity of infected ticks who transmit the disease to humans. . . . Thus, this case

36 *Tarasoff v. Regents of U. of Cal.* 529 P.2d 553, 557.

37 It should be noted that the Texas Supreme Court, faced with a factually similar case, declined to impose a common law duty on mental-health professionals to warn third parties of their patient's threats. See, *Thapar v. Zezulka*, 994 S.W.2d 635 (Tex. 1999). https://www.courtlistener.com/opinion/2454771/thapar-v-zezulka/. Accessed May 7, 2019.

38 *Bradshaw v. Daniel*, 854 S.W.2d 865 (Tenn. 1993).

39 *Bradshaw v. Daniel*, 854 S.W.2d 865 (Tenn. 1993) at p. 867.

is analogous to the Tarasoff line of cases adopting a duty to warn of danger and the contagious disease cases adopting a comparable duty to warn. Here, as in those cases, there was a foreseeable risk of harm to an identifiable third party, and the reasons supporting the recognition of a duty to warn are equally compelling here. *We, therefore, conclude that the existence of the physician-patient relationship is sufficient to impose upon a physician an affirmative duty to warn identifiable third persons in the patient's immediate family against foreseeable risks emanating from a patient's illness. Accordingly, we hold that . . . the defendant physician had a duty to warn his patient's wife of the risk to her of contracting Rocky Mountain Spotted fever . . .*[40] (Italics added.)

5.2.3. Pate v. Threlkel *(1994)*[41]

In 1987, Marianne New was treated for medullary thyroid carcinoma (MTC). This cancer "may occur . . . as a familial form . . . transmitted as an autosomal dominant trait."[42] In 1990, Heidi Pate, New's adult daughter, was also diagnosed with MTC. Subsequently, Pate sued the physicians who initially treated her mother for MTC, alleging that they knew or should have known of the likelihood that New's children would inherit the condition genetically and that they had a duty to warn New that her children should be tested for the disease. Pate argued that had New been warned in 1987, she (Pate) would have been monitored for the condition and been diagnosed earlier, when it was still curable.

The trial court dismissed Pate's complaint because Pate was not a patient of the defendant physicians and Florida law required "that there be a physician-patient relationship between the parties as a condition precedent to bringing a medical malpractice action."[43] The district court affirmed the trial court's dismissal.

The case went to the Florida Supreme Court, which was charged with answering the question, "Does a physician owe a duty of care to the children of a patient to warn the patient of the genetically transferable nature of the condition for which the physician is treating the patient?"

The court acknowledged that New's physicians certainly owed New a duty of due care but were noncommittal on the issue of whether that duty included a duty to warn her of the genetically transferable nature of her disease. The answer to that question, they wrote, depended upon whether "a reasonably prudent health care provider [would have] warn[ed] [the] patient of the genetically transferable nature of . . . [MTC],"[44] (a question of fact that would need to be answered by the trial court, to which the case would be remanded). The Florida Supreme Court went on to hold that, if the physicians' duty to New included a duty to warn her of the genetic nature and transmissibility of her disease, then that duty ran to her daughter Ms. Pate as an intended third-party beneficiary.[45]

Interestingly, the court went on in dictum to discuss how any possible duty to warn might be discharged:

> If there is a duty to warn, to whom must the physician convey the warning? Our holding should not be read to require

---

40 *Bradshaw v. Daniel*, 854 S.W.2d 865 (Tenn. 1993) at p. 872.

41 *Pate v. Threlkel*, 661 So.2d 278 (Fla. 1995).

42 Berkow R, Fletcher AJ, eds. *The Merck Manual of Diagnosis and Therapy*. 16th ed. Rahway, NJ: Merck Research Laboratories; 1992:1086.

43 *Pate v. Threlkel*, 661 So.2d 278 (Fla. 1995), at p. 280.

44 *Pate v. Threlkel*, 661 So.2d 278 (Fla. 1995), at p. 280.

45 Black's Law Dictionary 830 (abridged 6th edition), 1991, at p. 1029.

> the physician to warn the patient's children of the disease. In most instances the physician is prohibited from disclosing the patient's medical condition to others except with the patient's permission. Moreover, the patient ordinarily can be expected to pass on the warning. To require the physician to seek out and warn various members of the patient's family would often be difficult or impractical and would place too heavy a burden upon the physician. *Thus, we emphasize that in any circumstances in which the physician has a duty to warn of a genetically transferable disease, that duty will be satisfied by warning the patient.* (Internal citations omitted; italics added.)

In a factually similar New Jersey case in 1996, a New Jersey appellate court "decline[d] to hold . . . that, in all circumstances, the duty to warn will be satisfied by informing the patient,"[46] leaving open the possibility that in certain cases such a warning might have to be given directly to the patient's family.

CASE 5.D

Consider the *duty to warn third parties* as discussed in sections 5.2.1 through 5.2.4 and recall the *principles of biomedical ethics* discussed in Chapter 1. In which of the principles is the *duty to warn third parties* grounded? Be as specific as possible in your answer.

Answer: ______________________________

____

____

____

____

____

____

____

____

____

WRAP-UP

Chapter Summary

Confidentiality refers to one's duty in a *private* situation (e.g., the physician-patient relationship) not to divulge information to inappropriate parties. Interests in *utility* and *autonomy* underlie the doctrine of confidentiality. Violations or breaches of confidentiality implicate the moral rules prohibiting the breaking of promises, the breaking of the law, and the neglect of duty. The legal protection of confidentiality includes both common law and statutory protections (including HIPAA). The duty of confidentiality is not absolute; not all breaches of confidentiality are wrongful. Both common law and statutory exceptions to the duty of confidentiality exist. When one of these exceptions is applicable, confidentiality may—and in some cases must—be breached.

46 *Safer v. Estate of Pack*, 677 A.2d 1188 (N.J. 1996).

Review Questions

1. What is *confidentiality*? What is *privacy*? How are they related?
2. Why does the doctrine of *confidentiality* exist? How does it benefit society?
3. Why is it wrong to breach *confidentiality*? Explain your answer in terms of the principles of biomedical ethics, or the moral rules, or the internal morality of medicine.
4. How is *confidentiality* related to *professionalism*?
5. What is *common law*? What is *statutory law*? How do they differ? What is HIPAA? Why is it discussed in this chapter?
6. List three exceptions to the legal duty of *confidentiality*. List two different policy rationales underlying exceptions to the duty.
7. When should a health professional consider breaching *confidentiality*? What factors weigh in favor of such a breach?
8. How are *confidentiality* and *informed consent* related?

Case Analyses

Case 5.A Analysis

Yes, privacy was invaded in two ways. First, Sharp HealthCare arguably intruded upon the seclusion of the videotaped patients in this case. In general, this aspect of privacy is violated when the "defendant intrude[s] into the plaintiff's private affairs, seclusion or solitude . . . and [when the] intrusion would be objectionable to a reasonable person."[47] Patients have an expectation of privacy when they are in the operating room, an expectation that was frustrated in this case by the placement of hidden cameras that reasonable persons would find objectionable. Note that invading this aspect of privacy (*non-intrusion*) does NOT require that the details of the intrusion be communicated to a third party. In this case, however, it is alleged that Sharp "saved the video clips on computers available to many people, some without password protection." This is a violation of the third type of privacy (*control of information access*) discussed previously, protection of personal information, both on the part of Sharp HealthCare as well as the individuals who wrongfully accessed/viewed the videoclips.

Case 5.B Analysis

Multiple health professionals and health professionals-in-training breached their professional fiduciary duties to the patient in question. The health professionals responsible for precepting and serving as role models for the medical and nursing students involved failed miserably. Just as a health professional's access to a patient and his or her medical record is on a "need to know" basis,[48] access to the operating room in this case should have been restricted by the surgeon and nurse in charge to those persons who had legitimate

47 What is invasion of privacy? FindLaw.com https://injury.findlaw.com/torts-and-personal-injuries/what-is-invasion-of-privacy-.html. Accessed May 5, 2019.

48 Thus, it was reported in March 2008 that Britney Spears's medical confidentiality had been breached and

> . . . more than 25 employees of UCLA Medical Center face disciplinary action, according to The Associated Press. More than 13 employees are expected to be fired and 12 others, including several doctors, will be disciplined for looking at Spears' UCLA hospital records. There is no evidence that any employee leaked or sold information about Spears . . . . However, merely looking at the confidential records is a violation of state and federal medical privacy laws . . .

See Hospital says Britney's medical confidentiality violated. liveDaily. http://www.livedaily.com/blog/1734.html. Accessed May 22, 2008.

patient-care or pedagogical reasons to be there. The presence of superfluous personnel was an invasion of the patient's privacy (intrusion). The making of the video without the patient's consent violated the principle of *respect for autonomy* (see Chapter 1) and his right to informed consent/refusal (see Chapter 6), and its posting on YouTube was a most egregious invasion of his privacy (information access) and a violation of the duty of confidentiality. Even health professionals-in-training should have known better. The episode embarrassed the patient involved and undermined faith in the individual and institutional providers involved and in medicine in general. The so-called "canister scandal" resulted in the 90-day suspensions of two physicians and a nurse by the Department of Health. Reportedly, 12 other health professionals "faced an administrative case for grave misconduct."[49] Had this occurred in the United States, consequences might have included (1) discipline of the medical and nursing students involved, up to and including expulsion; (2) professional disciplinary actions against the involved licensed health professionals; (3) administrative action against the involved hospital; and (4) a private cause of action for monetary damages against any/all of the above.

Case 5.C Analysis

Certainly. In this case, Texas Children's Hospital (a covered entity) determined that the nurse (a hospital employee) posted enough information to make it possible to identify the child being treated,[50] and this would qualify as protected health information (PHI).[51] The nurse has arguably committed a HIPAA violation. Although not done maliciously, the violation was not accidental, and such violations usually result in disciplinary actions including dismissal and punishment by the board of nursing. In fact, the nurse in this case was dismissed four days after the hospital became aware of her posts.[52] Further, being fired for a HIPAA violation might make it difficult for this nurse to find other employment, since HIPAA-covered entities might be hesitant to hire someone who has been fired for violating HIPAA rules.[53] While criminal penalties can result in cases involving theft of PHI for personal gain or use of PHI with intent to cause harm, these were not issues in this case. Finally, "[t]here is no private cause of action in HIPAA. If a nurse violates HIPAA, a patient cannot sue the nurse for a HIPAA violation. There may be a viable claim, in some cases, under state laws."[54]

Case 5.D Analysis

The duty to warn third parties is grounded in the principle of *beneficence*, which refers to the obligation to help others further their important and legitimate interests. The duty to warn implicated in the cases is clearly *obligatory* as opposed to *ideal beneficence*, but is it grounded in *specific beneficence* or in *general beneficence*? Based on the language used in the opinions, I submit that the duty is grounded in specific beneficence. For

49 Ong G, Flores H. Canister scandal: 90-day suspension of 2 docs, nurse ends. Philstar Global. https://www.philstar.com/nation/2008/09/06/398622/canister-scandal-90-day-suspension-2-docs-nurse-ends. Accessed May 6, 2019.

50 How an innocent social media post can turn into a HIPAA Violation. Vital Health Law. http://vitalehealthlaw.com/how-an-innocent-social-media-post-can-turn-into-a-hipaa-violation/. Accessed May 6, 2019.

51 What is protected health information? HIPAA Journal. https://www.hipaajournal.com/what-is-protected-health-information/. Accessed May 6, 2019.

52 Texas Children's Hospital fires nurse who posted about boy with measles. Houston Chronicle. https://www.houstonchronicle.com/news/houston-texas/houston/article/Texas-Children-s-Hospital-fires-nurse-who-13189543.php. Accessed May 6, 2019.

53 What happens if a nurse violates HIPAA? HIPAA Journal. https://www.hipaajournal.com/what-happens-nurse-violates-hipaa/. Accessed May 6, 2019.

54 What happens if a nurse violates HIPAA? HIPAA Journal. https://www.hipaajournal.com/what-happens-nurse-violates-hipaa/. Accessed May 6, 2019.

example, in *Tarasoff*, the court writes, "courts have imposed a duty of care . . .[in] . . . cases in which the defendant stands in some *special relationship* to either the person whose conduct needs to be controlled or in a relationship to the foreseeable victim of that conduct."[55] (Italics added.) In *Bradshaw*, the court "conclude[s] that the existence of the *physician-patient relationship* is sufficient to impose upon a physician an affirmative duty to warn identifiable third persons in the patient's immediate family against foreseeable risks emanating from a patient's illness."[56] Both of these opinions imply that the duty owed to nonpatient third parties derives from or runs through the doctor-patient relationship. In *Pate*, the court explicitly referred to the nonpatient third parties as *third-party beneficiaries* of the physician-patient relationship.

55 *Tarasoff v. Regents of U. of Cal.* 529 P.2d 553, 557.
56 *Bradshaw v. Daniel*, 854 S.W.2d 865 (Tenn. 1993) at p. 872.

CHAPTER 6

Conflicts of Interest

LEARNING OBJECTIVES

1. Define the term *conflict of interest* (COI).
2. Learn to recognize COIs and potential COIs.
3. Explain why COIs are problematical for health professionals.
4. Recognize different categories of COIs.
5. List strategies for managing COIs.

More. *A man should go where he won't be tempted. Look, Richard, see this. [He hands him a silver cup.] Look . . . Look . . .*

Rich. *Beautiful.*

More. *Italian . . . Do you want it?*

Rich. *Why?*

More. *No joke; keep it; or sell it.*

Rich. *Well—Thank you, of course. Thank you! Thank you! But—*

. . . .

More. . . . *It was sent to me a little while ago by some woman. Now she's put a lawsuit into the Court of Requests. It's a bribe, Richard.*

Rich. *Oh . . . [Chagrined.] So you give it away, of course.*

More. *Yes! . . . . Richard, in office they offer you all sorts of things. I was once offered a whole village, with a mill, and a manor house, and heaven knows what else—a coat of arms, I shouldn't be surprised.*[1]

1 A man for all seasons. In: Corrigan RW, ed. *Laurel British Drama: The Twentieth Century.* New York, NY: Dell Publishing; 1965:365.

1. Introduction

Because health professionals are in special relationships with their patients, the health professionals are obligated to act in the best healthcare interests of those patients. However, health professionals sometimes have interests outside the therapeutic relationship that can affect that obligation. As it relates to health care, a *conflict of interest (COI)* is a situation in which a health professional's personal interests conflict with or appear to conflict with his or her responsibilities to the patient. Once a COI is recognized, it must be managed appropriately.

2. How Do COIs Arise?

Regarding the realm of patient care, the most important duty of health professionals is to provide care that is in the best medical interests of their patients. Some health professionals are engaged in outside activities as well, such as teaching or research; some may invest in or own biotechnology companies or lab testing or treatment facilities.[2] While such outside activities often benefit society, they also raise concerns about whether they might unduly influence the health professional's judgment regarding the professional's primary interest—the promotion and protection of patient welfare. For example, a health professional who owns a lab testing facility might benefit financially by referring patients there for lab tests, whether in fact medically necessary or not.[3]

3. COIs Defined

A COI may be defined as "a real or seeming incompatibility between a person's private interests and his or her public or fiduciary duties."[4]

3.1. The Elements That Constitute COIs

In 2009, the Institute of Medicine published a report entitled *Conflict of Interest in Medical Research, Education, and Practice* in which a COI was said to exist "when an individual or institution has a secondary interest that creates a risk of undue influence on decisions or actions affecting a primary interest."[5] Stated otherwise, "a COI is a set of circumstances that creates a risk that professional judgment or actions regarding a *primary interest* will be unduly influenced by a *secondary interest*" (italics added).[6]

3.1.1. Primary Interests

The *primary interest* varies according to the purpose of the professional activity involved. Thus, in the realm of patient care, the primary interest is in promoting and protecting the welfare of patients. In the realm of research, the primary interest is in promoting and protecting the integrity of research. In the realm of teaching, the primary interest is in promoting and protecting the quality of medical education.

3.1.2. Secondary Interests

The element that gives rise to the COI is the so-called secondary interest. As we saw previously (see section *2. How Do COIs Arise?*), secondary

---

2 Muth CC. Conflict of interest in medicine. *JAMA*. 2017;317(17):1812. doi:10.1001/jama.2017.4044. https://jamanetwork.com/journals/jama/fullarticle/2623608. Accessed September 9, 2019.

3 Muth CC. Conflict of interest in medicine. *JAMA*. 2017;317(17):1812. doi:10.1001/jama.2017.4044. https://jamanetwork.com/journals/jama/fullarticle/2623608. Accessed September 9, 2019.

4 *Blacks' Law Dictionary*. 9th ed. St. Paul, MN: West Publishing; 2009:207.

5 Lo B, Field MJ, eds. *Conflict of Interest in Medical Research, Education, and Practice*. Washington, DC: National Academies Press; 2009.

6 Lo B, Field MJ, eds. *Conflict of Interest in Medical Research, Education, and Practice*. Washington, DC: National Academies Press; 2009.

interests are not intrinsically evil; rather, they become problematic only when they eclipse the relevant primary interests in professional decision-making.

Secondary interests may be financial or nonfinancial.

3.1.2.1. Financial Secondary Interests. Financial secondary interests include, for example, reimbursement incentives and gifts.

3.1.2.1.1. Reimbursement Incentives. Managed care and fee-for-service (FFS) both create financial secondary interests in the form of reimbursement incentives. FFS "incentivizes doing more of the services for which there exist fees. This can create incentives for unnecessary tests and procedures . . . ."[7] Managed care, on the other hand, "incentivizes doing less of anything; once a patient is on your panel, the marginal revenue from actually doing anything for the patient is zero, and the marginal cost in terms of your time + materials/supplies/etc. is positive."[8] Managed care creates reimbursement incentives to avoid doing even medically necessary tests and procedures.

What about salaried health professionals? Are they, unlike their FFS and managed care brethren, free of reimbursement incentives? Danielle Ofri has written, "One beautiful thing about being salaried is that I have absolutely no financial conflict of interest with regard to my patients' care. Nothing that I recommend or prescribe alters my income."[9] But such an assertion seems simplistic.

> As a salaried employee . . . your job depends on the happiness of your boss (i.e., the practice owner), who could be . . . [a] physician or a hospital administrator. . . . This could mean restrictions on your ability to . . . do what you think is in your individual patient's best interest . . . .[10]

Recall Case 2.D in Chapter 2. In the case of *Sloan v. South Carolina Board of Physical Therapy Examiners*, the South Carolina legislature enacted a statute authorizing the South Carolina Board of Physical Therapy Examiners to

> refuse to renew the license of a licensed person . . . [or to] suspend, revoke, or otherwise restrict the license of a licensed person who:
>
> (1) requests, receives, participates or engages directly or indirectly in the dividing, transferring, assigning, rebating, or refunding of fees received for professional services or profits by means of a credit or other valuable consideration, including, but not limited to, wages, an unearned commission, discount, or gratuity with a person who referred a patient, or with a relative or business associate of the referring person; . . . .[11]

The Supreme Court of South Carolina in that case decided that the statute in question "prohibit[ed] a physical therapist from working

7 Are there financial conflicts of interest with salary-based physician payment? The Notwithstanding Blog. https://notwithstandingblog.wordpress.com/2010/04/16/are-there-financial-conflicts-of-interest-with-salary-based-physician-payment/#41610note1. Published April 16, 2010.

8 Are there financial conflicts of interest with salary-based physician payment? The Notwithstanding Blog. https://notwithstandingblog.wordpress.com/2010/04/16/are-there-financial-conflicts-of-interest-with-salary-based-physician-payment/#41610note1. Published April 16, 2010.

9 Ofri D. Salaried physicians become more politically progressive. KevinMD.com. https://www.kevinmd.com/blog/2010/04/salaried-physicians-politically-progressive.html. Published April 16, 2010.

10 Are there financial conflicts of interest with salary-based physician payment? The Notwithstanding Blog. https://notwithstandingblog.wordpress.com/2010/04/16/are-there-financial-conflicts-of-interest-with-salary-based-physician-payment/#41610note1. Published April 16, 2010.

11 *Sloan v. South Carolina Board of Physical Therapy Examiners*, 370 S.C. 452.

as an employee of a physician when the physician refers patients to the physical therapist for services."[12] The court opined that the legislature was concerned about "actual and potential conflicts of interest which are likely to lead to overuse of medical services by physicians who, for their own financial gain rather than their patients' medical needs, refer patients to entities in which the physicians hold a financial interest."[13] As we mentioned in Chapter 2, the legislature was likely also concerned about the effect of the profit motive on the physical therapists, since "therapists who work in POPT clinics may . . . feel pressured to over-utilize therapy services to promote profits, rather than patient wellbeing."[14]

Further, a salary payment model "eliminates an important incentive to increase performance. Patients are often told that the schedule is full. Why squeeze in a patient?"[15] As Kirsch has written, "docs [and presumably other health professionals] would rather read the *New York Times* than [practice medicine] for free."[16] Consider, for example, the 2014 Veterans Administration scandal involving the deaths of scores of veterans because of delays in treatment in the VA system.[17] One cannot help but wonder whether such delays would have occurred if reimbursement of VA healthcare providers was FFS-based as opposed to salaried.

3.1.2.1.2. Gifts. Gifts are another kind of financial secondary interest. Gifts might come from patients or from the pharmaceutical industry.

CASE 6.A

Reread Case 2.E, which was discussed in Chapter 2. What are the primary and secondary interests involved from a COI perspective?

Analysis: ______________________________

The propriety of accepting gifts from patients depends on a number of factors, including the patient's motive for the making of the gift (e.g., as an expression of gratitude—proper—versus as an attempt to influence care—improper) and the "gift's value relative to the patient's or physician's means."[18] Improper gifts represent a form of seduction. "Whether the intention is stated or implied, a lavish gift is a psychological (or actual)

12 *Sloan v. South Carolina Board of Physical Therapy Examiners,* 370 S.C. 452.

13 *Sloan v. South Carolina Board of Physical Therapy Examiners,* 370 S.C. 452.

14 Working in a physician-owned physical therapy clinic: arguments for and against. myPTsolutions. https://myptsolutions.com/working-physician-owned-physical-therapy-clinic-arguments/. Accessed May 21, 2021.

15 Fee-for-service or salaried medicine? Part I. MD Whistleblower. http://mdwhistleblower.blogspot.com/2010/01/fee-for-service-or-salaried-medicine.html. Published January 31, 2010.

16 Fee-for-service or salaried medicine? Part I. MD Whistleblower. http://mdwhistleblower.blogspot.com/2010/01/fee-for-service-or-salaried-medicine.html. January 31, 2010.

17 Pearson M. The VA's troubled history. CNN politics. https://www.cnn.com/2014/05/23/politics/va-scandals-timeline/index.htmlPe. Published May 30, 2014. Accessed Oct 28, 2019.

18 AMA Code of Medical Ethics Opinion 1.2.8. https://www.ama-assn.org/delivering-care/ethics/gifts-patients. Accessed October 31, 2019.

bribe and means that the patient expects lavish or special treatment."[19]

Similar considerations govern the propriety of accepting gifts from industry (e.g., pharmaceutical or medical device companies). Such gifts risk biasing—or being perceived as biasing—professional judgment and thus undermining professional integrity or public trust in medicine. Consider the following words of Marcia Angell, former editor of the *New England Journal of Medicine*:

> Similar conflicts of interest and biases exist in virtually every field of medicine, particularly those that rely heavily on drugs or devices. It is simply no longer possible to believe much of the clinical research that is published, or to rely on the judgment of trusted physicians or authoritative medical guidelines. I take no pleasure in this conclusion, which I reached slowly and reluctantly over my two decades as an editor of *The New England Journal of Medicine*.[20]

Regarding such gifts, the AMA Code of Medical Ethics asserts:

> Any gifts accepted by physicians individually should primarily entail a benefit to patients and should not be of substantial value . . . . Individual gifts of minimal value are permissible as long as the gifts are related to the physician's work (e.g., pens and notepads).[21]

According to the AAPA Guidelines for Ethical Conduct for the PA Profession:

> Acceptance of gifts, trips, hospitality, or other items is discouraged. Before accepting a gift or financial arrangement, PAs might consider the guidelines of the Royal College of Physicians, "Would I be willing to have this arrangement generally known?" or of the American College of Physicians, "What would the public or my patients think of this arrangement?"[22]

According to the Code of Ethics for the Physical Therapist, "Physical therapists shall not accept gifts or other considerations that influence or give an appearance of influencing their professional judgment."[23]

3.1.2.2. Nonfinancial Bias. Examples of nonfinancial secondary interests include, for example, the desire for professional advancement, or the desire for recognition and personal achievement.

Recall from Chapter 2 that under the Parsonian model of professionalism, not all nonfinancial secondary interests are created equal from a professionalism standpoint. The desire for political power is particularly pernicious.

> Professionals . . . must not be too strongly motivated by the desire for power, lest they attempt to achieve it by promoting social norms at the expense of individual liberty. On the other hand, they must not be too strongly motivated by profit, lest they allow their authority to be bought out by wealthy private [patients] seeking exemption from social norms. Instead . . . the professional project is successful only because professionals are motivated

19 Bruckman R. *How to Break Bad News: A Guide for Health Care Professionals*. Baltimore, MD: The Johns Hopkins University Press; 1992:160–161.

20 Angell, M. Drug companies & doctors: a story of corruption. *The New York Review of Books*. January 15, 2009. https://www.nybooks.com/articles/2009/01/15/drug-companies-doctorsa-story-of-corruption/. Accessed May 2, 2019.

21 Virtual Mentor. 2014;16(4):261–264. doi: 10.1001/virtualmentor.2014.16.4.coet2-1404.

22 Guidelines for ethical conduct for the PA profession. AAPA. https://www.aapa.org/wp-content/uploads/2017/02/16-EthicalConduct.pdf.

23 Code of ethics for the physical therapist. APTA. https://www.apta.org/siteassets/pdfs/policies/codeofethicshods06-20-28-25.pdf. Accessed June 8, 2021.

> primarily by the desire for status and reputation—both among their peers and in society at large—rather than by the desire for money or power.[24]

Thus, the desire for professional advancement, or for status and reputation are arguably not deleterious to professionalism, while the desire for political power is.

CASE 6.B

Consider the following narrative:

> An on-call gynecology resident rotating through a large private hospital is called in the middle of the night and asked to see a 20-year-old female patient on the gynecologic oncology unit who was having trouble sleeping. The resident, himself sleepy, sleep-deprived, and unhappy about being up again, makes his way to the nurses station and peruses the young woman's chart. She is dying of ovarian cancer and is experiencing intractable nausea and vomiting. He enters her room and notes that she is cachectic and profoundly short of breath despite nasal oxygen. The patient, whose name is Debbie, tells the resident, "Let's get this over with." The resident asks nursing to draw 20 mg of morphine sulfate into a syringe and then returns to the patient's bedside. He tells her that he is going to give her something that will let her rest and injects the contents of the syringe intravenously. As the resident stands by, the patient closes her eyes. Her breathing slows, becomes irregular, and ultimately ceases.[25]

Does the gynecology resident described potentially have a COI? If so, what is it?

Analysis: ______________________________

____

____

____

____

____

____

____

____

____

3.1.3. Undue Influence

"A COI exists whether or not a particular individual or institution is actually influenced by the secondary interest."[26] In other words, the finding of a COI does not require that primary interests actually be compromised; rather, all that is needed is there is an *undue risk* that the primary interest will be neglected as a result of pursuit of secondary interests.

Determining whether a risk of *undue influence* exists requires judgment and is a fact-intensive inquiry. Among the factors to be considered in making the determination are (1) the value of the secondary interest (the greater the value of the secondary interest, the more likely its influence and (2) how much latitude the arguably conflicted individual or institution enjoys in making the decision(s) or taking the action(s) affecting the primary interest at stake.

---

24 Latham SR. Medical professionalism: a Parsonian view. *Mount Sinai Journal of Medicine*. 2002;69(6):364.
25 Name Withheld by Request. It's over, Debbie. *JAMA* 1988;259(2):272.
26 Lo B, Field MJ, eds. *Conflict of Interest in Medical Research, Education, and Practice*. Washington, DC: National Academies Press; 2009:47. http://nationalacademies.org/hmd/reports/2009/conflict-of-interest-in-medical-research-education-and-practice.aspx

CASE 6.C

Again, reread Case 2.E, which was discussed in Chapter 2. Is there a COI?

Analysis: ______________________________

____

____

____

____

____

____

____

____

____

3.2. Distinguishing COIs from Related Concepts

3.2.1. Bias

"Bias is presenting information, drawing conclusions, or making recommendations that are not scientifically valid or supported by the weight of rigorous evidence."[27] Unlike random error, bias leads to systematic (i.e., predictable) deviations from underlying truth. How are bias and COIs related? Lo has written that "conflicts of interest resemble a screening test for bias, with imperfect sensitivity and specificity." Thus, bias can result even absent any COI (imperfect sensitivity)—for example, physicians are more likely to disregard heart-attack symptoms in younger female patients than in younger males.[28] This reflects a gender bias, with no COIs in sight. Conversely, a COI might exist and yet not result in bias (imperfect specificity). As an example, consider again Case 2.E in Chapter 2, discussed in Case 6.A and Case 6.C. Had Dr. Portes authorized the angiogram, or had the medical facts of the case been such that no reasonable physician would have authorized an angiogram under the circumstances, then one could have said that there was a COI present that did not result in bias.

3.2.2. Conflict of Obligation (COO)

A conflict of obligation (COO) refers to a conflict between competing primary interests.[29] *Tarasoff v. Regents of U. of Cal.* (1976), discussed in Chapter 5, section 5.2.1, illustrates a COO. Therein, the psychologist was faced with a conflict between two primary interests—maintaining the confidentiality of a patient and preventing that patient from harming someone else. "There is no conflict of interest in this example because both interests have plausible claims to be considered primary."[30]

3.2.3. Conflict of Commitment (COC)

A conflict of commitment (COC) refers to "a conflict between what institutions view as employees' primary responsibilities to the institution and the employees' outside commitments, such as voluntary community service, participation in a political campaign, or teaching or conducting

---

27 Lo B, Ott C. What is the enemy in CME, conflicts of interest or bias? *JAMA*. 2013;310(10):1019–1020.

28 Lichtman JH, Leifheit EC, Safdar B, et al. Sex differences in the presentation and perception of symptoms among young patients with myocardial infarction. *Circulation*. 2018;137(8):771–780.

29 Lo B, Field MJ, eds. *Conflict of Interest in Medical Research, Education, and Practice*. Washington, DC: National Academies Press; 2009:48.

30 Lo B, Field MJ, eds. *Conflict of Interest in Medical Research, Education, and Practice*. Washington, DC: National Academies Press; 2009:48.

research for another institution."[31] In COCs, the competing activities are conducted at or on behalf of different institutions.

CASE 6.D[32]

You are a PA in a Florida family medicine practice. A 35-year-old circumcised heterosexual male (let's call him Harry) presents as a new patient, concerned that he might have a sexually transmitted disease, and especially concerned about the possibility of HIV. He reports that on a business trip to Las Vegas 3 months ago he had three sexual encounters with prostitutes. He reports using condoms on each occasion. He denies any constitutional or genitourinary symptoms. His past medical history is unremarkable. He is living with a woman named Sally, who is also your patient, and reports being monogamous prior to the Vegas trip. His review of systems is negative. His physical exam is completely normal. He requests HIV testing and unfortunately is tested without an informed consent discussion. His HIV test result is unexpectedly positive. You bring him into the office and disclose the results to him. You ask him whether he has had unprotected sexual intercourse with Sally since returning from Vegas, and he says he has. You tell him that he needs to inform Sally of the results of his HIV test so that she, too, can be tested. He replies that he has not told her of his indiscretions and is not willing to at this point. He says that he is not ready to tell her of his HIV positivity and asks that you not tell her either. What is the nature of the conflict here, if any?

Analysis: ______________________________

____

____

____

____

____

____

____

____

____

4. Why Medical COIs Are Ethically Problematic

4.1. Consequences of COIs

For the sake of simplicity, let's limit our discussion in this section to the realm of patient care, where the primary interest involves promoting and protecting patient welfare.

From the standpoint of the consequentialist, COIs are problematic for two reasons. First, they threaten the integrity of medical judgment, increasing the likelihood that that patient welfare will be compromised in the pursuit of some secondary interest. Secondly, whether or not a COI actually affects the integrity of a medical judgment, a COI that is not appropriately managed threatens public confidence in the integrity of medical judgment. This loss of public confidence will itself negatively affect patient welfare.[33]

4.2. COIs and the Moral Rules

Failure to appropriately manage a COI is arguably a violation of the moral rule prohibiting the breaking of promises (Gert's seventh rule)—since health

31 Lo B, Field MJ, eds. *Conflict of Interest in Medical Research, Education, and Practice.* Washington, DC: National Academies Press; 2009:48.

32 This case is an abbreviated and modified version of Case 6.B, pp. 156-158 in Paola FA, Walker R, Nixon LL. *Medical Ethics and Humanities.* Sudbury, MA: Jones & Bartlett; 2010.

33 Lo B, Field MJ, eds. *Conflict of Interest in Medical Research, Education, and Practice.* Washington, DC: National Academies Press; 2009:49.

professionals both implicitly and explicitly promise to appropriately manage COIs—and of the moral rule prohibiting neglect of duty (Gert's tenth rule).

In cases in which the influence of a secondary interest results in an adverse outcome (i.e., harm to a patient), failure to appropriately manage the COI is a violation of the moral rule or rules that prohibit causing the harm (death, pain and suffering, disability, loss of freedom, or loss of pleasure)[34] suffered by the patient. This is so because, as per Bernard Gert, "if one violates one of the second five moral rules . . . [and] an evil results, this counts as violating one of the first five rules."[35] As suggested previously in section *4.1 Consequences of COIs,* even where a COI does not affect the integrity of a medical judgment, an inappropriately managed COI threatens public confidence in the integrity of that judgment and violates the second of Gert's moral rules, which prohibits the causing of pain/suffering.

4.3. How COIs Threaten Medical Professionalism

COIs implicate two of the four tenets of medical professionalism: *the medical professional's motivations* and *acts of profession*.

4.3.1. COIs and the Medical Professional's Motivations

Recall section 2.2.3 The Medical Professional's Motivations (see Chapter 2). While the term COI was not discussed previously, the concept of professionals' interests/motivations, proper and improper, was, and at least according to Parsons, not all secondary interests are created equal *from a professionalism standpoint*.

> Professionals . . . must not be too strongly motivated by the desire for power, lest they attempt to achieve it by promoting social norms at the expense of individual liberty. On the other hand, they must not be too strongly motivated by profit, lest they allow their authority to be bought out by wealthy private [patients] seeking exemption from social norms. Instead . . . the professional project is successful only because professionals are motivated primarily by the desire for status and reputation—both among their peers and in society at large—rather than by the desire for money or power. . . .[36]

It was suggested that professional self-regulation serves as a bulwark against secondary interests related to political power, if not against financial secondary interests:

> [Professionals'] interests . . . in status and reputation rather than in political power and wealth . . . affords a crucial counterbalance to the professionals' right of self-regulation: for while the right of self-regulation implies that professionals could not be induced by regulators into favoring the public interest over that of their private [patients], the non-pecuniary character of professionals' . . . interests helps guarantee that they could not be induced to favor private, moneyed interests over the interests of the public. . . . Professional institutions are not supposed to make physicians into saints. Parsons was adamant that professional self-regulation can work, and the interests of patients and society can be kept in balance, even if physicians are systematically and energetically self-interested. What is required is only that their self-interest be non-pecuniary in character. It is easier to turn aside short-term financial temptation if one is certain of one's high social status. The prospect of making another dollar will not distract the professional who is single-mindedly dedicated to achieving not only medical excellence, but also a

34 Recall that these harms correspond to Gert's first five moral rules.

35 Gert B. *Morality: Its Nature and Justification*. New York, NY: Oxford University Press; 1998:175.

36 Latham SR. Medical professionalism: a Parsonian view. *Mount Sinai Journal of Medicine*. 2002;69(6):364.

> reputation for medical excellence. . . . If physicians, through their professional organizations, can cultivate the proper interests—in status, in respect, in reputation for skill, in peer recognition—then their relentless competitive pursuit of these interests cannot hurt, and may even help, the rest of us.[37]

4.3.2. COIs and Acts of Profession

In section 2.2.4 Acts of Profession (see Chapter 2), we saw that health professionals profess both publicly (through the taking of an oath) and privately (in their daily encounters with patients) that they will use their medical expertise in the best medical interests of their patients.

The *Guidelines for Ethical Conduct for the PA Profession* specifically address the issue of COIs. They state:

> PAs should place service to patients before personal material gain and should avoid undue influence on their clinical judgment. Trust can be undermined by even the appearance of improper influence. Examples of excessive or undue influence on clinical judgment can take several forms. These may include financial incentives, pharmaceutical or other industry gifts, and business arrangements involving referrals. PAs should disclose any actual or potential conflict of interest to their patients.
>
> Acceptance of gifts, trips, hospitality, or other items is discouraged. Before accepting a gift or financial arrangement, PAs might consider the guidelines of the Royal College of Physicians, "Would I be willing to have this arrangement generally known?" or of the American College of Physicians, "What would the public or my patients think of this arrangement?"[38]

The *Code of Ethics for the Physical Therapist* includes the following provision: "3D. Physical therapists shall not engage in conflicts of interest that interfere with professional judgment."[39]

The *AARC Statement of Ethics and Professional Conduct* contains the following admonition: "Avoid any form of conduct that is fraudulent or creates a conflict of interest, and shall follow the principles of ethical business behavior."[40]

The *AOTA 2020 Occupational Therapy Code of Ethics* includes the following standard: "1L. Do not engage in conflicts of interest or conflicts of commitment in employment, volunteer roles, or research. (Principle: Fidelity; key words: conflict of interest)"[41]

The Code of Ethics of the American Speech-Language-Hearing Association (ASHA) also specifically addresses conflicts of interest. Principle of

CASE 6.E

Look again at the Hippocratic Oath (classical version in section *2.2.4 Acts of Profession* (see Chapter 2). Identify any provisions related to COIs and compare those provisions with the COI provisions in the *Guidelines for Ethical Conduct for the PA Profession*.

Analysis: ______________________________

____

____

---

37 Latham SR. Medical professionalism: a Parsonian view. *Mount Sinai Journal of Medicine*. 2002;69(6):367.

38 Guidelines for ethical conduct for the PA profession. AAPA. https://www.aapa.org/wp-content/uploads/2017/02/16-EthicalConduct.pdf. Accessed October 31, 2019.

39 Code of ethics for the physical therapist. APTA. https://www.apta.org/siteassets/pdfs/policies/codeofethicshods06-20-28-25.pdf. Accessed January 25, 2021.

40 AARC statement of ethics and professional conduct. AARC. https://www.aarc.org/wp-content/uploads/2017/03/statement-of-ethics.pdf. Accessed January 25, 2021.

41 AOTA 2020 occupational therapy code of ethics. AOTA. https://www.aota.org/-/media/Corporate/Files/Practice/Ethics/AOTA-2020-Code-of-Ethics.pdf. Accessed January 25, 2021.

Ethics III, Rule of Ethics B reads, "Individuals shall avoid engaging in conflicts of interest whereby personal, financial, or other considerations have the potential to influence or compromise professional judgment and objectivity."[42]

5. Managing COIs (Including COI Regs)

Health professionals may be involved in medical practice, medical education, or medical research, and COIs can occur in any or all of these areas. In order to appropriately navigate a COI, a health professional should be familiar with any relevant federal and/or state laws, rules or regulations, as well as any pertinent institutional or organizational COI policies.

"Most conflict of interest policies include the basic elements of the disclosure of financial relationships, the prohibition of certain relationships, and the management of conflicts of interest that have been identified. All of these elements are sometimes described under the general rubric of managing conflicts of interest."[43] These elements are sometimes referred to as the "three-D" approach to COIs—disclosure, disqualification (which includes recusal from participation in a specific decision), and divestiture.

5.1. Disclosure of COIs

COI policies typically require that a covered clinician or researcher disclose to his or her institution the existence of outside relationships giving rise to secondary interests. Some policies also require that financial secondary interests be disclosed to others who might be affected—e.g., research subjects, journal readers, students, or patients.

Besides organizational COI policies, the law has a role to play as well. For example, the Physician Payment Sunshine Act, part of the 2010 Affordable Care Act, requires all drug and device companies to publicly report their payments to healthcare providers. (A search tool used to search payments made by drug and medical device companies to physicians and teaching hospitals is available at https://openpaymentsdata.cms.gov/.) ProPublica[44] has been tracking drug company payments to doctors since 2010 through a project known as Dollars for Docs.[45] Consider the following piece, published in 2016:

> **Now There's Proof: Docs Who Get Company Cash Tend to Prescribe More Brand-Name Meds**
> by Charles Ornstein, Mike Tigas, and Ryann Grochowski Jones
> March 17, 2016, 5 a.m. EDT
> Doctors have long disputed that the payments they receive from pharmaceutical companies have any relationship to how they prescribe drugs.

42 Code of ethics. ASHA. https://www.asha.org/code-of-ethics/#sec1.4. Accessed June 8, 2021.

43 Lo B, Field MJ, ed. *Conflict of Interest in Medical Research, Education, and Practice.* Washington DC: National Academies Press; 2009:64. Admittedly, this use of forms of the word "manage" to signify multiple elements is confusing. To clarify, "managing" COIs includes the whole shebang (disclosure, prohibition, and management of COIs); "management" of COIs excludes disclosure and prohibition approaches.

44 ProPublica is an American "nonprofit newsroom that aims to produce investigative journalism in the public interest." See Wikipedia. https://en.wikipedia.org/wiki/ProPublica. Accessed January 26, 2020.

45 Dollars for docs. https://projects.propublica.org/docdollars/. Accessed January 26, 2020.

> There's been little evidence to settle the matter—until now.
>
> A ProPublica analysis has found for the first time that doctors who receive payments from the medical industry do indeed tend to prescribe drugs differently than their colleagues who don't. And the more money they receive, on average, the more brand-name medications they prescribe.
>
> We matched records on payments from pharmaceutical and medical device makers in 2014 with corresponding data on doctors' medication choices in Medicare's prescription drug program. . . .
>
> Doctors who got money from drug and device makers—even just a meal—prescribed a higher percentage of brand-name drugs overall than doctors who didn't, our analysis showed. Indeed, doctors who received industry payments were two to three times as likely to prescribe brand-name drugs at exceptionally high rates as others in their specialty.
>
> Doctors who received more than $5,000 from companies in 2014 typically had the highest brand-name prescribing percentages. Among internists who received no payments, for example, the average brand-name prescribing rate was about 20 percent, compared to about 30 percent for those who received more than $5,000.
>
> ProPublica's analysis doesn't prove industry payments sway doctors to prescribe particular drugs, or even a particular company's drugs. Rather, it shows that payments are associated with an approach to prescribing that, writ large, benefits drug companies' bottom line. . . .[46]

According to the National Academy of Sciences report on COIs, disclosure is a necessary part of COI policies, but it is not enough because, for example, "when a . . . conflict of interest is disclosed to individual patients, students, or research participants, they often lack the knowledge and perspective to assess the [COI] . . . and may have no satisfactory options if they have concerns about it."[47] Conflicts that are disclosed but not eliminated or managed can continue to pose risks to judgment and undermine public trust.[48]

5.2. Prohibiting or Eliminating COIs (AKA Disqualification)

Eliminating COIs (disqualification) is generally required where the outside relationship giving rise to the secondary interest poses a serious threat to the primary interest. The quintessential example is judicial recusal—"the process by which a judge is disqualified on objection of either party (or disqualifies himself or herself) from hearing a lawsuit because of self interest [*sic*], bias, or prejudice."[49] Thus, under Canon 3 of the Code of Conduct for United States Judges,

> A judge shall disqualify himself or herself in a proceeding in which the judge's impartiality might reasonably be questioned, including but not limited to instances in which . . . the judge knows that the judge . . . has a financial interest in the subject matter in controversy . . . .[50]

46 Ornstein C, Tigas M, Grochowski Jones R. Now there's proof: docs who get company cash tend to prescribe more brand-name meds. ProPublica. https://www.propublica.org/article/doctors-who-take-company-cash-tend-to-prescribe-more-brand-name-drugs. Published March 17, 2016. Accessed January 26, 2020.

47 Lo B, Field MJ, ed. *Conflict of Interest in Medical Research, Education, and Practice.* Washington DC: National Academies Press; 2009: 8. https://doi.org/10.17226/12598.

48 Lo B, Field MJ, ed. Conflict of Interest in Medical Research, Education, and Practice. Washington DC: National Academies Press; 2009:8. https://doi.org/10.17226/12598.

49 *Black's Law Dictionary.* Abridged 6th ed. St. Paul, MN: West Publishing; 1991:884.

50 Code of conduct for United States judges. United States Courts. https://www.uscourts.gov/judges-judgeships/code-conduct-united-states-judges. Accessed January 29, 2020.

5.3. Management of COIs (Divestiture)[51]

"The management of a conflict of interest is necessary when an assessment of an individual's financial relationships identifies a conflict of interest and when disclosure alone is inadequate but elimination [i.e., prohibition or disqualification] of the conflict is a requirement that is too severe."[52] Let's reconsider the above example of the judge faced with a financial secondary interest. Canon 3 of the Code of Conduct for United States Judges also provides:

> Notwithstanding the preceding provisions of this Canon, if a judge would be disqualified because of a financial interest in a party . . . disqualification is not required if the judge . . . divests the interest that provides the grounds for disqualification.[53]

WRAP-UP

Chapter Summary

As it relates to practicing health professionals, a COI is a situation in which a health professional's personal interests (so-called *secondary interests*) conflict with and create an *undue risk* of compromising his or her fiduciary responsibilities to the patient (the *primary interest*). Secondary interests can be but need not be financial. Determining whether a secondary interest poses an undue risk requires judgment and is a fact-intensive inquiry. The mere finding of a COI says nothing about the moral character or behavior of the conflicted individual—what matters is how the individual manages the COI. Depending on the nature of the COI, options include *disclosure* of the COI, *disqualification* (i.e., recusal) from the activity affecting the primary interest, and *divestiture* of the secondary interest giving rise to the conflict. COIs that are inappropriately managed violate the *internal morality of medicine* and undermine *medical professionalism*; they threaten both the integrity of medical judgment and public confidence in that integrity. COIs must be distinguished from conflicts of obligation (COO) and conflicts of commitment (COC).

Review Questions

1. Define the term *conflict of interest* (COI).
2. How do COIs arise? Are COIs intrinsically immoral?
3. What elements constitute COIs? Explain the concept of *undue influence* or *undue risk* as it relates to COI.

---

51 Admittedly, attaching multiple meanings to various forms of the word "manage" is confusing. To clarify, herein "managing" COIs includes the whole shebang (disclosure, prohibition, and management—i.e., finessing—of COIs); "management" of COIs excludes disclosure and prohibition approaches.

52 Lo B, Field MJ, ed. *Conflict of Interest in Medical Research, Education, and Practice.* Washington DC: National Academies Press; 2009:80. https://doi.org/10.17226/12598.

53 Code of Conduct for United States Judges. United States Courts. https://www.uscourts.gov/judges-judgeships/code-conduct-united-states-judges. Accessed January 29, 2020.

4. What kinds of *secondary interests* exist? Give examples of each.
5. How are bias and COI related?
6. Compare and contrast COI, COO, and COC. Give an example of each.
7. Explain why COIs are morally significant from the standpoint of the consequentialist. Explain why COIs are morally significant from a *moral rules* standpoint. Explain why COIs are morally significant from a *medical professionalism* standpoint.
8. List and explain the various options for managing COIs.

Case Analyses

Case 6.A Analysis

The case concerns medical practice, and so the primary interest at stake is promoting and protecting the medical welfare of Mr. Neade. As is true of practically all practicing clinicians, Dr. Portes has a secondary interest in financial gain. The financial arrangement between Dr. Portes and Chicago HMO created financial incentives for Dr. Portes to avoid referring member patients such as Mr. Neade for angiography. The incentives came in the form of both a carrot and a stick. On the carrot side, Dr. Portes would, assuming he were the sole full-time physician at Primary Care Family Center, receive 60% of any portion of the $75,000 (potentially $45,000) Medical Incentive Fund (MIF) not used for referrals or outside tests. On the stick side, if the $75,000 MIF was exhausted prior to the end of the year, Dr. Portes would be required to pay the costs of any additional consultations and/or medical testing.

Case 6.B Analysis

Yes, there is arguably a COI. Recall that a COI exists if the gynecology resident has a secondary interest that creates a risk of undue influence on decisions or actions affecting a primary interest. In this case, the primary interest refers to Debbie's best medical interests. While exactly what her best interests are is an important question, it is not relevant to the COI issue. Rather, this question tests your ability to recognize that the gynecology resident has a nonfinancial secondary interest at stake, one that might be unduly influencing his clinical actions vis-à-vis Debbie. In this case, the resident's secondary interest is in sleep:

> The call came in the middle of the night. As a gynecology resident rotating through a large, private hospital, I had come to detest telephone calls, because invariably I would be up for several hours and would not feel good the next day. . . . As I trudged along, bumping sleepily against walls and corners and not believing I was up again, I tried to imagine what I might find at the end of my walk.[54]

Quite apart from any effect that sleep-deprivation might have had on the resident's ability to think clearly, he/she had an understandable human interest in getting back to sleep as soon as possible, an interest that may have unduly influenced his/her actions vis-à-vis Debbie. How? First, it is not hard to imagine that, wanting to return to his/her bed ASAP, the resident rushed to judgment about what Debbie's best medical interests were; that rush to judgment culminated in the euthanasia of Debbie. A second way in which the resident's interest in sleep might have influenced his/her actions vis-à-vis Debbie is that he/she might simply have decided that euthanizing Debbie was the fastest way for him/her to get back to sleep and to have a chance of staying asleep.

54 Name Withheld by Request. It's over, Debbie. *JAMA*. 1988;259(2):272.

Case 6.C Analysis

Yes, there is an identifiable COI. As discussed in the Case 6.A analysis, the primary interest at stake is promoting and protecting the medical welfare of Mr. Neade. The secondary interest is Dr. Portes' interest in financial gain. The crucial issue is whether the circumstances described create a risk that Dr. Portes' professional judgment or his decision regarding authorization of an angiogram for Mr. Neade would be unduly influenced by his secondary interest in financial gain. Arguably yes. The factors to be considered in weighing the likelihood of undue influence include (1) the value of the secondary interest and (2) the extent of discretion/latitude enjoyed by Dr. Portes in making the decision regarding the angiogram. Regarding factor 1, the financial arrangement between Dr. Portes and Chicago HMO created powerful financial incentives for Dr. Portes to avoid referring member patients such as Mr. Neade for outside testing such as angiography. The incentives came in the form of both a carrot and a stick. On the carrot side, Dr. Portes would, assuming he were the sole full-time physician at Primary Care Family Center, receive 60% of any portion of the $75,000 (potentially $45,000) Medical Incentive Fund (MIF) not used for referrals or outside tests. Since in 1990—the year in which the events of *Neade v. Portes* took place—the average doctor's pre-tax earnings were $155,800 according to the American Medical Association (AMA),[55] the Medical Incentive Fund afforded Dr. Portes an opportunity to increase his income by 29%. On the stick side, if the $75,000 MIF was exhausted prior to the end of the year, Dr. Portes would be required to pay the costs of any additional consultations and/or medical testing, and these costs were potentially significant.[56] Regarding factor 2—the extent of discretion enjoyed by Dr. Portes in making the decision to approve (or not approve) the angiogram—it is probably safe to say that he enjoyed wide latitude in this regard. While Mr. Neade might have been able to seek a second opinion with another provider within the Chicago HMO network, one must wonder whether he would have been able to find one who was not similarly conflicted.

Case 6.D Analysis

The case involves patient care, and so the relevant primary interest is in promoting and protecting the welfare of patients. Here there is a conflict between two interests—Harry's interest in confidentiality and Sally's interest in being warned/protected from harm. Because both interests can be considered primary interests, we are faced with a conflict of obligations (COO) as opposed to a conflict of interests (COI).

Case 6.E Analysis

Regarding the Hippocratic Oath, the most relevant provision reads as follows: "Into whatever homes I go, I will enter them for the benefit of the sick, avoiding any voluntary act of impropriety or corruption, including the seduction of women or men, whether they are free men or slaves." In this provision, oath takers are promising that, when acting in a medical capacity, they will act in the best medical interests of their patients—or, in other words, in accordance with the *primary interest* (promoting and protecting the welfare of patients) as relates to the realm

55 Bencivenga J. Pay of physicians soaring since 1966. *The Christian Science Monitor.* November 21, 1991. https://www.csmonitor.com/1991/1121/21071.html.

56 Assuming the cost of a coronary angiogram to be $5,000–$10,000 in 2019 (How much does an angiogram cost. Costhelperhealth. Health Cost Helper. https://health.costhelper.com/angiograms.html. Accessed October 31, 2019). According to the *New York Times*, the average cost of a typical angioplasty in the United States is $32,000. (Sanger-Katz M. In the U.S., an angioplasty costs $32,000. Elsewhere? Maybe $6,400. *New York Times*. December 27, 2019. https://www.nytimes.com/2019/12/27/upshot/expensive-health-care-world-comparison.html?auth=login-email&login=email.) Healthcare costs have increased by a factor of about 4.8 between 1990 and 2019 (Amadeo K. The rising cost of health care by year and its causes. *The Balance*. June 25, 2019. https://www.thebalance.com/causes-of-rising-healthcare-costs-4064878. Accessed October 31, 2019.)

of clinical practice. Oath takers also promise to avoid improper or corrupt acts, presumably motivated by *secondary interests*, including but presumably not limited to sexual interests ("the seduction of women or men").

As they relate to COIs, the Guidelines for Ethical Conduct for the PA Profession are distinguishable from the Oath in a few ways. First, unlike the Oath, they explicitly use to term "conflict of interest." Second, they focus almost exclusively on financial COIs. Thirdly, and perhaps most importantly, the language employed in the Guidelines is aspirational ("should avoid," "should disclose," and "is discouraged") as opposed to prescriptive ("shall avoid," "shall disclose," and "is prohibited").[57] That seems oddly incommensurate.

57 Lon Fuller, in his book *The Morality of Law*, distinguished between the morality of aspiration and the morality of duty. See Fuller LL. *The Morality of Law*. New Haven and London: Yale University Press;1964.

CHAPTER 7

Informed Consent

LEARNING OBJECTIVES

1. Explain how *informed consent* relates to the *moral rules* and the principle of *respect for autonomy*.
2. Explain how the doctrine of informed consent relates to decisional capacity and voluntary choice.
3. Define *battery*, *tort*, and *intentional tort*.
4. List the elements that a plaintiff must prove in order to prevail in an action for *negligent informed consent*.
5. Given a scenario implicating consent, recognize whether it describes *battery*, or *negligence*, or neither.
6. Compare and contrast the *professional disclosure standard* and the *reasonable patient disclosure standard*.
7. List and explain the various exceptions to the rule requiring that consent be obtained prior to a medical touching.
8. Explain the concept of a *non-delegable duty* as it relates to *informed consent*.
9. Recognize and define *ghost surgery* and explain how it relates to *battery* and *consent*.
10. List, recognize and discuss some new disclosure obligations, including, e.g., financial conflicts of interest.

Michael: *My father made him an offer he couldn't refuse.*

Kay: *What was that?*

Michael: *Luca Brasi held a gun to his head, and my father assured him that either his brains or his signature would be on the contract.*[1]

1. Informed Consent: Its Ethical Basis

In the seminal case *Schloendorff v. Society of New York Hospital*, Justice Benjamin Cardozo penned the following oft-quoted formulation of the doctrine of informed consent:

Every human being of adult years and sound mind has a right to determine what shall be done with his own body; and a surgeon who performs an operation without his patient's consent commits an assault for which he is liable in damages . . . . This is true except in cases of emergency where the patient is

1 Puzo, Mario. The Godfather. New York: G. P. Putnam's Sons, 2022.

unconscious and where it is necessary to operate before consent can be obtained.[2]

1.1. Informed Consent and the Moral Rules

The obligation to obtain informed consent from patients prior to intervening medically is another example (see, e.g., confidentiality in Chapter 5) of a particular moral rule derived from the interplay between the general moral rules and the practice of medicine. In the case of informed consent, the general moral rules implicated are "do not deprive of freedom" and "do not neglect your duty." Because informed consent, like confidentiality, is a legal as well as a moral imperative, the general moral rule "obey the law" is also implicated.

1.2. Informed Consent and Autonomous Choice

In terms of the principles of biomedical ethics discussed in Chapter 1, informed consent is most closely related to the *principle of respect for autonomy/persons*, which asserts "first, that individuals should be treated as autonomous agents, and second, that persons with diminished autonomy are entitled to protection."[3] To treat individuals as autonomous agents means to allow them to exercise their right of self-determination, "free from both controlling interference by others and from limitations, such as inadequate understanding, that prevent meaningful choice."[4]

Autonomous choice requires that (1) the person deciding have decisional capacity, (2) the decision be voluntary, and (3) the decision be adequately informed. While strictly speaking the focus of informed consent is on the third prong of the autonomy trident, its connotation includes the first two as well. Therefore, we shall discuss all three elements here.

1.2.1. Decisional Capacity

Autonomous choice requires that the person choosing possesses *decisional capacity*.[5] Deciding that someone possesses capacity means that we are answering "yes" to the question, "Should we allow this person to make this decision under these circumstances?"

Recall that the principle of autonomy requires that individuals be treated as autonomous agents, but also that persons with diminished autonomy be protected. Whenever a patient makes a choice, the health professional must decide whether the patient has decisional capacity (and so should be allowed to choose) or whether the patient does not (and so must be protected). In making the capacity determination, one balances the risk of wrongfully denying the "competent" patient's self-determination against the risk of failing to protect from harm the "incompetent" patient who is unable to protect him or herself. Keep in mind that the law presumes, in the absence of evidence to the contrary, that persons have decisional capacity.

1.2.1.1. Formulations of Decisional Capacity. Gert et al. have proffered the so-called "ability to make a rational decision" formulation, under which a person has decisional capacity if and only if he has the ability to make a rational decision of a certain kind. Under this formulation, a person is said to have decisional capacity if he or she (1) does not have a cognitive disability interfering with either his/her ability to *understand* the information

2 *Schloendorff v. Society of New York Hospital,* 105 N.E. 92 (N.Y. 1914).

3 Beauchamp TL, Childress JF. Principles of Biomedical Ethics. 5th ed. Oxford University Press, 2001. http://ohsr.od.nih.gov/guidelines/belmont.html. Accessed June 11, 2008.

4 Beauchamp TL, Childress JF. *Principles of Biomedical Ethics.* 5th ed. Oxford University Press, 2001:58. http://ohsr.od.nih.gov/guidelines/belmont.html. Accessed June 11, 2008

5 While the term *competency* is sometimes used colloquially in place of decisional capacity, the two are not synonymous. *Incompetency* refers to a formal judicial finding that a person cannot make legally effective decisions regarding his/her own affairs. The law presumes that . . . Herein, when I intend competency in its colloquial sense, I will enclose it in quotation marks, e.g., "competent."

provided or his or her ability to *appreciate* that the information applies to him or her and (2) does not have a volitional or affective disability that interferes with his or her ability to make a *rational* decision.[6]

An alternative formulation advanced by Byron Chell holds that a person is considered to have decisional capacity if (1) he or she understands the situation and the consequences of his decision and 2) the decision is based upon adequate reasons.[7] Reasons are "conscious rational beliefs that can make some otherwise irrational actions, rational."[8]

These formulations have in common the following key components of decisional capacity: (1) *communication* by the patient of a treatment choice; (2) the patient's *understanding* his or her medical situation and the information provided by the clinician; (3) the patient's *appreciation* of the fact that the information applies to him or her; and (4) the choice is the product of *rationalization/reasoning* in which the patient weighs the pros and cons of the various options in reaching a decision consistent with his or her best interests and personal values.[9]

CASE 7.A

Consider the following scenario.

> A 79-year-old male with coronary artery disease, hypertension, non-insulin-dependent mellitus, moderate dementia, and chronic renal insufficiency is admitted after a fall evaluation. He is widowed and lives in an assisted living facility. He's accompanied by his niece, is alert, and oriented to person. He thinks he is in a clinic and is unable to state the year, but the remainder of the examination is unremarkable. His labs are notable for potassium of 6.3 mmol/L, BUN of 78 mg/dL, and Cr of 3.7 mg/dL. The niece reports that the patient is not fond of medical care, thus the most recent labs are from two years ago (and indicate a BUN of 39 and Cr of 2.8, with an upward trend over the past decade). You discuss possible long-term need for dialysis with the patient and niece, and the patient clearly states, "No." However, he also states that it is 1988. . . .
>
> The consulting nephrologist reviews their recommendations [for dialysis] with the patient and niece as well, and the patient consistently refuses. Having clearly communicated his choice, you ask the patient if he understands the situation. He says, "My kidneys are failing. That's how I got the high potassium." You ask him what that means. "They aren't going to function on their own much longer," he says. "I could die from it."
>
> You . . . ask him why he doesn't want dialysis. "I don't want dialysis because I don't want to spend my life hooked up to machines three times a week," the patient explains. "I just want to let things run their natural course." The niece says her uncle wouldn't have wanted dialysis even if it were 10 years ago, so she's not surprised he is refusing now.[10]

Does this patient possess decisional capacity? In other words, should he be allowed to make the decision to refuse dialysis?

---

6 Gert B, Culver CM, Clouser KD. *Bioethics: A Return to Fundamentals.* New York, NY: Oxford University Press; 1997:chapter 6.

7 Chell B. Competency: what it is, what it isn't , and why it matters. In: Monagle JF, Thomasma DC, eds. *Health Care Ethics: Critical Issues for the 21st Century.* Sudbury, MA: Jones and Bartlett; 2005.

8 Gert B. *Morality: Its Nature and Justification.* Oxford University Press; 1998:56. Gert uses the example that believing that having one's right arm amputated will save one's life is a reason for having one's arm amputated.

9 Dastidar JG, Odden A. How do I determine if my patient has decision-making capacity? *The Hospitalist.* 2011 August;2011(8). https://www.the-hospitalist.org/hospitalist/article/124731/how-do-i-determine-if-my-patient-has-decision-making-capacity. Accessed November 13, 2019.

10 Dastidar JG, Odden A. How do I determine if my patient has decision-making capacity? *The Hospitalist.* 2011 August;2011(8). https://www.the-hospitalist.org/hospitalist/article/124731/how-do-i-determine-if-my-patient-has-decision-making-capacity. Accessed November 13, 2019.

Analysis: ____________________

____

____

____

____

____

____

____

____

____

1.2.1.2. Religious Refusals. Consider the patient who refuses a lifesaving blood transfusion, stating "I am a Jehovah's Witness and I believe it is a violation of God's law to accept such blood. I understand the consequence of my refusal is death and I accept that result." Does such a patient have decisional capacity?

If you try to apply the above formulations of decisional capacity to such a patient, you will see that it is the *rationality* of the decision—the *adequacy of the reasons* given for refusing the transfusion—that is the crux of the issue. Is the belief that accepting a blood transfusion will have bad consequences for one in the afterlife a rational belief? Is it an adequate reason for refusing the transfusion? Gert et al. say yes:

> No rankings that are held by any significant religious, national, or cultural group count as irrational. The ranking by Jehovah's Witnesses of the harms that would be suffered in an afterlife as worse than dying decades earlier than one would if one accepted a transfusion is not an irrational ranking. Similarly, psychiatrists do not regard any beliefs held by any significant religious, national, or cultural group as delusions or irrational beliefs. The belief by Jehovah's Witnesses that accepting blood transfusions will have bad consequences for one's afterlife is not regarded as an irrational belief or delusion.[11]

Byron Chell (see above), on the other hand, argues that religious beliefs are irrational but that persons holding such beliefs should be deemed competent (i.e., to possess decisional capacity so long as the religious belief involved is "within our common religious experience or common notions of religion and do not appear to us 'crazy' or 'nonreligious.'"[12] And, in fact, "most of the [legal] cases that have considered this issue have concluded that [otherwise] competent Jehovah's Witnesses may choose to forgo medical treatment, whatever the results of those decisions may be . . ."[13]

1.2.2. Voluntary Choice

A decision is *voluntary* if "proceeding from the free and unrestrained will of the person."[14] An *involuntary* decision is one made against the expressed wishes of the decisionmaker, usually "under duress, force, or coercion."[15] The paradigmatic example of such an involuntary act is the *coercive* contractual release secured by Don Vito Corleone in *The Godfather* as recounted in the quotation that opened this chapter.

11 Gert B, Culver CM, Danner Clouser KD. Bioethics: A Return to Fundamentals. New York, NY: Oxford University Press; 1997: 28.

12 Chell B. Competency: what it is, what it isn't, and why it matters. In: Monagle JF, Thomasma DC, eds. Health Care Ethics: Critical Issues for the 21st Century. Sudbury, MA: Jones and Bartlett; 2005.

13 Furrow BR, Greaney TL, Johnson SH, Jost TS, Schwartz RL. *Health Law: Cases, Materials and Problems.* 7th ed. St. Paul, MN: West Publishing; 2013.

14 *Black's Law Dictionary.* 6th ed. St. Paul, MN: West Publishing; 1994:1088.

15 *Black's Law Dictionary.* 6th ed. St. Paul, MN: West Publishing; 1994:574.

Of course, not all attempts to influence the decisions of others undermine voluntariness—consider *persuasion*, for example. To persuade someone is to "cause (a person) to believe or do something by reasoning with him."[16] Indeed, much of the practice of medicine involves attempts to convince patients to do something—e.g., undergo a necessary diagnostic test or therapeutic procedure, or adopt a more salutary lifestyle—through the use of reason.

Manipulation lies somewhere on the continuum between persuasion (permissible) and coercion (impermissible), depending on the specifics of the case. "A statement or action can be counted manipulative to the extent that it does not sufficiently engage or appeal to people's capacity for reflective and deliberative choice."[17] Some forms of manipulation are egregious—consider, for example, subliminal advertising.[18] Other forms are less so. Consider the following:

> Suppose that public health officials try to persuade people to engage in certain behavior with the help of relative risk information: "If you do not do X, your chances of death from heart disease will triple!" But suppose that for the relevant population, the chance of death from heart disease is very small – say, one in 100,000 – and that people are far more influenced by the idea of "tripling the risk" than they would be if they learned that if they do not do X, they could increase a 1/100,000 risk to a 3/100,000 risk (to say the least, a modest increase). The relative risk frame is far more attention grabbing than the absolute risk frame; a tripling of a risk sounds alarming, but if the increase is by merely 2/100,000, people might not be much concerned. It is certainly reasonable to take the choice of the relative risk frame (which suggests a large impact on health) is an effort to frighten people and thus to manipulate them (at least in a mild sense).[19]

1.2.3. Informed Choice

For a choice to be autonomous it must be adequately informed. In the context of medical decision making, the patient must be informed about his/her medical situation and the foreseeable consequences of his/her decision. While we shall have more to say about the content of adequate informed consent below, it is generally true that:

> Under the doctrine of informed consent, it is generally held that a physician who performs a diagnostic, therapeutic, or surgical procedure has a duty to disclose to a patient of sound mind, in the absence of an emergency that warrants immediate medical treatment, (1) the diagnosis, (2) the general nature of the contemplated procedure, (3) the material risks involved in the procedure, (4) the probability of success associated with the procedure, (5) the prognosis of the procedure is not carried out, and (6) the existence of any alternatives to the procedure . . . [20]

16 *Oxford American Dictionary.* Heald Colleges edition. New York, NY: Oxford University Press; 1980:666.

17 Sunstein CR. Fifty shades of manipulation. *J. Marketing Behav.* 1:31. https://papers.ssrn.com/sol3/papers.cfm?abstract_id=2565892. Accessed November 25, 2019.

18 Bullock A. Subliminal advertising: the secret sales pitch. http://www.subliminalsex.com/subliminal%20advertising%20example.htm. Accessed November 25, 2019.

19 Sunstein, CR. Fifty shades of manipulation. *J Marketing Behav.* 1:14. https://papers.ssrn.com/sol3/papers.cfm?abstract_id=2565892. Accessed November 25, 2019.

20 *Hook v. Rothstein,* 281 S.C. 541, 316 S.E. (2d) 690 (1984).

2. Informed Consent: Its Legal Basis

The modern legal approach to cases involving consent issues is to distinguish between those in which a medical intervention takes place without consent, and those in which consent is obtained but is somehow substandard or flawed. The former cases are treated as *battery*; the latter are treated as cases of *negligence*.

> In the typical informed consent claim, the patient has given technical consent to being "touched" by the defendant but argues that consent would not have been given if appropriate disclosures had been made. Courts generally reject battery claims because the patient has "consented" to the touching. In most jurisdictions, battery claims are reserved for those situations in which (1) the patient has not consented to any procedure at all, (2) the health care provider performs a completely different procedure than that for which consent was given, (3) the health care provider performs a procedure on the wrong area of the body, or (4) a different, unconsented-to provider performs the procedure.[21]

Whether a suit is brought against you in battery or in negligence may matter a great deal. First, statutes of limitations often differ between the two. Second, punitive damages are almost never available to plaintiffs in negligence suits but may be in cases involving battery. Third, under the terms of some medical malpractice insurance policies, intentional torts such as battery may be excluded from coverage.

2.1. Battery as a Legal Basis

Battery is an *intentional tort* and is defined as the intentional,[22] unconsented to, harmful or offensive contact with the person of another. A *tort* is "a legal wrong committed upon the person or property [of another] independent of contract."[23] An *intentional tort* is a "tort or wrong perpetrated by one who intends to do that which the law has declared wrong . . . ."[24] Let's look at some actual cases to see how the definition of battery applies to the real world.

In *Mohr v. Williams*,[25] Mrs. Mohr consulted Dr. Williams about a right ear disorder. Dr. Williams examined the ear and attempted to examine the left ear too, but was unable to do so completely because of cerumen. Mrs. Mohr submitted to general anesthesia on the understanding that Dr. Williams would operate on the diseased right ear. After examining both ears under general anesthesia, Dr. Williams decided that the condition of the left ear was worse than that of the right, and so operated on the left ear only. When she awakened and learned what had happened, Mrs. Mohr sued Dr. Williams in battery.

Did the surgery involve *intentional, unconsented to, harmful or offensive* contact with the patient? Yes. Dr. Williams argued that the contact was neither harmful nor offensive since it ameliorated her left ear disorder; but while the court found that "the operation complained of was skillfully performed and of a generally beneficial nature," it nonetheless decided that unconsented-to medical contact is offensive. Nor did it matter that Dr. Williams did not intend any harm or offense—what matters is that he intended the contact. Finally, Dr. Williams also argued that Mrs. Mohr consented to the surgery. He argued, first, that her consent was *express*, in that she consented to surgery on her more diseased ear, which is what he performed.

---

21 Hall MA, Bobinski MA, Orentlicher D. *Health Care Law and Ethics*. 7th ed. Austin, TX: Aspen Publishers; 2007:215.
22 The law of battery does NOT require that the defendant have intended to produce harm or offense.
23 *Black's Law Dictionary*. Abridged 6th ed. St. Paul, MN: West Publishing; 1994:104.
24 *Black's Law Dictionary*. Abridged 6th ed. St. Paul, MN: West Publishing; 1994:104.
25 *Mohr v. Williams*, 95 Minn. 261, 104 N.W. 12 (Sup. Ct. Minn. 1905).

The court, while rejecting the argument, wrote that the "contention [was] not without merit." Alternatively, Dr. Williams argued that Mrs. Mohr's consent was *implied* by law under either of two doctrines—the *emergency doctrine* and the *extension doctrine*.

> If a person should be injured to the extent of rendering him unconscious, and his injuries were of such a nature as to require prompt surgical attention, a physician called to attend him would be justified in applying such medical or surgical treatment as might reasonably be necessary for the preservation of his life or limb, and consent on the part of the injured person would be implied. And again, if, in the course of an operation to which the patient consented, the physician should discover conditions not anticipated before the operation was commenced, and which, if not removed, would endanger the life or health of the patient, he would, though no express consent was obtained or given, be justified in extending the operation to remove and overcome them.[26]

The court held that neither exception was applicable.

Next consider the case of *Perna v. Pirozzi*,[27] which affords us an opportunity to explore further the scope of a patient's consent. Dr. Pirozzi, a urologist, advised his patient Mr. Perna to have surgery for removal of kidney stones. Mr. Perna agreed, requesting that Dr. Pirozzi perform the surgery, and signed a consent form naming Dr. Pirozzi as the operating surgeon and authorizing him to operate with the help of unnamed "assistants." Two days later the surgery was performed by Drs. Del Gaizo and Ciccone, partners of Dr. Pirozzi, who was not present. Mr. Perna sues Drs. Del Gaizo and Ciccone for battery.

Was this a battery? Yes, it was. The crucial legal issue was whether Mr. Perna's consent to surgery by Dr. Pirozzi authorized other surgeons to operate in his place. In answer, the court wrote, "the performance of the operation by a physician other than the one named in the consent form . . . [is] 'ghost surgery'" and is a battery because consent is nontransferable. Absent an emergency, patients have the right to determine not only whether surgery is to be performed on them, but who shall perform it."[27]

Finally, consider the case of *Tisdale v. Pruitt*,[28] which further elucidates the nature of consent. Ms. Tisdale was told by her family physician that she needed a dilatation and curettage (D&C) for a missed abortion. Her insurer required a second opinion and referred her to Dr. Pruitt. Ms. Tisdale informed Dr. Pruitt's receptionist that she was there only for a second opinion, who noted this on the chart in two places. Dr. Pruitt, however, did not read the chart. He placed Ms. Tisdale on the exam table, examined her and proceeded to do the D&C. The procedure lasted about five minutes, during which Ms. Tisdale was upset and crying. It was an unsatisfactory D&C, and a second one was needed, and was done by her family physician in the hospital under general anesthesia. Ms. Tisdale sued Dr. Pruitt for battery. In his own defense, Dr. Pruitt testified that Ms. Tisdale was "just absolutely docile I guess, and I just assumed that she was acquiescing, but I thought that I had her consent and her . . . very informed consent."[28] He testified, in essence, that Ms. Tisdale's consent to the D&C was implied (see *Mohr v. Williams*, above) by her passivity and silence.[29]

---

26 *Mohr v. Williams,* 95 Minn. 261, 104 N.W. 12 (Sup. Ct. Minn. 1905), at 269.

27 *Perna v. Pirozzi,* 92 N.J. 446, 457 A.2d 431 (Sup. Ct. N.J. 1983).

28 *Tisdale v. Pruitt,* 394 S.E.2d 857 (Ct. App. S.C. 1990).

29 The relevant legal maxim is "qui tacet, consentire videtur," which translates as "he who is silent is taken to agree. See, e.g., Bolt R. *A Man For All Seasons.* Act 2. See also Silence procedure. Wikipedia. https://en.wikipedia.org/wiki/Silence_procedure. Accessed November 27, 2019.

Was this a battery? Clearly the crucial issue in this case is, what happens when the health professional is mistaken about consent—believing that the patient has given consent when she in fact has not? The legal rule is, "If it *reasonably* seemed to the . . . [health professional] that the . . . [patient] consented, consent will be held to exist regardless of the . . . [patient's] subjective state of mind. That is, it is the *objective* manifestations by the . . . [patient] that are taken into account . . . "[30] (Italics added) Where the defendant's mistaken belief that the patient has consented is unreasonable—concluding that a plaintiff has consented when no reasonable person would so conclude under the circumstances—then a battery will be held to have occurred. So the question becomes, "Was Dr. Pruitt's belief that Ms. Tisdale had impliedly consent—by her silence and passivity—reasonable under the circumstances?" No. As indicated above, Dr. Pruitt's receptionist had indicated in two places on Ms. Tisdale's chart that she was there for a second opinion. In order to characterize Dr. Pruitt's mistake regarding consent as reasonable, one would have to argue that it is reasonable for a doctor not to read a patient's chart before doing a procedure on that patient. Therefore, this was a battery.

2.2. Negligence as a Legal Basis

The tort of negligence, in contrast, is one in which the wrong-doer or tortfeasor "fails to exercise . . . care in doing what is otherwise permissible."[31] We shall deal extensively with negligence in Chapter 11, but for now suffice it to say that in order to prevail in an action for negligent informed consent against a health professional, the plaintiff must prove that: 1) the treatment, or its refusal, carried a risk that was not disclosed to the patient; 2) the failure to disclose the risk breached the applicable standard of care (see Chapter 11); and 3) the patient was injured as a result of the nondisclosure (i.e., the nondisclosure caused the patient's injury). To prevail on this third element, the patient must prove both that the undisclosed risk materialized and that, had the risk of the treatment (or its refusal) been disclosed, the patient would have made a different treatment choice and thus avoided the injury.

2.2.1. *Standards of Disclosure*

To say that a "failure to disclose the risk breached the applicable standard of care" is to say that the health professional failed to disclose a risk that he/she should have disclosed; but how was the health professional who is being sued supposed to know whether a particular risk should have been disclosed? After all, presumably he/she disclosed to the patient those risks he/she thought warranted disclosure. Alas, legally speaking, he/she doesn't get to decide what should have been disclosed. Who does? The answer depends on the state in which you practice.

2.2.1.1. Professional Disclosure Standard. About half of the fifty states apply the so-called *professional disclosure standard*, requiring practitioners to disclose information/risks that would be disclosed by a reasonably competent practitioner under comparable circumstances.[32] This standard is deferential to medical practitioners and somewhat disadvantageous to plaintiff patients, since it requires an expert (another medical practitioner) to testify that the defendant practitioner did not meet the standard of care as it relates to his/her disclosure.

2.2.1.2. Reasonable Patient Standard. The other states apply the so-called *reasonable patient standard*, under which the medical practitioner must disclose information that a reasonable patient

30 Emanuel S. *Torts*. 3rd ed. Larchmont, NY: Emanuel Law Outlines; 1988:9–14.

31 *Black's Law Dictionary*. Abridged 6th ed. St. Paul, MN: West Publishing; 1994:104.

32 Furrow BR, Greaney TL, Johnson SH, et al. *Health Law*. 3rd ed. St. Paul, MN: West Publishing; 2014: 123.

would consider to be *material*, or important. You might ask, Who gets to decide what a reasonable patient would consider to be important? The answer is that the jury gets to decide. This standard is, as you might imagine, less deferential to medical providers and more advantageous to plaintiff patients.

2.2.2. Information to Be Disclosed

While the precise substance of the information that must be disclosed as part of informed consent depends on the above standards, in general practitioners must disclose "(1) the nature of the procedure, (2) the risks and hazards of the procedure, (3) the alternatives to the procedure, and (4) the anticipated benefits of the procedure."[33]

2.2.3. When Must Informed Consent Be Obtained?

Contrary to what you might believe, informed consent is required not only when a patient undergoes surgery or some other invasive procedure, but anytime a clinical intervention is undertaken or forgone—anytime a clinical decision point is reached.

Consider, for example, the case of the patient with a urinary tract infection that you have decided to treat with a fluoroquinolone. The FDA has mandated a black box warning regarding the fluoroquinolones, which reads in part:

> Systemic quinolones have been associated with disabling and potentially irreversible serious adverse reactions such as tendinopathy, including tendinitis and tendon rupture requiring surgical repair or resulting in prolonged disability. These reactions can occur within hours to weeks after starting these agents in patients of any age, with or without pre-existing risk factors. . . . Tendon rupture typically involves the Achilles tendon; however, ruptures of the hand, shoulder, biceps, thumb, and other tendons have also been reported. Tendinitis and tendon rupture can occur bilaterally. Rupture can occur during therapy or up to a few months after therapy has been stopped.[34]

Your patient develops tendonitis as a result of the fluoroquinolone and suffers an Achilles tendon rupture requiring surgical repair. He sues you, his physician assistant (PA), in negligence for failing to disclose the risk of tendon rupture to him. If in fact you failed to disclose the risk of tendon rupture to him, then even if your prescribing a fluoroquinolone was medically proper, you may well lose the case because you did the right thing in the wrong way.

Let me stress again that you need to think about informed consent anytime a clinical intervention is undertaken or forgone. Consider the following case.

CASE 7.B

Mrs. Truman died at the age of 30 in 1970 of cervical cancer. Dr. Thomas, a family physician engaged in general practice, had seen Mrs. Truman frequently from 1964 to 1969, but never performed a Pap smear on her. Mrs. Truman's two children sued Dr. Thomas for what they alleged was his negligent failure to perform a Pap smear on their mother. They argued, "It is the duty of a physician to disclose to his patient all relevant information to enable the patient to make an informed decision regarding the submission to or refusal to take a diagnostic test . . . Dr. Thomas breached his duty of care to Mrs. Truman when he failed to inform her of the potentially fatal

33 *DeGennaro v. Tandon,* 873 A.2d 191, 196 (Conn. App. 2005).

34 Ciprofloxacin drug summary. Prescribers' Digital Reference. https://www.pdr.net/drug-summary/Ciprofloxacin-Tablets-ciprofloxacin-3144. Accessed March 1, 2020.

consequences of allowing cervical cancer to develop undetected by a pap smear."[35] Dr. Thomas testified that he did not specifically inform Mrs. Truman of the risk involved in refusing to undergo such a test, but rather told her "You should have a Pap smear." He further testified, "I am sure we discussed it with her so often that she couldn't fail to realize that we wanted her to have a complete examination . . . ." Mrs. Truman's children prevail in their lawsuit. How? Explain how this case implicates the doctrine of informed consent.

Analysis: ______________________________

____

____

____

____

____

____

____

____

____

2.2.4. Exceptions to the Duty to Elicit Informed Consent

There are circumstances under which the normal requirements of informed consent are relaxed.

The first exception is when consent is *implied*, as discussed in relation to the *Mohr v. Williams* case considered above (recall the *emergency doctrine* and the *extension doctrine*).

The second exception is that a patient may *waive* his/her right to give informed consent. He/she may say, "I trust you, doctor, just do what you think is best." The waiver exception makes sense, since patients cannot be forced to receive information that they do not want; but to protect patient autonomy, the law requires that such waivers be unambiguous.

The third exception is that information need not be disclosed as part of the informed consent process where that information is *common knowledge*. As stated in *Canterbury v. Spence*, ". . . there is no obligation to communicate those [dangers] of which persons of average sophistication are aware."[36] For example, it seems likely that in 2022 it is common knowledge that cigarette smoking increases a patient's risk of developing lung cancer.

The fourth exception is that information need not be disclosed as part of the informed consent process where the patient has prior or *actual knowledge*. For example, if this is the second thoracentesis a patient has undergone in the past month, it is likely that he/she will be found to have prior or actual knowledge of its risks (assuming he/she was adequately informed the first time).

Finally, the last exception is that of *therapeutic privilege*, which theoretically permits a provider to withhold information from a patient when disclosing it would pose a serious threat to the patient's well-being. Imagine, for example, a hospital patient with severe inoperable three-vessel coronary artery disease and coexisting severe anxiety disorder who develops intractable chest pain whenever he is given even the slightest bad news. He was hospitalized with chest pain precipitated by the news that his LDL cholesterol was above target. His cardiac enzymes reveal that he has suffered a myocardial infarction (MI). His wife implores you to treat him as you must, but not to disclose this to the patient because she fears "he will drop dead if he knows he's had a heart attack." If you decide to withhold this information from the patient, your argument for doing so would be the therapeutic privilege. You should know, however, that this is a strongly criticized exception, and that I can cite no case in which a court relied on it.

35 *Truman v. Thomas,* 611 P.2d 902 (Sup. Ct. Cal. 1980).
36 *Canterbury v. Spence,* 464 F .2d 772 (D.C. Dir. 1969).

CASE 7.C

Consider the following case:

> A 70-year-old man with a history of chronic obstructive pulmonary disease and diabetes is brought into the emergency department with a change in mental status (unconsciousness). Exam reveals a tattoo on his chest that reads "Do Not Resuscitate," accompanied by his signature. Labs reveal an elevated blood alcohol content. Subsequently, he becomes hypotensive and is found to have an anion-gap metabolic acidosis with a pH of 6.81. Efforts to restore him to a mental status adequate to discuss goals of care are unsuccessful, and so the social work department was consulted to assist in contacting next of kin.[37]

While the next of kin are being sought, do you think the tattoo should be honored?

Analysis: ______________________________

____

____

____

____

____

____

____

____

____

2.2.5. Informed Consent as a Non-delegable Duty

An important issue that we have not yet addressed is, Who is responsible for obtaining informed consent? The answer is that the responsibility belongs to the clinician to whose intervention the patient is consenting or refusing. Thus, in *Valles v. Albert Einstein Med. Ctr.*,[38] the Supreme Court of Pennsylvania held that the duty to obtain a patient's informed consent is a *non-delegable duty* owed by the physician conducting the surgery or treatment. We shall take up the concept of the non-delegable duty further in Chapter 11.

2.2.6. Expanding Frontiers of Informed Consent

Traditionally the focus of informed consent cases has been on whether the provider adequately disclosed to the patient information intrinsic to the procedure in question (e.g., nature, risks, benefits, alternatives). More recent case law suggests that a provider's disclosure obligations might extend beyond the scope of the procedure itself and might encompass material risks that emanate from the provider him/herself. As the name of the section suggests, these are developing areas in the law of informed consent.

2.2.6.1. Health Care Provider Experience. In *Johnson v. Kokemoor*, the defendant neurosurgeon exaggerated his surgical experience during the informed consent process.[39] The patient underwent basilar bifurcation aneurysm surgery and was rendered an incomplete paraplegic. In the suit that followed, defendant Dr. Kokemoor argued that informed consent required that he reveal only those risks inherent in the surgical

37 Holt GE, Sarmento B, Kett D, Goodman KW. An unconscious patient with a DNR tattoo: [letter]. *New Eng J Med*. 2017;377(22):2192–2193.

38 *Valles v. Albert Einstein Medical Center,* 805 A.2d 1232 (Pa. 2002). https://www.courtlistener.com/opinion/1425414/valles-v-albert-einstein-medical-center/. Accessed November 10, 2019.

39 *Johnson v. Kokemoor,* 545 N.W.2d 495 (Wis.1996). Dr. Kokemoor, when asked, reportedly "replied that he had performed the surgery . . . 'several' times; asked what he meant by several, [he] said 'dozens' and 'lots of times.' In fact . . . the defendant . . . had operated on basilar bifurcation aneurysms only twice and had never operated on a . . . basilar bifurcation aneurysm [as large as] . . . the plaintiff's . . . ."

procedure, and that he was not obligated to disclose (even if asked by the patient) information about his surgical experience. The Supreme Court of Wisconsin disagreed, holding that Kokemoor's surgical experience was material to the issue of informed consent.

Johnson v. Kokemoor has been followed in a number of other jurisdictions[40] and rejected in others[41] that have grappled with the issue.

2.2.6.2. Infectivity of the Provider. Do health care providers have a legal duty to disclose to patients risks that result from their (the providers') possible infectivity?

In *Estate of Behringer v. Medical Center at Princeton*,[42] the plaintiff Behringer was an otolaryngologist (ENT) on the medical staff of the Medical Center when he was diagnosed with the Acquired Immunodeficiency Syndrome (AIDS). Upon learning of his diagnosis, the Medical Center suspended his surgical privileges. As a condition of lifting the suspension, the board of trustees of the Medical Center voted to require the use of a special "informed consent form" to be presented to patients about to undergo surgery by HIV-positive surgeons, which read as follows:

> I have on this date executed a consent, which is attached hereto, for (Procedure) to be performed by Dr.____. In addition, I have also been informed by Dr.____, that he has a positive blood test indicative of infection with HIV (Human Immunodeficiency Virus) which is the cause of AIDS. I have also been informed of the potential risk of transmission of the virus. (witness) _ (signature of patient)[43]

Following his death, Dr. Behringer's estate sued the Medical Center alleging that "1) the risk of transmission of HIV from surgeon to patient is too remote to require informed consent, and 2) the law of informed consent does not require disclosure of the condition of the surgeon."[44] The Court rejected both arguments and held that the Medical Center had properly required Dr. Behringer to disclose his HIV positive status in obtaining informed consent from prospective surgical patients as a condition of lifting the temporary suspension of his surgical privileges. Regarding the first argument, the Court wrote, "The ultimate risk to the patient is so absolute—so devastating—that it is untenable to argue

---

40 E.g., *Barriocanal v. Gibbs*, 697 A.2d 1169 Del. 1997); *Goldberg v. Boone*, 396 Md. 94, 912 A.2d698 (Md. 2006); *Andersen v. Khanna*, 913 N.W.2d 526, 2018 Iowa Sup. LEXIS 62, 2018 WL 2999519

41 E.g., *Duttry v. Patterson*, 565 Pa. 130, 771 A.2d 1255, (Pa. 2001);*Duffy (Estate of Warren) v. Flagg*, 279 Conn. 682, 905 A.2d 15, 2006 Conn. LEXIS 312.

42 *Estate of Behringer v. Medical Ctr. at Princeton*, 249 N.J. Super. 597, 592 A.2d 1251, 1991 N.J. Super. LEXIS 165, 55 Fair Empl. Prac. Cas. (BNA) 1145, 1 Am. Disabilities Cas. (BNA) 1773, 55 Empl. Prac. Dec. (CCH) P40,779, 56 Empl. Prac. Dec. (CCH) P40,779 (Superior Court of New Jersey, Law Division, Mercer County April 25, 1991, Decided). https://advance-lexis-com.ezproxylocal.library.nova.edu/api/document?collection=cases&id=urn:contentItem:3S3J-WGS0-003C-P0SR-00000-00&context=1516831.

43 According to the opinion of the court, "All parties recognized that in the absence of patients willing to undergo invasive procedures by HIV-positive surgeons, this was a 'de facto prohibition' from surgical practice." In fact, after being diagnosed with AIDS Dr. Behringer never again operated at the medical center. Subsequently, in reliance on an opinion by the Council on Ethical and Judicial Affairs (CEJA) of the American Medical Association (AMA) suggesting that physicians with infectious diseases should not engage in activities creating a risk of disease transmission to others, the Medical Center adopted a new policy for HIV seropositive healthcare workers (HCWs). Under that policy, physicians or healthcare providers with known HIV seropositivity would be permitted to treat patients at the Medical Center but would not be permitted to perform procedures posing any risk of HIV transmission to patients.

44 *Estate of Behringer v. Medical Ctr. at Princeton*, 249 N.J. Super. 597, 651 A.2d 1251, 1991 N.J. Super..

against informed consent."[45] Regarding the second argument, the Court wrote, "The informed consent cases are not so narrow as to support that argument."[46] In the opinion of the Court, informed consent case law supports required disclosure of "any attendant substantial risks."[47]

2.2.6.3. Payment Incentives/Financial COIs. Do health care providers have a duty to disclose to patients payment incentives or material risks that result from existing financial conflicts of interest (COIs)?

In *Shea v. Esensten*,[48] plaintiff Patrick Shea consulted his primary care physician (PCP) about chest pains for which he had been hospitalized while on an overseas business trip. Notwithstanding Shea's extensive family history of heart disease, his physician told him that referral to a cardiologist was unnecessary. Mr. Shea died within a few months of heart failure.

Mr. Shea had been an employee of Seagate Technologies, which provided health care benefits to employees by contracting with a health maintenance organization (HMO) called Medica. Medica required Seagate's employees to choose one of their authorized PCPs (of whom Dr. Esensten was one) and required a written referral from that PCP before a patient could see a specialist such as a cardiologist.

> Unknown to Mr. Shea, Medica's contracts with its preferred doctors created financial incentives that were designed to minimize referrals. Specifically, the primary care doctors were rewarded for not making covered referrals to specialists, and were docked a portion of their fees if they made too many. According to Mr. Shea's widow . . . , if her husband would have known his doctor could earn a bonus for treating less, he would have disregarded his doctor's advice, sought a cardiologist's opinion at his own expense, and would still be alive today.[48]

Shea's widow sued, arguing among other things, that Medica's non-disclosure of its financial incentives violated its fiduciary duties. The district court dismissed the complaint, but on appeal the U.S. Court of Appeals reversed:

> Although the district court acknowledged Medica's duty of loyalty, the court felt the compensation arrangements between Medica and its doctors were not material facts requiring disclosure. We disagree. From the patient's point of view, a financial incentive scheme put in place to influence a treating doctor's referral practices . . . is certainly a material piece of information. . . . Thus, we conclude Mr. Shea had the right to know Medica was offering financial incentives that could have colored his doctor's medical judgment about the urgency for a cardiac referral.[48]

Other courts faced with the financial COI issue have decided differently. (See, for example, *Neade v. Portes*,[49] the facts of which were presented in Case 2.D, discussed in Chapter 2 and in Chapter 6.)

---

45 Estate of Behringer v. Medical Ctr. at Princeton, 249 N.J. Super. 597, 657 A.2d 1251, 1991 N.J. Super. The court wrote, "It is the court's view that the risk of [HIV] transmission is not the sole risk involved. The risk of a surgical accident, i.e., a needlestick or scalpel cut, during surgery performed by an HIV-positive surgeon, may subject a previously uninfected patient to months or even years of continual HIV testing. Both of these risks are sufficient to . . . require[e] disclosure. . . . If there is to be an ultimate arbiter of whether the patient is to be treated invasively by an AIDS-positive surgeon, the arbiter will be the fully informed patient."

46 Estate of Behringer v. Medical Ctr. at Princeton, 249 N.J. Super. 597, 654 A.2d 1251, 1991 N.J. Super..

47 Estate of Behringer v. Medical Ctr. at Princeton, 249 N.J. Super. 597, 654 A.2d 1251, 1991 N.J. Super.

48 *Shea v. Esensten,* 107 F.3d 625 (8th Cir. 1997).

49 *Neade v. Portes,* 739 NE2d 496 (Ill. 2000).

WRAP-UP

Chapter Summary

The duty to obtain *informed consent* from patients is an example of a particular moral rule derived from the interplay between the general moral rules (in this case, "do not deprive of freedom," "do not neglect your duty," and "obey the law") and the practice of medicine. *Informed consent* is most closely related to the *principle of respect for autonomy/persons*. The focus of informed consent is on the informational prong of the autonomy trident, assuming as it does that the patient/decisionmaker has *decisional capacity* and that his/her choice is *voluntary*. The modern legal approach to cases involving consent issues is to distinguish between those in which a medical intervention takes place without consent (*battery*) and those in which consent is obtained but is somehow substandard or flawed (*negligence*). *Battery* is the intentional, harmful or offensive touching of another without his or her consent. Medical providers can be sued for battery if: the patient has not consented at all; the medical provider performs a procedure other than the one to which the patient consented (including, for example, the right procedure on the wrong part of the body); or an unconsented-to medical provider performs the procedure. Patient consent to medical procedures may be express or *implied*, as, for example, under the *emergency* or the *extension doctrines*. Where a medical provider mistakenly believes that consent has been obtained, the outcome of the case depends on the reasonableness of the mistake. Where the provider's mistake is reasonable, consent will be found and there is no battery. Where the defendant's mistake is unreasonable, then a battery will have occurred. Because modern cases treat *informed refusal* and *informed consent* as two sides of the same coin, patients refusing a recommended test or procedure must be informed of all material risks and benefits of the refusal and alternatives thereto. The frontiers of informed consent law have expanded of late, with courts considering whether medical providers have a legal duty to disclose to patients material risks that result not from the procedure being consented to, but from some characteristic of the medical provider him/herself.

Review Questions

1. How did Justice Cardozo formulate the doctrine of informed consent in the famous *Schloendorff* case?
2. Which of the *moral rules* discussed in Chapter 1 are implicated by the doctrine of informed consent?
3. Explain the relationship between the *doctrine of informed consent* and the *principle of respect for autonomy/persons*.
4. What are the four key components of *decisional capacity*?
5. Explain how *coercion*, *persuasion*, and *manipulation* relate to *informed consent*.
6. What is a *battery?* When health professionals are sued for issues involving consent, when does the law treat them as battery cases? When does it treat them as *negligence* cases?
7. Is consent for a health care provider to perform a medical procedure transferable to another provider?
8. How does the law handle situations in which a health professional makes a mistake about consent, believing he/she had obtained consent from a patient who did not mean to consent, performs a medical procedure on that patient?

9. If a hospitalized patient for whom you are caring wishes to sign out against medical advice (AMA), what should you tell him/her? How does this situation relate to the doctrine of *informed consent*?
10. Your supervising physician asks you to obtain informed consent from a patient for an abdominal paracentesis that he/she will be performing. How should you respond?
11. As part of the informed consent process, is a health professional legally obligated to disclose to the patient the extent of his/her experience with a diagnostic or therapeutic procedure for which consent is being obtained? Is he/she ethically obligated? Does it matter whether the patient makes specific inquiry?

Case Analyses

Case 7.A Analysis

Yes, the patient has decisional capacity and should be allowed to refuse dialysis. He has clearly and consistently *communicated* a choice to refuse dialysis. Despite his azotemia and moderate dementia, he *understands* the information that has been provided him by his clinicians ("My kidneys are failing. That's how I got the high potassium.") and *appreciates* that the information applies to him ("They aren't going to function on their own much longer," he says. "I could die from it."). Finally, his choice appears to be the product of rationalization/reasoning in which he weighed the pros and cons of dialysis in reaching a decision consistent with his personal values ("I don't want dialysis because I don't want to spend my life hooked up to machines three times a week," the patient explains. "I just want to let things run their natural course.").

Case 7.B Analysis

You might think that this is a run of the mill negligence case, since the plaintiffs are alleging that Dr. Thomas was negligent in not performing a Pap smear. But Dr. Thomas' reason for not performing the test seems like a good one—Mrs. Truman refused to consent to it! At first glance, that refusal would seem to be protected by the principle of *respect for autonomy*. The plaintiffs, however, go on to argue that their mother refused the potentially life-saving Pap smear because Dr. Thomas' disclosure regarding the Pap smear was inadequate or substandard—that, in other words, her refusal was not "informed"—because he "failed to inform her of the potentially fatal consequences of allowing cervical cancer to develop undetected by a pap smear."[50] If her refusal was not adequately "informed," then Dr. Thomas cannot use her refusal as a justification for not performing the Pap. Unlike most informed consent cases, here the patient was injured not as a result of the procedure but rather as a result of her *refusing* the procedure. This case is therefore more accurately characterized as being about *informed refusal*, and the issue in the case is whether Mrs. Truman's refusal of the Pap was an informed one. The court finds that it was not, that once Mrs. Thomas refused the Pap, Dr. Thomas had a duty to advise Mrs. Thomas of the material risks (including invasive cervical cancer and death) that would ensue from that refusal.

Case 7.C Analysis

The overarching issue in this case is whether the principle of respect for autonomy applies to the DNR tattooed on the patient's chest—whether, in other words, we should conclude that it represents an autonomous choice on his part and therefore honor it. A finding of autonomous choice requires that a choice be made and communicated; that

50 *Truman v. Thomas*, 611 P.2d 902 (Sup. Ct. Cal. 1980).

the person choosing have *decisional capacity*; that the choice be *voluntary*; and that the choice be adequately *informed*. So, the first subsidiary issue is whether the tattoo represents a current choice or something else. It might, for example, not represent a choice at all, but simply a tattoo that the patient thought would look cool; or it might be the remains of a choice that he once made and later regretted. The former seems unlikely; and had the patient changed his mind, it seems likely that he would have taken some step(s) to communicate that change (perhaps a tattooed line through "Do Not"). Regarding the second subsidiary issue (did the patient have *decisional capacity*), recall that in the absence of evidence to the contrary the law presumes that persons have decisional capacity (see *1.2.1 Decisional Capacity*). The elevated blood alcohol level does not constitute such evidence unless the tattoo was applied during this episode of intoxication, and there is nothing in the case report to suggest that it was a brand-new tattoo. Likewise, there is nothing to suggest that the tattoo was involuntarily applied (third subsidiary issue). The final subsidiary issue is whether the patient's DNR decision was adequately *informed* when he decided on the DNR tattoo.[51] Based on the case report, we simply don't know; and while informed decision-making, unlike *decisional capacity*, cannot be presumed,[52] neither can it be presumed that the decision-making was not informed. Yet even in the absence of any controlling presumption, we must decide; and because this case involves a prospective decision (shall we resuscitate him or not?) as opposed to the retrospective decisions characterizing most informed consent cases (was the patient who was not resuscitated given adequate information by his PA or physician before he refused resuscitation?), our decision will determine whether or not the patient's wishes are carried out. So, does it seem likely that the patient, at the time he decided on his DNR tattoo, was unaware of some *material* information that would have caused him to decide otherwise?[53] It seems unlikely; the facts of this case report suggest no unanticipated circumstances such as those described in footnote 53.

51 Note that here, unlike most of the informed consent cases discussed in this chapter, we are not scrutinizing the adequacy of the information given to a patient by a physician or PA; rather, we are scrutinizing the adequacy of the information available to patient.

52 Vearrier L. Do-not-resuscitate tattoos: are they valid? ACEPNow. April 10, 2018. https://www.acepnow.com/article/do-not-resuscitate-tattoos-are-they-valid/. Accessed March 1, 2020.

53 What material risks, you might ask, are associated with a DNR? One such risk is that the patient might not be resuscitated under circumstances in which he would want to be resuscitated. Consider, for example, a patient with stage IV COPD who has a DNR because he wishes to avoid intubation and mechanical ventilation because of progressive COPD. Imagine that patient presents to the ER with a mild community acquired pneumonia. He is treated with IV antibiotics and experiences an anaphylactic reaction requiring resuscitation. If he is resuscitated, our expectation is that he will walk out of the hospital; yet he has a DNR order. Would he have agreed to a DNR order if he knew that there was a risk he would not be resuscitated under these circumstances?

SECTION 3

Ethical and Legal Issues in Contemporary Health Care Practice

In this, the final section of the text, we cover a number of ethical and legal issues in contemporary healthcare practice.

In Chapter 8, we discuss a variety of interactions among healthcare professionals—including dyadic relationships between allied healthcare professionals (AHCPs) and physicians and between diverse AHCPs. This chapter affords us an opportunity to discuss the concepts of *direct*, *derivative*, and *vicarious liability*.

In Chapter 9, we discuss ethical and legal issues surrounding life's beginning, including the moral and legal standing of tiny humans, and the maternal-fetal dyad.

In Chapter 10, we discuss medical decision making at life's end, including questions regarding who gets to make those decisions and limitations regarding the right to refuse or to demand treatment.

Finally, in Chapter 11, we discuss malpractice. We intentionally left this topic until the end of the book, for it has been our experience that the law is relatively overemphasized in bioethics education, often preempting or short-circuiting bioethical analysis. Students often ask what the law has to say about whatever bioethics topic is being discussed, in an effort to cut to the chase.[1] We hope that the material that we have presented so far and the placement of this chapter at the book's end will discourage this.

---

1 Paola F. Law, humanities, and equipoise in the ethics education of PAs. *The Internet Journal of Allied Health Science and Practice*. 2006;4(2):1–6.

CHAPTER 8

Interactions Among Health Care Professionals

Janet K. Sparker, Ed.D., R.N., PA-C
Frederick Adolf Paola, M.D., J.D.

LEARNING OBJECTIVES

1. Define the term *dyad* and recognize examples of dyadic relationships involving health professionals.
2. Identify different models of *dyadic* relationships.
3. Explain the various steps involved in the formation and maintenance of dyadic relationships.
4. Explain the term *appraisal respect*.
5. Define, recognize, and differentiate *direct liability*, *derivative liability*, and *vicarious liability*, and explain how each relates to dyadic relationships involving health professionals.
6. Define and recognize *respondeat superior*, and explain how it relates to vicarious liability.

The Greeks observed a paradox about the dyad: While it appears separate from unity, its opposite poles remember their source and attract each other in an attempt to merge and return to the state of unity. The dyad simultaneously divides and unites, repels and attracts, separates and returns.[2]

—**Priya Hemenway**, in *Divine Proportion: Phi in Art, Nature, and Science*

While in previous chapters we have explored the relationship between the health professional and the patient, in this chapter we consider relationships among health professionals. As we shall see, many such relationships are *dyadic*. The adjective *dyadic* refers to the sociological interaction between individual members of a pair and includes physician-physician pairs as well as physician-nonphysician and nonphysician-nonphysician pairs.[3] These collegial relationships in clinics and hospitals form

2 Hemenway P. Chapter 2: Pythagoras and the mystery of numbers. In: Hemenway P. *Divine Proportion: Phi in Art, Nature, and Science*. Union Square; 2005:52.

3 Liden R, Anand S, Vidyarthi P. Dyadic relationships. *Annual Review of Organizational Psychology and Organizational Behavior.* 2016;3:139–166.

the basic units that coalesce into healthcare teams responsible for patient outcomes. The *Marcus Welby, M.D.* television model (1969–1976) of the kindly but authoritative physician who made all decisions unilaterally has evolved into one in which teams make decisions—an arguably more manageable approach to caring for rising numbers of patients in the increasingly complex landscape of modern medicine.[4]

1. Dyadic Relationships Involving Health Professionals

Herein we shall discuss selected dyadic relationships involving health professionals. In our discussion of these dyadic relationships, we will use the legal scheme created by Florida's Medical Practice Act[5] as an example and a jumping off point. Since time and space preclude a discussion of all the various health professionals, we shall limit our discussion to dyads involving four types: physician assistants (PAs); physical therapy (PT) practitioners; occupational therapy (OT) practitioners; and respiratory care (RC) practitioners. The reader should note that the themes that we discuss have broad applicability, but that the particulars may vary from state to state, consistent with what we discussed in Chapter 4.

1.1. The Physician–PA Dyad

1.1.1. PAs as Dependent Practitioners

The American Academy of PAs (AAPA) defines PAs as "medical professionals who diagnose illness, develop and manage treatment plans, prescribe medications, and often serve as a patient's principal healthcare provider."[6] That sounds a lot like the definition of a physician. However, because PA education/training is far shorter than physician education/training (about 2 years of PA school as opposed to 4 years of medical school plus anywhere from 3 to 7 years of residency, depending on one's specialty), the practice of medicine by PAs requires a degree of physician supervision that varies by state. For example, under section 458.347 of the Florida Statutes, "'Physician assistant' means a person who is a graduate of an approved program or its equivalent or meets standards approved by the boards and is licensed to perform medical services *delegated by the supervising physician*"[7] (italics added). The Florida Statute goes on to specify:

> (f) "Supervision" means responsible supervision and control. Except in cases of emergency, supervision requires the easy availability or physical presence of the licensed physician for consultation and direction of the actions of the [PA]. . . .
>
> (3) PERFORMANCE OF SUPERVISING PHYSICIAN.—Each physician . . . supervising a licensed [PA] must be qualified in the medical areas in which the [PA] is to perform and shall be individually or collectively responsible and liable for the performance and the acts and omissions of the [PA].
>
> (15) LIABILITY.—Each supervising physician using a [PA] is liable for any acts or omissions of the [PA] acting under the physician's supervision and control.[8]

4 *Marcus Welby, M.D.* https://www.imdb.com/title/tt0063927/fullcredits. Accessed on May 5, 2020.

5 The reader will recall that we discussed medical practice acts in Chapter 4.

6 What is a PA? American Association of Physician Assistants Web site. https://www.aapa.org/what-is-a-pa/. Accessed on June 20, 2020

7 Florida Statutes 458.347 Physician Assistants, at (2) (e). http://www.leg.state.fl.us/statutes/index.cfm?App_mode=Display_Statute;Search_String=&URL=0400-0499/0458/Sections/0458.347.html. Accessed January 25, 2021.

8 Florida Statutes 458.347 Physician assistants.—. http://www.leg.state.fl.us/statutes/index.cfm?App_mode=Display_Statute;Search_String=&URL=0400-0499/0458/Sections/0458.347.html. Accessed January 25, 2021.

PAs are, therefore, *dependent practitioners*, and this dependency (this supervision requirement) immediately places the PA in a dyadic relationship with the supervising physician.

What does the statute tell us about how the Florida Legislature conceptualizes the physician-PA dyad? Well, first of all it should be clear that the fact that the physician is in a supervisory position relative to the PA reflects his/her more extensive training and greater *expert authority (see section 2.2, Parsonian Model of Professionalism, Chapter 2)* since, as mentioned previously, PAs start their careers with only a fraction of the training afforded physicians. This supervisory position is reinforced by holding the supervising physician *vicariously liable* (see section 3. *Direct, Derivative and Vicarious Liability*) for the medical acts and omissions of the PA.

1.1.2. Moral Agency as a Limit to Dependency

The supervising physician possesses greater medical expertise than the PA being supervised. As we shall see next, this is generally true of all supervisory relationships (e.g., PT–PTA, OT–OTA, OTA–OT aide, etc.). However, the concept of *expert authority* does not apply in the moral arena. The supervisor's *expert authority* does not extend to moral matters. As stated in Chapter 1, there is no such thing as a moral authority, and as we have written elsewhere, "our concern is that PAs or their supervising physicians might confuse the professional or medical expert authority of the physician with physician authority in the moral arena which . . . does not exist."[9]

Indeed, the law reinforces the notion that PAs remain responsible for their actions since under the law they remain directly liable for their medical acts and omissions.[10,11] We will discuss the concept of *direct liability* in greater detail next.

1.2. Dyads Involving PTs

Again, let's use the Florida Statutes as an example of state regulation of the physical therapy profession.

In Florida, physical therapy practitioners are regulated by the Board of Physical Therapy Practice under Chapter 486 of Title XXXII of the Florida Statutes. That chapter reads in part:

> 486.021 Definitions.—As used in this chapter, unless the context otherwise requires, the term:
>
> . . . .
>
> (5) "Physical therapist" [PT] means a person who is licensed and who practices physical therapy in accordance with the provisions of this chapter.
>
> (6) "Physical therapist assistant" [PTA] means a person who is licensed in accordance with the provisions of this chapter to perform patient-related activities, including the use of physical agents,

---

9 Paola FA, Carr MF, Gianola FJ, O'Neil JA, Perry C. Ethics education of PA students: Avoiding the procrustean bed. *Journal of Physician Assistant Education*. 2006; 17(2):21–25.

10 McLean TR. Crossing the quality chasm: autonomous physician extenders will necessitate a shift to enterprise liability coverage for health care delivery. *Health Matrix: Journal of Law-Medicine*. 2002;12:239. https://advance-lexis-com.ezproxylocal.library.nova.edu/api/document?collection=analytical-materials&id=urn:contentItem:4784-2P90-00CV-3015-00000-00;context=1516831. See p. 270.

11 See, for example, *Drew v. Knowles,* 511 So. 2d 393, 1987 Fla. App. LEXIS 9515, 12 Fla. L. Weekly 1798 (Court of Appeal of Florida, Second District, July 24, 1987, Filed). https://advance-lexis-com.ezproxylocal.library.nova.edu/api/document?collection=cases;id=urn:contentItem:3RRR-6C00-003D-X3YY-00000-00&context=1516831. At page 396, the court writes, "We agree that a nurse acting under the direction and orders of a physician in matters involving medical professional skill and judgment is absolved from liability for the acts so performed, absent independent negligence upon the part of the nurse, and absent a performance of those acts or duties a nurse is called upon to perform at a level of performance below that which is expected of a similarly qualified nurse. Similarly, where a nurse is called upon to exercise professional judgment or to perform discretionary ministerial acts and does so negligently, the nurse may be liable."

whose license is in good standing, and whose activities are performed *under the direction of a [PT]* as set forth in rules adopted pursuant to this chapter. Patient-related activities performed by a [PTA] for a board-certified orthopedic physician or physiatrist licensed pursuant to chapter 458 [an allopath] or chapter 459 [an osteopath] or a practitioner licensed under chapter 460 [a chiropractor] shall be under the general supervision of a [PT], but *shall not require onsite supervision by a [PT]*. Patient-related activities performed for all other health care practitioners licensed under chapter 458 or chapter 459 and those patient-related activities performed for practitioners licensed under chapter 461 or chapter 466 *shall be performed under the onsite supervision of a [PT]*. [Italics added.]

(7) "Physical therapy practitioner" means a [PT] or a [PTA] who is licensed and who practices physical therapy in accordance with the provisions of this chapter.

(9) "Direct supervision" means supervision by a [PT] who is licensed pursuant to this chapter. Except in a case of emergency, direct supervision requires the physical presence of the licensed [PT] for consultation and direction of the actions of a [PT] or [PTA] who is practicing under a temporary permit and who is a candidate for licensure by examination.

(10) "Physical therapy assessment" means observational, verbal, or manual determinations of the function of the movement system relative to physical therapy . . . for the purpose of physical therapy treatment.

(11) "Practice of physical therapy" means the performance of physical therapy assessments and the treatment of any disability, injury, disease, or other health condition of human beings, or the prevention of such disability, injury, disease, or other health condition, and the rehabilitation of such disability, injury, disease, or other health condition by alleviating impairments, functional movement limitations, and disabilities by designing, implementing, and modifying treatment interventions through therapeutic exercise; functional movement training in self-management and in-home, community, or work integration or reintegration; manual therapy; massage; airway clearance techniques; maintaining and restoring the integumentary system and wound care; physical agent or modality; mechanical or electrotherapeutic modality; patient-related instruction; the use of apparatus and equipment in the application of such treatment, prevention, or rehabilitation; the performance of tests of neuromuscular functions as an aid to the diagnosis or treatment of any human condition; or the performance of electromyography as an aid to the diagnosis of any human condition only upon compliance with the criteria set forth by the Board of Medicine.

(a) A [PT] may implement a plan of treatment developed by the [PT] for a patient or provided for a patient by a practitioner of record . . . . The [PT] shall refer the patient to or consult with a practitioner of record if the patient's condition is found to be outside the scope of physical therapy. If physical therapy treatment for a patient is required beyond 30 days for a condition not previously assessed by a practitioner of record, the [PT] shall have a practitioner of record review and sign the plan. . . .[12]

12 Florida Statutes, Title XXXII Chapter 486 Physical Therapy Practice. http://www.leg.state.fl.us/statutes/index.cfm?App_mode=Display_Statute&URL=0400-0499/0486/0486ContentsIndex.html;StatuteYear=2020&Title=%2D%3E2020%2D%3EChapter%20486. Accessed January 30, 2021.

1.2.1. PTAs

It should be apparent (see 486.021 (6), above) that PTAs are dependent practitioners and in a dyadic relationship with their supervising PTs. What about PTs?

1.2.2. PTs

Under 486.021 (11)(a) of the Florida Statutes, PTs may practice physical therapy independently of physicians (i.e., are independent practitioners, free of any requirement for supervision by physicians), although their independence is subject to certain provisos.[13]

CASE 8.A

Consider the following case, a fact pattern we initially encountered in Case 4.C in Chapter 4:

> On January 6, 1986, Douglas Smith, a [high school] student . . . injured his right ankle at basketball practice. After putting ice on the ankle, the athletic coach, Robin Becker, brought Smith to Lavergne's office to have Lavergne look at the injury. Lavergne [a PT] volunteered his services to the local high schools to screen injuries incurred during athletic events. Lavergne examined the ankle, performed a heel strike test and concluded the ankle was not likely broken. Lavergne told Smith to keep the ice on the ankle, try to put weight on it and if pain persisted, he should see his family physician or return to Lavergne's office and Lavergne would refer him to a physician.
>
> A complaint was filed with the Louisiana State Board of Medical Examiners against Lavergne and a formal administrative hearing was held on November 18, 1986. The board ruled against Lavergne, reprimanded him for . . . "engaging in the practice of physical therapy in excess of the scope of physical therapy practice as defined by the Physical Therapy Practice Act of Louisiana, La. R.S. 37:2401-2418 . . . by undertaking and purporting to diagnose and prescribe appropriate treatment for an acute athletic injury" [and placed him on probation for two years].
>
> La. R.S. 37:2410(A) in pertinent part reads as follows: "Initial evaluation or consultation of a screening nature to determine the need for physical therapy may be performed without referral, but implementation of physical therapy treatment to individuals for their specific condition or conditions shall be based on the prescription or referral of a person licensed to practice medicine, surgery, dentistry, or podiatry."
>
> . . . . While we recognize the statutory duty imposed upon the board to sanction violators of the act, we do not agree with the Board's conclusion that, under the statute, a clear distinction can be drawn between medical diagnosis and physical therapy evaluation in the instant case.
>
> . . . . The statute is clear that a physical therapist can only implement physical therapy on a patient for a specific condition after the patient has received a prescription for such therapy or referral from a licensed physician, surgeon, dentist or podiatrist. The statutory provision fails to emphasize that an initial evaluation or consultation of a screening nature can only be conducted on a patient who has an injury which has been previously

---

13 "Twenty-eight states have direct access laws by which patients can seek physical therapy directly without a doctor's prescription. Florida is one such state. Patients in Florida can go directly to physical therapists; however, this direct access does not allow physical therapists to implement treatment plans in acute care settings. The condition must be within the physical therapist's scope of practice. If it is not, the physical therapist can consult with a qualified healthcare practitioner or refer the patient, and if the care plan exceeds 30 days, a practitioner of record must review and sign off on the plan." See, (March 26, 2020 Thursday). If Suffering from Back Pain, See a Physical Therapist First – Get Started Without a Doctor's Prescription. Global English (Middle East and North Africa Financial Network). https://advance-lexis-com.ezproxylocal.library.nova.edu/api/document?collection=news&id=urn:contentItem:5YHM-BKF1-F04Y-T048-00000-00&context=1516831. Accessed January 28, 2021.

diagnosed by a physician. If that was the intent of the legislature . . . then it is not evident from reading the statute.

. . . . The Board reprimanded and sanctioned Lavergne because it found he undertook and determined the nature and cause of Smith's injury and prescribed appropriate treatment . . . . After reviewing the record in this matter, we conclude these findings are not correct. The testimonial evidence is overwhelming that Lavergne told Smith that he should see a physician about his ankle . . . . As far as prescribing medical treatment for an acute athletic injury, Lavergne simply told Smith to continue to keep ice on the ankle. Ostensibly, this is what any reasonable person, one not necessarily trained in first aid or in a medically related field, would have suggested. Should Lavergne be sanctioned because he was a licensed physical therapist and suggested the same? Does the Physical Therapy Practice Act expressly prohibit a physical therapist from offering such reasonable advice? We think not.

. . . . We are not convinced that, under the wording of the statute, Mr. Lavergne's actions constituted a medical diagnosis or prescription for treatment. To so hold would substantially prejudice the rights of Lavergne. La. R.S. 49:964(G). For the foregoing reasons, the judgment of the lower court affirming the decision of the Louisiana State Board of Medical Examiners in the Matter of Oday John Lavergne, Jr., L.P.T. is hereby reversed.[14]

(1) What is the main legal issue in this case, and why do the Board and the appellate court differ in their answers to this question? (2) How does this case relate to the dyadic relationships we have been discussing?

Analysis: ______________________________

____

____

____

____

____

____

____

____

____

1.3. Dyads Involving Occupational Therapy Practitioners

In Florida, occupational therapy practitioners are regulated by the Board of Occupational Therapy Practice under Part III of Chapter 468, Title XXXII.[15] That chapter reads in part:

> 468.203 Definitions.—As used in this act, the term: . . . .
>
> (3) "Occupational therapist" [OT] means a person licensed to practice occupational therapy as defined in this act and whose license is in good standing.
>
> (4) "Occupational therapy" means the use of purposeful activity or interventions to achieve functional outcomes.
>
> (a) For the purposes of this subsection:

14 *Lavergne v. Louisiana State Bd. of Medical Examiners,* 539 So. 2d 656, 1989 La. App. LEXIS 110 (Court of Appeal of Louisiana, Fourth Circuit January 30, 1989, Decided). https://advance-lexis-com.ezproxylocal.library.nova.edu/api/document?collection=cases;id=urn:contentItem:3S3K-46Y0-008T-X08M-00000-00;context=1516831.

15 The 2020 Florida Statutes. http://www.leg.state.fl.us/statutes/index.cfm?App_mode=Display_Statute&URL=0400-0499/0468/0468PartIIIContentsIndex.html&StatuteYear=2020;Title=%2D%3E2020%2D%3EChapter%20468%2D%3EPart%20III. Accessed January 30, 2021.

1. "Achieving functional outcomes" means to maximize the independence and the maintenance of health of any individual who is limited by a physical injury or illness, a cognitive impairment, a psychosocial dysfunction, a mental illness, a developmental or a learning disability, or an adverse environmental condition.

2. "Assessment" means the use of skilled observation or the administration and interpretation of standardized or nonstandardized tests and measurements to identify areas for occupational therapy services.

(b) Occupational therapy services include, but are not limited to:

1. The assessment, treatment, and education of or consultation with the individual, family, or other persons.

2. Interventions directed toward developing daily living skills, work readiness or work performance, play skills or leisure capacities, or enhancing educational performance skills.

3. Providing for the development of: sensory-motor, perceptual, or neuromuscular functioning; range of motion; or emotional, motivational, cognitive, or psychosocial components of performance.

These services may require assessment of the need for use of interventions such as the design, development, adaptation, application, or training in the use of assistive technology devices; the design, fabrication, or application of rehabilitative technology such as selected orthotic devices; training in the use of assistive technology; orthotic or prosthetic devices; the application of physical agent modalities as an adjunct to or in preparation for purposeful activity; the use of ergonomic principles; the adaptation of environments and processes to enhance functional performance; or the promotion of health and wellness. . . .

(5) "Occupational therapy aide" [OT aide] means a person who assists in the practice of occupational therapy, who works under the direct supervision of a licensed [OT] or occupational therapy assistant [OTA], and whose activities require a general understanding of occupational therapy . . .

(6) "Occupational therapy assistant" [OTA] means a person licensed to assist in the practice of occupational therapy, who works under the supervision of an [OT], and whose license is in good standing. . . .

(8) "Supervision" means responsible supervision and control, with the licensed [OT] providing both initial direction in developing a plan of treatment and periodic inspection of the actual implementation of the plan. Such plan of treatment shall not be altered by the supervised individual without prior consultation with, and the approval of, the supervising [OT]. The supervising [OT] need not always be physically present or on the premises when the assistant is performing services; however, except in cases of emergency, supervision shall require the availability of the supervising [OT] for consultation with and direction of the supervised individual.[16]

1.3.1. Dyads Involving OTAs and OT Aides

It should be clear that 468.203 anticipates that OTAs and OT aides will function as part of a dyad, with OTAs supervised by OTs, and OT aides supervised by either OTAs or OTs.

16 Florida Statutes Title XXXII Chapter 468.203. http://www.leg.state.fl.us/statutes/index.cfm?App_mode=Display_Statute;Search_String=&URL=0400-0499/0468/Sections/0468.203.html. Accessed January 30, 2021.

1.3.2. Dyads Involving OTs

Besides functioning as the supervisory half of dyads involving OTAs or OT aides, are OTs required to function as part of a physician–OT dyad? According to the Florida Board of Occupational Therapy, the answer would seem to be a qualified "no."

> Does an occupational therapist need a signed prescription from a physician authorizing OT services in the state of Florida?
>
> In many jurisdictions, the practice of occupational therapy is contingent upon the prescription or referral of a physician, however, the Florida Occupational Therapy Practice Laws and Rules are silent on this issue, not stating that a physician's prescription is required to provide OT services. The regulations only state a licensed Florida OT and OTA with an active unencumbered license can provide occupational therapy services in the state. See Chapter 468.203, (4) Definitions, Florida Statutes.
>
> NOTE: However, there may be, and often are, facilities, company policies, insurances, HMO's, and/or billing requirements that may mandate a physician's prescription for occupational therapy services, including other regulatory entities such as the Agency for Health-Care Administration (Facility Regulations), Medicare, Medicaid, etc.[17]

1.4. Dyads Involving Respiratory Care Practitioners

In Florida, respiratory care practitioners (RCPs) are regulated by the Board of Respiratory Care under Part V of Chapter 468, Title XXXII.[18] That chapter reads in part:

> 468.352 Definitions.—As used in this part, the term:
>
> . . . .
>
> (2) "Certified respiratory therapist" [CRT] means any person licensed pursuant to this part who is certified by the National Board for Respiratory Care or its successor; who is employed to deliver respiratory care services, *under the order of a physician* licensed pursuant to chapter 458 [an allopath] or chapter 459 [an osteopath], in accordance with protocols established by a hospital or other health care provider or the board; *and who functions in situations of unsupervised patient contact* requiring individual judgment. [Italics added.] . . . .
>
> (5) "Direct supervision" means practicing under the direction of a licensed, registered, or certified respiratory therapist who is physically on the premises and readily available, as defined by the board.
>
> (6) "Physician supervision" means supervision and control by a physician licensed under chapter 458 or chapter 459 who assumes the legal liability for the services rendered by the personnel employed in his or her office. Except in the case of an emergency, physician supervision requires the easy availability of the physician within the office or the physical presence of the physician for consultation and direction of the actions of the persons who deliver respiratory care services.
>
> (7) "Practice of respiratory care" or "respiratory therapy" means the allied health specialty associated with

---

17 Florida Board of Occupational Therapy FAQs. https://floridasoccupationaltherapy.gov/occupational-therapy-faqs/. Accessed January 30, 2021.

18 The Florida 2020 Statutes. http://www.leg.state.fl.us/statutes/index.cfm?App_mode=Display_Statute&URL=0400-0499/0468/0468PartVContentsIndex.html&StatuteYear=2020&Title=%2D%3E2020%2D%3EChapter%20468%2D%3EPart%20V. Accessed January 30, 2021.

the cardiopulmonary system that is practiced *under the orders of a physician* licensed under chapter 458 or chapter 459 and in accordance with protocols, policies, and procedures established by a hospital or other health care provider or the board, including the assessment, diagnostic evaluation, treatment, management, control, rehabilitation, education, and care of patients in all care settings. [Italics added.]

(8) "Registered respiratory therapist" [RRT] means any person licensed under this part who is registered by the National Board for Respiratory Care or its successor, and who is employed to deliver respiratory care services *under the order of a physician* licensed under chapter 458 or chapter 459, in accordance with protocols established by a hospital or other health care provider or the board, *and who functions in situations of unsupervised patient contact* requiring individual judgment. [Italics added.]

(9) "Respiratory care practitioner"[19] means any person licensed under this part who is employed to deliver respiratory care services, under direct supervision, pursuant to the order of a physician licensed under chapter 458 or chapter 459.

(10) "Respiratory care services" includes:

(a) Evaluation and disease management.

(b) Diagnostic and therapeutic use of respiratory equipment, devices, or medical gas.

(c) Administration of drugs, as duly ordered or prescribed by a physician licensed under chapter 458 or chapter 459 and in accordance with protocols, policies, and procedures established by a hospital or other health care provider or the board.

(d) Initiation, management, and maintenance of equipment to assist and support ventilation and respiration.

(e) Diagnostic procedures, research, and therapeutic treatment and procedures, including measurement of ventilatory volumes, pressures, and flows; specimen collection and analysis of blood for gas transport and acid/base determinations; pulmonary-function testing; and other related physiological monitoring of cardiopulmonary systems.

(f) Cardiopulmonary rehabilitation.

(g) Cardiopulmonary resuscitation, advanced cardiac life support, neonatal resuscitation, and pediatric advanced life support, or equivalent functions.

(h) Insertion and maintenance of artificial airways and intravascular catheters.

(i) Education of patients, families, the public, or other health care providers, including disease process and management programs and smoking prevention and cessation programs.

(j) Initiation and management of hyperbaric oxygen.

The main differences between a CRT and an RRT involve the level of education, experience, and advanced clinical skills.[20]

Chapter 468.352 contemplates that all RCPs function as part of a dyad with a physician since all RCPs deliver respiratory care services pursuant to the order of a licensed physician, in

19 According to the National Board for Respiratory Care, besides CRTs and RRTs, other credentialed respiratory care practitioners include the certified pulmonary function technologist; registered pulmonary function technologist; adult critical care specialist; neonatal/pediatric specialist; and sleep disorders specialist. https://www.nbrc.org/. Accessed January 31, 2021.

20 ClubStaffing. From CRT to RRT: How and Why You Should Advance. Published October 8, 2019. https://www.clubstaffing.com/allied-corner/rrt-to-crt-career-advancement/#:~:text=What%20is%20the%20difference%20between,the%20TMC%20examination%20for%20certification. Accessed January 30, 2021.

contradistinction to the situations involving PT and OT. On the other hand, 468.352 provides for unsupervised practice by CRTs and RRTs; presumably, lower-level RCPs require direct supervision by a CRT, an RRT, or a physician (see 468.352 (5) and (6), noted previously).

2. Fundamental Aspects of Dyadic Relationships

In sociology, a *dyad* signifies a group of two people. A dyad "is arguably the fundamental unit of interpersonal interaction and interpersonal relations."[21,22] Dyadic relationships in the workplace are of various types, including *leader–follower* dyads, *mentor–protégé* dyads,[23] and *coworker–coworker* (or *teammate–teammate*) dyads. *Leader–follower* and *mentor–protégé* dyads are referred to as vertical dyads, since the statuses of the two members are not equal.

2.1. Formation of Dyadic Relationships

All dyadic relationships begin with *person perception* on the part of both parties to the new dyad.

Persons form initial impressions of each other that tend to be remarkably accurate.[24,25] These initial impressions—including judgments regarding trustworthiness (see Chapter 1, section 2.3 The Moral Virtues/Vices)—are based on nonverbal cues, such as facial expressions, and are used in deciding whether an investment of time and effort in the would-be dyadic relationship is justified.[26]

While first impressions are dominated by nonverbal cues, verbal interaction enables each party to assess the personality, attitudes, and values of the other. "An established finding from social psychology is that people tend to be attracted to individuals who express similar attitudes and values."[27,28]

Admiration and respect are important determinants of the formation and maintenance of dyadic relationships.

> In work settings, individuals viewed as being technically or professionally skilled tend to be respected by others. Grover[29] refers to this as "appraisal respect." Indeed, professional respect . . . [is] a key . . . [determinant of] the quality of dyadic relationships . . . . And . . . quality relationships require that both parties of the dyad . . . demonstrate this respect for their partners.[30]

---

21 Liden R, Anand S, Vidyarthi P. Dyadic relationships 2016. *Annual Review of Organizational Psychology and Organizational Behavior.* 2016;3(1):139–166.

22 Kenny DA, Kashy DA, Cook WL. *Dyadic Data Analysis.* New York: Guilford Press; 2006.

23 The mentor–protégé model applies, for example, to physician–physician dyads throughout medical education, including undergraduate medical education, internship, residency, and fellowship training.

24 Ambady N, Hallahan M, Rosenthal R. On judging and being judged accurately in zero-acquaintance situations. *J Pers Soc Psychol.* 1995;69(3):518–529

25 Ambady N, Rosenthal R. Thin slices of expressive behavior as predictors of interpersonal consequences: a meta-analysis. *Psychol Bull.* 1992;111:256–274

26 Liden R, Anand S, Vidyarthi P. Dyadic relationships 2016. *Annual Review of Organizational Psychology and Organizational Behavior*. 2016;3(1):139–166, at 140.

27 Byrne D. *The Attraction Paradigm.* New York: Academic; 1971.

28 Liden R, Anand S, Vidyarthi P. Dyadic relationships 2016. *Annual Review of Organizational Psychology and Organizational Behavior.* 2016;3(1):139–166, at p. 141.

29 Grover SL. Unraveling respect in organization studies. *Hum Relat.* 2014;67(1):27–51, at 27.

30 Liden R, Anand S, Vidyarthi P. Dyadic relationships 2016. *Annual Review of Organizational Psychology and Organizational Behavior.* 2016;3(1):139–166, at 141.

2.2. Evolution of Dyadic Relationships

Role-taking occurs when a person enters the dyad.[31] In a vertical dyad (e.g., *mentor–protégé* or *leader–follower*), the supervisor would use this time to assess the knowledge and skills of the subordinate. So, for example, an OTA joins an OT practice and during this initial role-taking period is evaluated by the OTA's supervising OT based on the OTA's performance on tasks (*sent-roles*) assigned by the supervisor.

Role-making and *role-routinization* refer to the evolution and maturation of the role that results from the ongoing give-and-take between the higher status member (the supervisor) and the lower status member (the supervisee). Supervisees who prove themselves to be trustworthy, hard-working, knowledgeable, and skilled, and who share the values held by the supervisor are likely to gain his or her respect; they are said to belong to the *in-group* and are likely to be given the most challenging and interesting work and to be offered opportunities for additional training and advancement.[32,33]

CASE 8.B

A nationally acclaimed electrophysiologist (Dr. T) with decades of experience treating highly complex patients with life-threatening arrhythmias collaborated regularly with his PA partner. The PA performed tasks described in the medical model—determining the chief complaint, obtaining the history, and educating the patient regarding the disease process and the tests needed to confirm the preliminary diagnosis. These tasks were performed in a manner that patients could understand and that promoted their participation in the decision-making process. Typically Dr. T joined the patient interaction (now a triad?) as the expert in the final decision-making process after the groundwork had been laid for the patient to give informed consent (or refusal) to the proposed plan. This dyadic interaction was reassuring and empowering to patients, who praised the dyad to other potential patients.

One day a new patient phoned the practice, specifically requesting a consultation with the PA. This was not typical of tertiary care specialty clinics in the 1990s, where autonomous PA practice did not exist. Dr. T was delighted and made the incident public, proclaiming that never in his career had anyone specifically requested the PA's consultation.[29]

Which of the dyadic models is described in this example? How is the physician's response an example of *appraisal respect*?

Analysis: ______________________________

____

____

____

____

____

____

____

____

____

2.3. Fly in the Ointment: Employer–Employee Relationships

Dyadic relationships do not exist in a vacuum. They exist in the real world, and economic realities

31 The Leader-Member Exchange Theory. Mindtools. https://www.mindtools.com/pages/article/leader-member-exchange.htm. Accessed February 3, 2021.

32 Liden R, Anand S, Vidyarthi P. Dyadic relationships 2016. *Annual Review of Organizational Psychology and Organizational Behavior.* 2016;3(1):139–66, at p. 140.

33 The Leader-Member Exchange Theory. Mindtools. https://www.mindtools.com/pages/article/leader-member-exchange.htm. Accessed February 3, 2021.

often intervene, adding levels of complexity to dyadic relationships.

Consider, for example, a physician–PA dyad. Depending on the specifics of this particular dyad, it might be a *leader–follower* dyad, a *mentor–protégé* dyad, or a *teammate–teammate/coworker–coworker* dyad. Ok, simple enough. But what if the physician, instead of employing the PA, is employed by the PA to be his/her supervising physician? Such a situation might fundamentally change the nature of the dyad. (And, as we saw in Chapter 6, it might create a conflict of interest.)

3. Direct, Derivative, and Vicarious Liability[34]

Here we consider the two-way link between dyadic relationships and liability.

3.1. Direct Liability

Direct liability "refers to a situation in which a person . . . becomes liable to another on the basis of their own act or omission."[35] As we saw previously, each member of a healthcare professional dyad remains directly liable for his or her own acts or omissions. This result is the inevitable consequence of the fact that members of a dyad retain their status as moral agents.

3.2. Derivative Liability

Derivative liability is on display in the case *Darling v. Charleston Community Memorial Hospital*.[36] In that case, an 18-year-old suffered a broken leg playing football. Dr. Alexander, an independent contractor (not a hospital employee) on emergency call that day, placed the leg in a plaster cast. The patient complained of leg pain and swelling and discoloration of the toes were noted. Three days after the casting Dr. Alexander "split the sides of the cast with a Stryker saw; in the course of [doing so] the plaintiff's leg was cut . . . . Blood and other seepage were observed . . . , and there was a stench in the room, which one witness said was the worst he had smelled since World War II."[37] The patient ultimately required an above-the-knee amputation. In an action against the hospital, the hospital was held liable on either or both of two grounds: (1) for failing to "have a sufficient number of trained nurses for bedside care of all patients at all times capable of recognizing the progressive gangrenous condition . . . and of bringing [it] to the attention of the hospital administration and of the medical staff . . .";[38] and/or (2) for failing "to require consultation with or examination by members of the hospital surgical staff skilled in such treatment; or to review the treatment rendered . . . and to require consultants to be called in as needed."[39] The hospital's liability in *Darling* is an example of what is called *derivative liability*:

> Unlike cases involving pure vicarious liability, cases of derivative liability, such as the wrongful hiring of an incompetent employee, involve wrongful conduct both by the person who is derivatively liable and the actor whose wrongful conduct was the direct cause of injury to another. The liability is derivative because it depends upon a subsequent wrongful act or omission. As one court explained in a negligent entrustment setting:

---

34 This section is included here because of its connection with and importance to an understanding of dyadic relationships in health care. Admittedly, though, this section will be more readily appreciated by the reader who has an understanding of the material covered in Chapter 11. The reader might, therefore, wish to refer to Chapter 11 at this point. Additionally, much of the material in this section is drawn from Chapter 16 My brother's keeper? allocating legal responsibility among medical providers. In: Paola FA, Walker R, Nixon LL, eds. *Medical Ethics and Humanities*. Sudbury, MA: Jones and Bartlett Publishers; 2010.

35 Insuranceopedia. https://www.insuranceopedia.com/definition/1561/direct-liability. Accessed January 31, 2021.

36 *Darling v. Charleston Community Memorial Hospital,* 33 Ill.2d 326, 211 N.E.2d 253 (Sup. Ct. Ill. 1965).

37 *Darling v. Charleston Community Memorial Hospital,* 33 Ill.2d 326, 211 N.E.2d 253 (Sup. Ct. Ill. 1965).

38 *Darling v. Charleston Community Memorial Hospital,* 33 Ill.2d 326, 211 N.E.2d 253 (Sup. Ct. Ill. 1965).

39 *Darling v. Charleston Community Memorial Hospital,* 33 Ill.2d 326, 211 N.E.2d 253 (Sup. Ct. Ill. 1965).

> Obviously, an owner who is negligent in entrusting his vehicle is not liable for such negligence until some wrong is committed by the one to whom it is entrusted. Even if the owner's negligence in permitting the driving were gross, it would not be actionable if the driver was guilty of no negligence. The driver's wrong, in the form of legal liability to the plaintiff, first must be established, then by negligent entrustment liability for such wrong is passed on to the owner.

> Derivative liability is thus predicated on the tortious conduct of the defendant personally. However, like vicarious liability, there is no liability without the subsequent tortious conduct of another. (Internal footnotes omitted; italics added.)[40]

In *Darling*, the hospital itself behaved wrongfully by understaffing itself with nurses or by failing to supervise the quality of medical care being delivered by its medical staff. Still, the hospital's wrongful behavior would not have given rise to a legal action if not for the negligence of Dr. Alexander, and that is why the hospital's liability is said to be derivative.

3.3. Vicarious Liability

Vicarious liability refers to that legal rule under which "the person who is being held responsible for the conduct of the . . . [wrongdoer] has engaged in no wrongful conduct personally, but is liable because of his or her relationship with the actor who engaged in the wrongful conduct."[41] Stated otherwise, "'Imputed negligence' [aka *vicarious liability*] means that, [where A is negligent and B is not,] by reason of some relation existing between A and B, the negligence of A is to be charged against B, although B has played no part in it, . . . or indeed has done all that he possibly can to prevent it."[42]

As we saw in our discussion in section 1. *Dyadic Relationships Involving Health Professionals*, some dyadic relationships in health care involve supervision of one provider by another—e.g., a PA supervised by a physician; a PTA supervised by a PT; an OTA supervised by an OT; or a RCP supervised by an RRT. Involvement in such relationships entails legal consequences.

CASE 8.C: *Yorston v. Penell*[43]

The plaintiff Yorston accidentally shot himself in the leg with a nail gun. He was brought to the hospital and became a patient of Dr. Pennell, an attending surgeon on the medical staff but NOT a hospital employee. Also involved in the care of the patient were Dr. Hatemi, the surgical resident, and Mr. Rex, a surgical subintern [usually a third or fourth year medical student], both of whom were hospital employees. Mr. Rex was instructed to do the admitting history and physical examination (H&P) by Dr. Hatemi. During the course of the exam, the patient advised Mr. Rex that he was allergic to penicillin, but Mr. Rex neglected to note this in his written H&P. Subsequently, Dr. Hatemi, on the instructions of Dr. Pennell, operated on Yorston. Postoperatively, in reliance on Rex's H&P Dr. Hatemi prescribed 600,000 units of penicillin to Yorston, who experienced an allergic reaction. Yorston sued Dr. Pennell and won a judgment. There was no allegation made that Dr. Pennell had done anything wrong or that he was in any way negligent in supervising Dr. Hatemi or Mr. Rex. How did Yorston prevail against Dr. Pennell?

Analysis: ______________________

____

---

40 Underwood WD, Morrison MD. Apportioning responsibility in cases involving claims of vicarious, derivative, or statutory liability for harm directly caused by the conduct of another. 55 *Baylor L. Rev.* 617, 620 (2003).

41 Underwood WD, Morrison MD. Apportioning responsibility in cases involving claims of vicarious, derivative, or statutory liability for harm directly caused by the conduct of another. 55 *Baylor L. Rev.* 617, 618 (2003).

42 *Crowell v. City of Philadelphia*, 531 Pa. 400, 407, 613 A.2d 1178, 1181 (Sup. Ct. Pa. 1992), quoting Prosser and Keeton on Torts §69 (5th ed. 1984).

43 *Yorston v. Pennell*, 397 Pa. 28; 153 A.2d 255 (Sup. Ct. Pa. 1959).

The specific type of *vicarious liability* at work in *Yorston v. Pennell* is known as *respondeat superior*, which translates as "let the master answer" or "let the higher up answer."[44] *Respondeat superior* most commonly applies in the employer–employee context—that is to say, the employer is vicariously liable for the acts of the employee. (The employee is liable as well, though in his case liability is direct.) The policy rationale underlying the doctrine is that the employer, having both a "deeper pocket" than the employee and a right to control the employee, is better situated both to pay for the plaintiff's damages and to prevent future potential plaintiffs from being damaged.

WRAP-UP

Chapter Summary

A *dyad* refers to an interaction between a pair of individuals. Dyadic relationships can generally be classified as *leader–follower*, *mentor–protégé*, *coworker–coworker*, or *teammate–teammate*, and the nature of dyadic relationships involving health professionals depends in part on whether they are *dependent* or *independent* practitioners. Successful dyads are characterized by trust and by *appraisal respect*, which refers to the respect that ensues from an individual being viewed as technically or professionally skilled. Each member of a dyad is directly liable for his or her acts and omissions. A member of a dyad who is in a supervisory position may be vicariously liable for the acts/omissions of his or her supervisee under the doctrine of *respondeat superior*.

Review Questions

1. Define *dyad*.
2. List three models of dyadic relationships, and try to provide an example of each.
3. Define vicarious liability and explain how it relates to the physician-health professional dyad.
4. What is direct liability?
5. What is derivative liability, and how does it differ from vicarious liability?

44 Other types of vicarious liability exist, including apparent or ostensible agency, non-delegable duty, partnerships, and joint enterprises. See, for example, My brother's keeper? Allocating legal responsibility among medical providers. In: Paola FA, Walker R, Nixon LL, eds. *Medical Ethics and Humanities*. Sudbury, MA: Jones and Bartlett Publishers; 2010.

Case Analyses

Case 8.A Analysis

(1) The issue in this case is whether the physical therapist (Lavergne) was practicing outside the scope of PT practice (as defined by the State of Louisiana in its Physical Therapy Practice Act) in his clinical encounter with Smith. In deciding affirmatively, the Board's position was that Lavergne's actions in "evaluating" and "treating" Smith constituted the unauthorized practice of medicine. The court disagreed. On the question of evaluation, the court found the wording of the relevant statute to be ambiguous or vague and decided that it would therefore be unfair to sanction Lavergne for doing something that was arguably permitted under a reasonable interpretation of that statute. On the question of treatment, the court points out that:

> Lavergne simply told Smith to continue to keep ice on the ankle. Ostensibly, this is what any reasonable person, one not necessarily trained in first aid or in a medically related field, would have suggested. Should Lavergne be sanctioned because he was a licensed physical therapist and suggested the same? Does the Physical Therapy Practice Act expressly prohibit a physical therapist from offering such reasonable advice? We think not.[45,46]

(2) This case relates to the dyadic relationships we have been discussing so far in that the Board's opinion is that the actions of Lavergne would have been within the scope of PT practice only if they were carried out in the context of a dyadic relationship of sorts comprising a physician of record and the physical therapist.

Case 8.B Analysis

The model that best characterizes the dyad between a supervising physician and a recent PA school graduate who is being trained by the supervising physician is the *mentor–protégé* model. It appears from the scenario, however, that the PA involved is experienced in the field of electrophysiology, and it appears that this dyad has progressed through the role-taking, role-making, and role-routinization stages. The two providers appear to demonstrate *appraisal respect* for each other's abilities. The employment relationship between the two providers is not specified (e.g., was the PA the employee of the physician?), but that aside, the *teammate–teammate* or *coworker–coworker* model would seem to fit the dyad existing between these two experienced practitioners.

Case 8.C Analysis

One possibility is that Dr. Pennell is being held liable by the court for failing to adequately supervise Rex and Hatemi. That would be a form of *derivative liability*, but in fact the case was not submitted to the jury on that theory. It turns out that Dr. Pennell's liability is completely divorced from any wrongdoing on his part. His liability is said to be vicarious; the negligence of someone else (Rex) is being imputed to him. Pennell's liability is not contingent upon any wrongful act or omission of his own, but rather on the wrongful act(s) or omission(s) of other healthcare providers.

45 *Lavergne v. Louisiana State Bd. of Medical Examiners,* 539 So. 2d 656, 1989 La. App. LEXIS 110 (Court of Appeal of Louisiana, Fourth Circuit January 30, 1989, Decided). https://advance-lexis-com.ezproxylocal.library.nova.edu/api/document?collection=cases;id=urn:contentItem:3S3K-46Y0-008T-X08M-00000-00;context=1516831.

46 There is a classic scene in *The Noose Hangs High*, a Universal Pictures film starring Budd Abbott and Lou Costello. In that scene, Abbott humorously reprimands Costello for recommending to him that he take aspirin for a headache: "Have you a license to practice medicine?" https://www.youtube.com/watch?v=9b8oEcFmQD0. Accessed January 29, 2021. For information regarding the film, see https://en.wikipedia.org/wiki/The_Noose_Hangs_High. Accessed January 29, 2021.

CHAPTER 9

Ethical Issues at Life's Beginning

Stephanie Lolita Anderson, M.D., J.D.
Frederick Adolf Paola, M.D., J.D.

LEARNING OBJECTIVES

1. Identify and distinguish *presently existing actual moral agents*, *future actual moral agents*, and *presently existing moral agents* and how each of these relates to the scope of morality.
2. Explain the *human stock definition of personhood*.
3. Identify criteria of personhood.
4. List approaches that ground *moral standing* in something other than personhood, and explain each approach.
5. Explain *viability* and its significance to abortion jurisprudence.
6. Explain what is meant by the *maternal–fetal dyad* and the *two-patient obstetric model*.
7. Explain Judith Jarvis Thomson's *defense of abortion*.

Vitae Summa Brevis Spem Nos Vetat Incohare Longam

They are not long, the weeping and the laughter,
Love and desire and hate:
I think they have no portion in us after
We pass the gate.

They are not long, the days of wine and roses:
Out of a misty dream
Our path emerges for a while, then closes
Within a dream.

—**Ernest Dowson**[1]

1 Poets.org. https://poets.org/poem/vitae-summa-brevis-spem-nos-vetat-incohare-longam. Accessed June 24, 2020.

Many voices are speaking at once about what is meant by the beginning of life. Yet, as Gazzaniga has written, "The fertilized egg represents the starting point for the soon-to-be dividing entity that will grow into a fetus and finally into a baby. *It is a given* that a fertilized egg is the beginning of the life of an individual." (italics added)[2] So, the issue is less about when life begins and more about when life begins to matter in a moral sense; in other words, at what point in human development/ontogeny is that human entitled to the protection of the moral rules? (See Chapter 1, section 1. *Ethics and Morality*.) This is a question about which reasonable people disagree, and this disagreement underlies many of the bioethical controversies with which society has grappled in recent years, including abortion, management of frozen embryos,[3] pregnant women exposing their fetuses to risk,[4] and human cloning.[5]

1. Human Development and Moral Standing

Gert has written, "No one disagrees that all *presently existing [actual moral agents]* and *future actual moral agents* are protected by the moral rules. Common morality also includes all those who have been actual moral agents and are still conscious." (italics added)[6] Infants and children belong to neither of these categories; rather, they are considered *presently existing potential moral agents*. Gert has written that while it is not rationally required for infants and children to be accorded the protection of morality, there is substantial agreement for doing so. Embryos and fetuses are also *presently existing potential moral agents*, and yet the issue of whether they should be accorded the protection of morality is more controversial.

Why? What are the criteria that people consider in deciding whether or not a human at a particular developmental stage is entitled to the protection of morality? To date we have not yet reached such a consensus, so we will consider the competing approaches.

1.1. The Personhood Approach to Moral Standing

One approach has been to equate moral standing with personhood. Under this approach, a human life begins to matter in a moral sense when it becomes a *person*. But what is a person, and when does a human life become a person?

1.1.1. Human Stock[7] Definition of Personhood

According to the fifth century philosopher Boethius, a person is an individual belonging to a species whose goal is the attainment of rationality (e.g., *Homo sapiens*). Membership in the species is sufficient to bestow personhood on the individual; it is not necessary that the individual in question possess rationality in order to

---

2 Gazzaniga MS. The ethical brain. *New York Times*. June 19, 2005. https://www.nytimes.com/2005/06/19/books/chapters/the-ethical-brain.html?auth=login-email;login=email. Accessed June 25, 2020.

3 Should there be legal limits on how many embryos can be transferred into a woman who wants to be pregnant? In Kaebnick GE, ed. *Taking Sides*. 15th ed. New York, NY: McGraw-Hill; 2014:157–169.

4 Should a pregnant woman be punished for exposing her fetus to risk? In Kaebnick GE, ed. *Taking Sides*. 15th ed. New York, NY: McGraw-Hill; 2014:172–192.

5 Human cloning and human dignity: an ethical inquiry. The President's Council on Bioethics. July 2002. https://bioethicsarchive.georgetown.edu/pcbe/reports/cloningreport/. Accessed June 25, 2020.

6 Gert B. *Morality*. p. 141. He argues that the addition of former actual moral agents "is supported by noting that all rational persons who are moral agents would want to retain the protection of the moral rules if they were to lose their capacity to act as moral agents and could still suffer harms."

7 This chapter does not deal with ethical issues raised by genetics, many of which appear at the beginning of life. The interested reader is referred, for example, to: Anderson SL. The human genome project. In: Sanbar SS, Firestone MH, Fiscina S, LeBlang TR, Wecht CH, Zaremski MJ, eds. *Legal Medicine*. 7th ed. Philadelphia, PA: Mosby Elsevier; 2007:193–200.

be considered a person. Stated otherwise, some maintain that "a person . . . is an individual of a living species [i.e., *Homo sapiens*] some of whose members demonstrate the capacities to think, choose, reason . . . ."[8] But consider the following:

> . . . a human being (and, thus, a "person") is the reproductive product of other human beings. Even if we accept this "human stock" definition of person, however, the inquiry remains open. Does that human stock become a person, for tort law or other purposes, upon conception? Upon quickening? Upon viability? Upon birth? A year after birth? Upon physical maturity?[9]

At one end of the spectrum, some maintain that personhood attaches at the moment the ovum is fertilized.[10] Others, on the other hand, have argued

> Individuation within the human species is a necessary . . . condition for personhood . . . . I would argue . . . that an individual developing into a member of the human species is not a human individual until such time as the embryo cannot potentially become more than one individual of the human species through twinning . . . .[11]

1.1.2. Personhood as a Criterial Concept

Mary Anne Warren has proposed five criteria of personhood:

> . . . I suggest that the traits which are most central to the concept of personhood, or humanity in the moral sense, are, very roughly, the following:
>
> 1. Consciousness (of objects and events external and/or internal to the being), and in particular the ability to feel pain;
> 2. Reasoning (the *developed* capacity to solve new and relatively complex problems);
> 3. Self-motivated activity (activity which is relatively independent of either genetic or direct external control);
> 4. The capacity to communicate, by whatever means, messages of an indefinite variety of types . . .; [and]
> 5. The presence of self-concepts, and self-awareness . . . .[12]

Similarly, bioethicist Joseph Fletcher proposed a list of 15 such attributes, listed here in no rank order: (1) minimum intelligence; (2) self-awareness; (3) self-control; (4) a sense of time; (5) a sense of futurity; (6) a sense of the past; (7) the capability to relate to others; (8) concern for others; (9) communication; (10) control of existence; (11) curiosity; (12) change and changeability; (13) balance of rationality and feeling; (14) idiosyncrasy; and (15) neocortical function. Regarding the latter, Fletcher writes:

> In a way, this is the cardinal indicator, the one all the others are hinged upon. Before cerebration is in play, or with its end, in the absence of the synthesizing function of the cerebral cortex, the

---

8 McCartney JJ. Embryonic stem cell research and respect for human life: philosophical and legal reflections. 65 *Alb. L. Rev.* 597 (2002).

9 Furrow BR, Greaney TL, Johnson SH, Jost TS, Schwartz RL. *Bioethics: Health Care Law and Ethics.* 5th ed. St. Paul, MN: West; 2004:32.

10 Evangelicum Vitae (The Gospel of Life), encyclical letter of John Paul II (March 25, 1995).

11 McCartney JJ. Embryonic stem cell research and respect for human life: philosophical and legal reflections. 65 *Alb. L. Rev.* 597 (2002).

12 Warren MA. On the moral and legal status of abortion. *The Monist.* 1973;57(1):43–61. In applying these, she writes, "We needn't suppose that an entity must have all of these attributes to be . . . considered a person; (1) and (2) may be sufficient . . . . [But] any being that satisfies none of (1)–(5) is certainly not a person."

> person is nonexistent. Such individuals are objects but not subjects.[13]

Warren concludes that a fetus may be aborted because the fetus is not a person under this criterial approach. One problem with her argument is that it also leads to the conclusion that neither are infants persons and that therefore infanticide is morally permissible.

1.2. Nonpersonhood Approaches to Moral Standing

These approaches recognize that while personhood entitles one to the protection of morality, nonpersons might still be entitled to moral protection. Thus, as you saw in section 1. *Human Development and Moral Standing*, humans who have irrevocably lost the attributes of personhood but who remain conscious[14] are protected by the moral rules.[15] Consider the following example:

> Personhood is important as an inclusion criterion for moral equality: any theory which denies equal moral status to certain persons must be rejected. But personhood seems somewhat less plausible as an exclusion criterion, since it appears to exclude infants and mentally handicapped individuals who may lack the mental and social capacities typical of persons.[16]

So, under nonpersonhood approaches to moral standing, where is that standing to be grounded?

1.2.1. Moral Standing Grounded in the Intrinsic Value of Human Life

Ronald Dworkin has argued that what he calls the *detached* objection to abortion is independent of any fetal rights or interests; rather,

> . . . human life has an intrinsic, innate value; that human life is sacred just in itself; and that the sacred nature of human life begins when its biological life begins, even before the creature whose life it is has movement or sensation or interests or rights of its own. Accordingly . . . abortion is wrong . . . because it . . . insults the intrinsic value, the sacred character, of . . . human life.[17]

This is referred to as the *detached* view because it does not presuppose any fetal rights or interests.

1.2.2. Moral Standing Grounded in Sentience

"Sentience is the capacity to have experiences . . . . However, the capacity to have pleasurable and painful experiences seems particularly relevant to moral status."[18] This should come as no surprise to anyone who has read section 2.1 *The Moral Rules* in Chapter 1. Recall that the moral rules include "Do not cause pain/suffering" and "Do not deprive of pleasure."

---

13 Fletcher J, Humanness. In: *Humanhood: essays in biomedical ethics*. Buffalo, NY: Prometheus Books; 1979:12–16.

14 Bender A, Jox RJ, Grill E, Straube A, Lulé D. Persistent vegetative state and minimally conscious state. *Dtsch Arztebl Int*. 2015;112:235–242. https://www.ncbi.nlm.nih.gov/pmc/articles/PMC4413244/pdf/Dtsch_Arztebl_Int-112-0235.pdf. Accessed June 25, 2020.

15 In the words of Gert, "Common morality also includes all those who have been actual moral agents and are still conscious."

16 Warren MA. Abortion. In: Singer P, ed. *A Companion to Ethics*. Cambridge, MA: Basil-Blackwell; 1991:303–314 at 311.

17 Dworkin R. *Life's Dominion*. New York, NY: Vintage Books; 1993:11.

18 Warren MA. Abortion. In: Singer P, ed. *A Companion to Ethics*. Cambridge, MA: Basil-Blackwell; 1991:303–314 at 308.

> The sentience criterion suggests that, other things being equal, it is morally worse to kill a sentient than a non-sentient organism. The death of a sentient being, even when painless, deprives it of whatever pleasurable experiences it might have enjoyed in the future. Thus, death is apt to be a misfortune for that being in a way that the death of a non-sentient organism is not.[19]

The sentience criterion helps explain why late term abortion or partial birth abortion is more objectionable from a moral standpoint than first trimester abortion; however, it does not explain why it is morally worse to kill a human being than a sentient animal such as a fish or a fly.

1.2.3. Moral Standing Grounded in Potential Personhood

Some would ground moral standing not in personhood, but in the potential for personhood. For example, Marquis[20] has argued that the best explanation as to why killing a human adult or child is presumptively wrong is that

> . . . it deprives an individual of that individual's future of valuable experiences and activities—a "future like ours" [FLO]. From this, Marquis thinks it follows that abortion is in most cases as wrong as murder and for the same reason: it deprives an individual of that individual's valuable "future like ours" [FLO]. Thus "fetuses can be victims of abortion in exactly the same way as adults or children can be victims of murder."[21]

Stated otherwise, "since killing adult humans is wrong because it deprives them of a future of value and [since] the fetus has a future of value, killing fetuses is wrong in the same way that killing adult human beings is wrong."[22]

2. Human Development and Legal Standing

Recall that in section 1.1.1. *Human Stock Definition of Personhood*, we asked, "When does human stock become a person, for tort law or other purposes, upon conception? Upon quickening? Upon viability? Upon birth? A year after birth? Upon physical maturity?"[23] Let's revisit this question with a focus on the law.

2.1. Constitutional Rights and the Viability Approach

The majority opinion in *Roe v. Wade* brought the notion of *viability* into our law. In that case, the U.S. Supreme Court held that the unborn are not "persons" under the U.S. Constitution and therefore not protected by that provision of the 14th Amendment that prohibits depriving persons of life without due process of law.[24] The *Roe* holding established a three trimester approach to abortion. Because during the first trimester abortion was found to be safer for the pregnant woman than childbirth, any laws interfering with first trimester abortions would be presumptively

19 Warren MA. Abortion. In: Singer P, ed. *A Companion to Ethics*. Cambridge, MA: Basil-Blackwell; 1991:303–314 at 308.

20 Marquis D. Why abortion is immoral. *J Philos* 1989;86:183–202.

21 Kuflik A. The "future like ours" argument and human embryonic stem cell research. *J Med Ethics*. 2008;34:417–421.

22 Brown M. A future like ours revisited. *J Med Ethics*. 2002;28(3):192–195. doi: 10.1136/jme.28.3.192. https://www.ncbi.nlm.nih.gov/pmc/articles/PMC1733571/. Accessed June 25, 2020.

23 Furrow BR, Greaney TL, Johnson SH, Jost TS, Schwartz RL. *Bioethics: Health Care Law and Ethics*. 5th ed. St. Paul, MN: West; 2004:32.

24 The 14th Amendment states in part "nor shall any state deprive any person of life, liberty, or property, without due process of law . . . ." See Legal Information Institute, Cornell Law School, XIV Amendment. https://www.law.cornell.edu/constitution/amendmentxiv. Accessed June 25, 2020.

unconstitutional. During the second trimester, states would be permitted to regulate abortion only to protect the health of the pregnant woman. With the onset of the third trimester and with it fetal viability (the ability of the unborn child to live on its own outside the woman's womb), the "State's important and legitimate interest in potential life" becomes "compelling," and the state can restrict or limit abortions except where abortion was necessary to preserve the woman's life or health. "This is so because the fetus then presumably has the capability of meaningful life outside the mother's womb."[25]

Under *Roe*, the pregnant woman had a *legal* right to choose abortion up until the onset of the third trimester (which *Roe* equated with fetal viability), a right protected by that provision of the 14th Amendment that prohibits depriving persons of liberty without due process of law. Following the onset of viability, the state's interest in protecting potential human life became compelling and states were permitted to prohibit abortion, although *Roe* did not recognize any rights of the unborn themselves.[26]

In the 1992 decision *Planned Parenthood v. Casey*, the U.S. Supreme Court reaffirmed a woman's constitutional right to abort a fetus before viability without "undue" state interference as well as the state's right to restrict or prohibit abortion after viability except to preserve the life or health of the woman. However, *Casey* abandoned the *Roe* trimester framework, a concession to the fact that advances in obstetrics and neonatology had in the interim moved the point of fetal viability back from between the 24th and 28th weeks of gestation to before the 23rd week.[27]

Ronald Dworkin (see previous section 1.2.1 *Moral Standing Grounded in the Intrinsic Value of Human Life* in this chapter) has written that at about the point of viability, a *derivative* objection to abortion comes into play:

> At about the time of fetal viability . . . the brain may have developed sufficiently so that a primitive form of sentience is possible. A fetus might then . . . be said to have interests of its own.[28]

Dworkin calls this objection *derivative* because it is derived from—as is the government's responsibility to protect the viable fetus—the rights/interests of the viable fetus in question.

In 2022, the US Supreme Court overruled *Roe v. Wade* and progeny in the case *Dobbs v. Jackson Women's Health Organization*[29], holding that the Constitution does not confer a right to abortion. The legal effect of *Dobbs* was to return the authority to regulate abortion to the people and their elected representatives, the legal situation that had existed from the adoption of the Constitution in 1788 through the *Roe* decision in 1973. In essence, the Court decided that the abortion decision was a *political question* (see Section 3.3 Justiciability in Chapter 4 on US law).

---

25 *Roe v. Wade,* 410 U.S. 113 (1973). It is not self-evident why the fetus' physical dependence on the mother precludes its being considered a person.

26 Paola F. Fetal interests. In: Sanbar S, Gibofsky A, Firestone MH, LeBlang TR, eds. *Legal Medicine*. 3rd ed. St Louis, MO: Mosby; 1995:364–371.

27 *Planned Parenthood v. Casey,* 505 U.S. 833 (1992). https://supreme.justia.com/cases/federal/us/505/833/. Accessed June 27, 2020. For years doctors estimated that the earliest premature survivors had to reach 28 weeks' gestation and weigh 2.2 pounds or more. Over the past 40 years, progress has meant that some babies delivered at 24, 23 or even 22 weeks survive, even as they weigh less than one pound. The survival of infants less than 22 weeks has improved in some facilities, from 3.6% to 20% over the past decade.

28 Dworkin R. *Life's Dominion.* New York, NY: Vintage Books; 1993:169.

29 Supreme Court of the United States. *Dobbs state health officer of the Mississippi Department of Health, et al. v. Jackson Women's Health Organization et al.* No. 19-1392. Argued December 1, 2021–Decided June 24, 2022. Accessed July 20, 2022 at https://www.supremecourt.gov/opinions/21pdf/19-1392_6j37.pdf

2.2. Fetal Interests/Rights Under Criminal Law and Tort Law

As we suggested previously, the answer to the question, "When does human stock become a person?" might depend on the reason for asking the question. Are we asking for constitutional purposes? Are we asking for reasons that have to do with the tort law? (See Chapter 10, *Medical Malpractice Law and the PA*.) Reasons that have to do with the criminal law? While a discussion of fetal interests under tort law and criminal law is beyond the scope of this text,[30] the case of *Keeler v. Superior Court* demonstrates this point.

> [Robert] and Teresa Keeler . . . [were divorced] on September 27, 1968. They had been married for 16 years. Unknown to petitioner, Mrs. Keeler was then pregnant by one Ernest Vogt, whom she had met earlier that summer. She subsequently began living with Vogt in Stockton, but concealed the fact from [RK]. [RK] was given custody of their two daughters, aged 12 and 13 years, and under the decree Mrs. Keeler had the right to take the girls on alternate weekends.
>
> On February 23, 1969, Mrs. Keeler was driving on a narrow mountain road in Amador County after delivering the girls to their home. She met [RK] driving in the opposite direction; he blocked the road with his car, and she pulled over to the side. He walked to her vehicle and . . . said, "I hear you're pregnant. If you are you had better stay away from the girls and from here." [When Mrs. Keeler exited her vehicle, RK] . . . then looked at her abdomen and became "extremely upset." He said, "You sure are. I'm going to stomp it out of you." He pushed her against the car, shoved his knee into her abdomen, and struck her in the face with several blows. She fainted, and when she regained consciousness petitioner had departed.
>
> . . . police and medical assistance were summoned. [Mrs. Keeler] had suffered substantial facial injuries as well as extensive bruising of the abdominal wall. A Caesarian section was performed and the fetus was examined in utero. Its head was found to be severely fractured, and it was delivered stillborn. The pathologist gave as his opinion that the cause of death was skull fracture with consequent cerebral hemorrhaging, that death would have been immediate, and that the injury could have been the result of force applied to the mother's abdomen. . . .
>
> Upon delivery the fetus weighed five pounds . . . . Both Mrs. Keeler and her obstetrician testified that fetal movements had been observed prior to February 23, 1969. The evidence was in conflict as to the estimated age of the fetus; the expert testimony on the point, however, concluded "with reasonable medical certainty" that the fetus had developed to the stage of viability, i.e., that in the event of premature birth on the date in question it would have had a 75 percent to 96 percent chance of survival.[31]

Besides being charged with battery upon his ex-wife, RK was charged with the murder of "Baby Girl" Vogt under California Penal Code section 187, which provides: "Murder is the unlawful killing of a human being, with malice aforethought." As the Court wrote, "The dispositive question is whether the fetus which petitioner is accused of killing was, on February 23, 1969,

30 The interested reader is referred, for example, to: Paola FA. Fetal interests. In: Sanbar SS, Gibofsky A, Firestone MH, LeBlang TR, eds. *Legal Medicine*. 4th ed. St Louis, MO: Mosby; 1998:315–322.

31 *Keeler v. Superior Court*, 470 P.2d 617 (1970).

a "human being" *within the meaning of the statute*" (italics added).

The Court held that the Vogt fetus was not a human being within the meaning of the statute and that, consequently, the murder charge could not be sustained. How did the Court reach this legal conclusion? It began by "inquiring into the intent of the [California] Legislature in 1850 when it first defined murder as the unlawful and malicious killing of a 'human being.'" The Court reviewed legal history and that, by 1850, an infant could not be the subject of homicide unless: (1) quickening had occurred (i.e., fetal movements had been detected), and (2) the fetus was born alive, dying subsequently. The Court therefore concluded that "in declaring murder to be the unlawful and malicious killing of a 'human being' the Legislature of 1850 intended that term to have the settled common law meaning of a person who had been born alive, and did not intend the act of feticide—as distinguished from abortion—to be an offense under the laws of California."[32] Further, while other U.S. states had enacted statutes criminalizing feticide, California had not. Subsequent to the events of *Keeler*, the California Legislature modified section 187 to read, "Murder is the unlawful killing of a human being, *or a fetus*, with malice aforethought."

CASE 9.A

Consider the facts of the *Keeler* case in which the Vogt fetus was adjudged not to have been entitled to the protection of the *law* prohibiting killing. Was the Vogt fetus entitled to the protection of the moral rule "do not kill"?

Analysis: ____________________

____

3. The Maternal–Fetal Dyad

A *dyad* is a relationship or continual interaction between two parties.[33] (The reader will recall that we considered professional dyads in Chapter 8, *Interactions Among Health Care Professionals*.)

3.1. The Shift From One-Patient to Two-Patient Obstetric Model

Mattingly has written that traditionally "physicians conceptualized the *maternal–fetal dyad* as one complex patient, the gravid female, of which the fetus was an integral part."[34] The development of high-resolution ultrasonography and other modern diagnostic tools, as well as in utero medical and surgical procedures, have "shifted the emphasis from unity to duality"—to a new two-patient obstetric model. The implications of this shift are illustrated by the following passage:

32 *Keeler v. Superior Court,* 470 P.2d 617, at 628 (1970).

33 Dyad. Dictionary.com. https://www.dictionary.com/browse/dyad?s=t. Accessed June 26, 2020.

34 Mattingly SS. The maternal-fetal dyad. *Hastings Center Report.* 1992;22(1):13.

> In cases where maternal and fetal burdens associated with fetal therapy are relatively small and prospective benefits to the fetus are substantial, the physician's duty of beneficence on the one-patient obstetric model is clearly to recommend treatment . . . even if treatment offers no medical benefits, only burdens, to the woman . . . . When the maternal-fetal dyad is regarded as [a] . . . whole, what matters is that combined maternal-fetal benefits outweigh combined maternal-fetal burdens. Distributions of benefits and burdens between fetal and maternal components of the [dyad] . . . are not ethically relevant.
>
> [Under the two-patient obstetric model] . . . however, it is no longer appropriate to consider effects of treatment on the two combined. Physicians are to decide what is medically best for each patient considered separately. When fetal benefits outweigh fetal burdens of intervention, beneficence dictates recommending therapy for the fetal patient. But when . . . caring for the fetal patient imposes some degree of discomfort, harm, or risk on the maternal patient with no offsetting therapeutic benefits to her . . . [the principle of] maleficence requires recommending against treatment for the maternal patient.
>
> Here is an ethical two-patient problem for the physician . . . : treatment medically indicated for one patient is contraindicated for the other, yet both must be treated (or not treated) alike.[35]

3.2. Decision-Making Under the Two-Patient Obstetric Model

How, then, should health professionals proceed under the two-patient obstetric model when the interests of the two patients are not concordant? Traditionally, the duty of *nonmaleficence* we owe the maternal patient would constrain our ability to act with *beneficence* toward the fetal patient (recall *primum non nocere*—first, do no harm—in section 3.2.2 Nonmaleficence in Chapter 1).

Mattingly points out, however, that while "conflicts between duties of beneficence and nonmaleficence to multiple patients are rare in medicine," they are not unprecedented. Examples outside of obstetrics include live-donor tissue transplantation and nontherapeutic research; in such cases, a careful relaxation of the nonmaleficence constraints is allowed, permitting providers to treat some patients nontherapeutically in order to benefit others under certain conditions. The conditions that must be met are:

> First, the medical burdens inflicted must be smaller in relation to anticipated benefits than they are when they accrue to one and the same patient. Second, patients treated nontherapeutically must be volunteers. Recommending nontherapeutic treatment remains unethical, although providing it is permissible at the subject's or donor's request.[36]

Mattingly argues that the two-patient obstetric model bifurcates the process of making medical recommendations. First, the health professional recommends beneficial fetal therapy for the fetal patient. This, in turn, "requires a maternal proxy decision on behalf of the incompetent-fetal patient." The pregnant woman's responsibility for fetal well-being is relevant here, and Mattingly suggests that health professionals are morally authorized to challenge a proxy decision that is contrary to the [fetal] patient's best interests. However, even if a substitute proxy (the father of the fetus, or a court-appointed legal guardian) consents to therapy on behalf of the fetus, there remains a second hurdle to be overcome. In this second step, the physician invites and encourages

35 Mattingly SS. The maternal-fetal dyad. *Hastings Center Report.* 1992;22(1):13.
36 Mattingly SS. The maternal-fetal dyad. *Hastings Center Report.* 1992;22(1):13.

the pregnant woman to submit voluntarily to burdensome (to her) treatment for the sake of proportionate fetal benefits. Should the woman refuse the invitation (in effect declining treatment of the maternal–fetal dyad) to submit to treatment that is contrary to her medical best interests, disregarding that refusal would constitute "not medical paternalism but medical maleficence."

CASE 9.B

Consider the following case:

> A.C. was diagnosed with leukemia when she was thirteen years old. . . . [S]he underwent a number of major surgical procedures, therapy, and chemotherapy. When she was twenty-seven years old, after her cancer had been in remission for three years, A.C. married. At the time she became pregnant, she had not undergone chemotherapy for more than a year. . . .
>
> When A.C. was approximately twenty-five weeks pregnant, she went to her regularly scheduled prenatal visit complaining of shortness of breath and some pain in her back. Her physicians subsequently discovered that she had a tumor mass in her lung which was most likely a metastatic oxygenic carcinoma. She was admitted to the hospital on June 11 and her prognosis was terminal.
>
> On June 15, during A.C.'s twenty-sixth week of pregnancy, A.C., her physicians, her mother, and her husband discussed the possibility of providing A.C. with radiation therapy or chemotherapy to relieve her pain and to continue her pregnancy. Her physicians believed that her unborn child's chances of viability would be greatly increased if it were delivered when it had reached twenty-eight weeks gestational age. By June 16, the date on which the hospital sought the declaratory order in the Superior Court, A.C. had been heavily sedated so that she could continue to breathe. Her condition was declining, and the attending medical staff concluded that passive treatment was appropriate because the mother would not survive and the child's chances of survival were grim. The hospital administration then . . . [sought a declaratory judgment] in the Superior Court [the trial court].
>
> The trial court appointed counsel for A.C. and the fetus, respectively. The District of Columbia was permitted to intervene for the fetus as parens patriae. A hearing was held at the hospital . . . .
>
> There was some dispute about whether A.C. would have chosen to have a caesarean section on June 16. Before she was sedated, A.C. indicated that she would choose to relinquish her life so that the fetus could survive should such a choice present itself at the fetus' gestational age of twenty-eight weeks. Her physicians never discussed with her what her choice would be if such a choice had to be made before the fetus reached the twenty-eight-week point. The fetus was suffering oxygen starvation and resultant rapid heart rate. There was at that point less than 20 percent chance that it would be afflicted with cerebral palsy, neurological defects, deafness and blindness. There was not a clear medical consensus on the course of A.C.'s treatment. Those physicians who objected to the proposed surgery did so because A.C. refused her consent to the procedure, not because the surgery was medically objectionable. One physician testified that he believed that A.C. would not have wanted to deliver a baby that might have to undergo the pain of having handicaps that are associated with premature delivery. Another physician believed that A.C. would not have refused permission for the caesarean section to be performed. During the course of her pregnancy, however, A.C. was aware that a number of medications she was taking might harm the fetus. Nevertheless, she expressed a desire to her physicians to be kept as comfortable as possible throughout her pregnancy and to maintain the quality of her life.
>
> The trial court determined that the fetus was viable and that the District of Columbia had an interest in protecting the potential life of the fetus. . . . [T]he court decided that the caesarean section should be performed.

Shortly after the trial judge made his decision, A.C. was informed of it. She stated, during a period of lucidity, that she would agree to the surgery although she might not survive it. When another physician went to A.C. to verify her decision, she apparently changed her mind, mouthing the words, "I don't want it done." There was no explanation for either decision. . . .

[A] telephonic hearing was had before a hastily assembled division of the court. The trial judge's findings were read to us, and we heard from counsel and an attending physician. The latter answered questions respecting the relative chances of survival of both A.C. and the fetus with and without the surgery. He also informed us of the rapid decline of A.C. and the need to proceed promptly with the surgery, if it was decided to do so. . . .

The court based its decision to deny a stay on the medical judgment that A.C. would not survive for a significant time after the surgery and that the fetus had a better, though slim, chance if taken before A.C.'s imminent death. If A.C. died before delivery, the fetus would die as well. Though A.C. might have lived twenty-four to forty-eight hours, the surgery might have hastened her death. . . . [The caesarean operation was performed, and the child and mother died soon thereafter.][37]

Was the court's decision to authorize the caesarean section appropriate from a *moral* standpoint? Give reasons supporting your position.

Analysis: ______________________________

____

____

____

____

____

____

____

____

3.3. Abortion as Self-Defense

Judith Jarvis Thomson penned a famous essay in 1971 entitled "A Defense of Abortion."[38] In it, she assumes, for the sake of argument, that a fetus is a person from the moment of conception; even so, she argues, in a thought experiment, it does not necessarily follow that aborting a fetus is morally impermissible. The essay was meant as a defense of abortion but is discussed here because of its relevance to the maternal–fetal dyad. Specifically, while sections 3.1 and 3.2 consider the moral implications of maternal refusal of treatment of the dyad, this section considers the implications of a pregnant woman acting affirmatively in a way that benefits her at the expense of the fetus. The thought experiment goes as follows:

> You wake up in the morning and find yourself back to back in bed with an unconscious violinist. A famous unconscious violinist. He has been found to have a fatal kidney ailment, and the Society of Music Lovers has canvassed all the available medical records and found that you alone have the right blood type to help. They have therefore kidnapped you, and last night the violinist's circulatory system was plugged into yours, so that your kidneys can be used to extract poisons from his blood as well as your own. The director of the hospital tells you, "Look, we're sorry the Society of Music Lovers did this to you—we would never have permitted

37 In Re AC. 533 A.2d 611 (1987). Justia US Law. https://law.justia.com/cases/district-of-columbia/court-of-appeals/1987/87-609-0-0.html. Accessed June 28, 2020.

38 Thomson J. A defense of abortion. *Philosophy and Public Affairs*. 1971;1(1): 47–66.

> it if we had known. But still, they did it, and the violinist now is plugged into you. To unplug you would be to kill him. But never mind, it's only for nine months. By then he will have recovered from his ailment, and can safely be unplugged from you." Is it morally incumbent upon you to accede to this situation?[39]

Thomson answers in the negative—that it is not impermissible for the woman to unplug herself from the violinist even though this will cause his death. This is so because there are limits to the right to life, and that right does not include the right to use another person's body without their permission. You would be behaving in a way consistent with the *moral ideal* "preserve life" if you allowed the violinist to go on using your kidneys (see section 2.2 The Moral Ideals in Chapter 1). We might even say that you were exemplifying the *moral virtue* of kindness (see section 2.3 The Moral Virtues/Vices in Chapter 1) in so doing, but morality does not require that you do so.

CASE 9.C

Consider Thomson's thought experiment above, which is meant as a defense of abortion. In what ways is the violinist unlike the fetus?

Analysis: ______________________________

____

____

____

____

____

____

____

____

____

WRAP-UP

Chapter Summary

Many of the ethical issues encountered at life's beginning derive from disagreements among reasonable people about the scope of morality—specifically, disagreements about the point in human development/ontogeny at which a human is or should be entitled to the protection of morality (i.e., who has *moral standing*). Common morality protects all *presently existing actual moral agents*, *future actual moral agents*, and all those who have been actual moral agents and are still conscious. Children (both unborn and born) are considered *presently existing potential moral agents*.

In terms of deciding what beings have *moral standing*, some take a *personhood* approach. Some proponents of this approach define a personhood by membership in the species *Homo sapiens* (*human stock* approach). Other proponents of the personhood approach define personhood by the presence of certain criteria. Still others reject the personhood approach to moral standing and ground that standing in the intrinsic value (sanctity) of human life, in a being's sentience, or in a being's potential personhood. In terms of deciding when humans develop legal stand-

39 Thomson J. A defense of abortion. *Philosophy and Public Affairs.* 1971;1(1):47–66.

ing, under *Roe v. Wade* and progeny fetal viability marked the point at which the state's interest in potential life becomes compelling, and the states had the right to restrict or prohibit abortion after viability except to preserve the life or health of the pregnant woman. In the 2022 case *Dobbs v. Jackson Women's Health Organization*, the US Supreme Court overruled *Roe v. Wade*, holding that the Constitution does not confer a right to abortion. The legal effect of *Dobbs* was to return the authority to regulate abortion to the people and their elected representatives. In essence, the Court decided that the abortion decision was a *political question*.

The pregnant woman and her fetus have been referred to as the maternal–fetal dyad. Mattingly has written that the development of modern imaging, as well as in utero medical and surgical procedures, have shifted the emphasis from unity to duality, from a one-patient obstetric model to a new two-patient obstetric model. This shift has ethical implications.

Review Questions

1. Give an example of each of the following: a *presently existing actual moral agent*, a *future actual moral agent*, and a *presently existing potential moral agent*.
2. Explain how each of the following terms relates to moral and legal status: conception, *quickening*, *viability*, and birth.
3. What is *quickening*?
4. How do criterial approaches to personhood differ from the human stock approach?
5. List the criteria of personhood as proposed by Mary Anne Warren.
6. What do approaches to moral standing grounded in the *intrinsic value of human life*, in *sentience*, and in *potential personhood* have in common?
7. Why does *viability* matter?

Case Analyses

Case 9.A Analysis

The Vogt fetus was a *presently existing potential moral agent*, and as such (see section 1. *Human Development and Moral Standing*, in this chapter) whether she was entitled to the protection of the moral rules is disputed. Let's consider first arguments in favor of protecting her. Those who ground moral standing in the *human stock definition of personhood* could argue that the Vogt fetus was a person and therefore entitled to the protection of morality. The Vogt fetus was, after all, pretty far along on the developmental continuum—past the point of *quickening* and the point of *viability*. Only those who would insist on birth or some postnatal milestone as a condition of personhood would deny that the Vogt fetus was a person at the hour of her death (see section 1.1.1 *Human Stock Definition of Personhood* in this chapter). Likewise, those who ground moral standing in the intrinsic value of human life (see section 1.2.1 *Moral Standing Grounded in the Intrinsic Value of Human Life* in this chapter), or in sentience (see section 1.2.2 *Moral Standing Grounded in Sentience* in this chapter), or in potential personhood (see section 1.2.3 *Moral Standing Grounded in Potential Personhood* in this chapter) would be in favor of according the protection of morality to the Vogt fetus. Now let's consider arguments against according the Vogt fetus the protection or morality. As mentioned previously, some who subscribe to the human stock definition of personhood might nevertheless argue that the Vogt fetus was not a person because she was not yet born at the time of her death. Additionally, those who ground moral standing in personhood but subscribe to the view that personhood is a criterial concept, such as Mary Anne Warren and

Joseph Fletcher (see section 1.1.2 *Personhood as a Criterial Concept* in this chapter), might argue that the Vogt fetus did not meet sufficient criteria for personhood.

Case 9.B Analysis

The focus of the question is on moral as opposed to legal considerations. A number of analytic approaches might be employed by students in answering this question. Here we approach the question using Mattingly's *two-patient obstetric model* (see section 3.2 *Decision Making Under the Two-Patient Obstetric Model* in this chapter). The proposed treatment (a caesarean section) might benefit A.C.'s fetus but will not benefit A.C. and will likely shorten her already very short life expectancy. Under the model, the physicians should recommend caesarean section for the fetus and invite or encourage A.C. to submit to caesarean for the sake of proportionate fetal benefits, which in effect they did. What was A.C.'s response? We are told that:

> A.C. indicated that she would choose to relinquish her life so that the fetus could survive should such a choice present itself at the fetus' gestational age of twenty-eight weeks. Her physicians never discussed with her what her choice would be if such a choice had to be made before the fetus reached the twenty-eight-week point.[40]

Before they could ask A.C. about her wishes regarding a caesarean for a twenty-six week fetus, she lost decisional capacity. We are told that:

> The trial court determined that the fetus was viable and that the District of Columbia had an interest in protecting the potential life of the fetus. . . . [T]he court decided that the caesarean section should be performed.
>
> Shortly after the trial judge made his decision, A.C. was informed of it. She stated, during a period of lucidity, that she would agree to the surgery although she might not survive it. When another physician went to A.C. to verify her decision, she apparently changed her mind, mouthing the words, "I don't want it done." There was no explanation for either decision. . . .[41]

So, did A.C. consent to caesarean or refuse it? Her statement that she would "agree to the surgery" after being told that the court had already authorized it anyway raises questions about whether her going along was truly *voluntary*. Further, because of her overall medical condition, the fact that she was being sedated for pain, the fact that she gave no reasons for her decisions, and the fact that she was by all accounts slipping in and out of decisional capacity, we need to be concerned about whether she possessed *decisional capacity* at the time she made her statements. The appropriate next step would have been for the court to determine—one way or the other—what A.C. had decided and whether that decision was *autonomous* (i.e., voluntary, informed, and made by one with decisional capacity). If the court had decided that her choice (either to consent to a caesarean or to refuse it) was an autonomous one, it should have honored that choice. If, on the other hand, the court had decided that her choice was not an autonomous choice, it should have employed a substituted judgment standard in order to ascertain what A.C. would have decided about a caesarean at twenty-six weeks of gestation if she were able. Again, that choice should probably have been honored. Some students might want to argue that even if the court determined that A.C had refused, or would have refused, a caesarean

40 In Re AC. 533 A.2d 611 (1987). Justia US Law. https://law.justia.com/cases/district-of-columbia/court-of-appeals/1987/87-609-0-0.html. Accessed June 28, 2020.

41 In Re AC. 533 A.2d 611 (1987). Justia US Law. https://law.justia.com/cases/district-of-columbia/court-of-appeals/1987/87-609-0-0.html. Accessed June 28, 2020.

section, her refusal should be overridden because of the fact that she is near death and her fetus has its whole life ahead of it. This will be a more difficult argument to make, and such students will need to answer the following question: if you are correct, why doesn't society harvest organs from dying patients against their will to save others?

Case 9.C Analysis

You will recall from Chapter 1 that the principle of justice requires that we treat equals equally and unequals unequally but in proportion to their relevant inequalities. To the extent that the fetus is analogous to the violinist, Thomson's abortion defense holds; but to the extent that they are distinguishable, it does not. The violinist differs in a number of ways from the fetus. First, the violinist in Thomson's thought experiment finds himself attached to the woman as the result of a crime against the woman—kidnapping and battery. This is not true of the fetus unless it was conceived as the result of rape. In most cases, pregnancy results from a voluntary act on the part of the woman (consensual intercourse), sometimes (though not always) in spite of her efforts at contraception. Voluntary intercourse arguably constitutes implied consent for the fetus' presence and therefore its presence is no trespass.[42] A second distinction between the violinist and the fetus is that the fetus is the pregnant woman's child, whereas the violinist is a stranger to the woman. As you should recall from Chapter 1, under the principle of *specific beneficence* we owe a duty to further the important and legitimate interests of select others with whom we are in a special relationship (see section 3.2.3. *Beneficence*, in Chapter 1). The parent–child relationship is such a relationship. In contrast, there is no special relationship existing between the woman and the violinist. It is through the lens of *general beneficence* (an *ideal*, and almost never obligatory) that the Thomson's violinist must be viewed. Third, regarding the violinist Thomson writes, "To unplug you would be to kill him." But arguably to unplug the violinist is not killing him but rather analogous to removing life support (i.e., "allowing him to die") and is justifiable under the *rule of the double effect* (see Section 3.2.2.1 *The Rule of the Double Effect*, in Chapter 1) whereas abortion directly and intentionally kills the fetus.[43] Fourth, in Thomson's thought experiment the link between the violinist and the woman is medicalized. We are told that the violinist has a *malady* ("ailment") and that the "director of the hospital" is involved. But medicalizing the link—in essence treating it like a malady—is question-begging because it *assumes* that interrupting the link furthers some legitimate medical goal. In the case of the fetus, one can argue that electively aborting a normal fetus furthers no legitimate medical goal.

42 Warren M. On the moral and legal status of abortion. *Monist.* 1973;57(1):43–61.
43 Schwarz S. *The Moral Question of Abortion.* Chicago: Loyola University Press; 1990: ch. 8.

CHAPTER 10

Ethical Issues at Life's End

Robert M. Walker, M.D.

LEARNING OBJECTIVES

1. Define *advance directive*.
2. Define *physician-assisted death*.
3. Explain the principle of *double effect*, especially with reference to the use of morphine at the end of life.
4. Distinguish between the right to refuse treatment and the right to die.
5. Distinguish between the right to refuse treatment and the right to hasten death.
6. Explain the difference, if any, between withholding and withdrawing medical interventions.
7. Distinguish between the right to refuse treatment and the right to demand it.
8. Distinguish between tube feeding as a medical treatment versus the provision of a basic human need.
9. Discuss whether advance directives must be followed, or whether they can be overridden by substitute decision-makers.
10. Recognize and distinguish between two different ethical approaches to treating patient in times of plentiful versus scarce healthcare resources.

The educated person seeks exactness in each area to the extent that the nature of the subject allows; for apparently it is just as mistaken to demand demonstrations from a rhetorician as to accept [merely] persuasive arguments from a mathematician.[1]

—**Aristotle**, Nicomachean Ethics

Medical care at life's end is fraught with ethical issues that can challenge the most experienced health professionals. While there are many ways to organize these issues, the most direct way is to frame them as questions. Who decides? Can patients refuse any treatment? Can a patient/family demand treatment that providers think is medically inappropriate or futile? Is tube feeding a medical treatment or basic care? Must advance directives be followed? Is there a difference between withholding and withdrawing treatment? Should physicians and physician assistants (PAs) be involved in physician-assisted death? Is the principle of double effect just another form of euthanasia? How should we act when faced with scarce medical resources at the end of life?

1 Aristotle, *Eth. Nic.* I.iii.1–4, 1094b.

1. Who Decides?

This question is often put forward more dramatically, e.g., Who lives? Who dies? Who decides?[2,3] When applied to individual cases, these questions boil down to asking who the appropriate decision-maker is. If a patient has decision-making capacity, then the patient decides what medical interventions to accept or reject. Matters become more complicated when a patient permanently loses decisional capacity, for example, in the event of severe stroke. In that case, providers would turn to an appropriate substitute decision-maker for help. In the best scenario, the patient would have already completed an advance directive designating someone to serve as their decision-maker. If there is no designated decision-maker, the "next of kin" is typically turned to, with many states having a specific hierarchy or preference list specified by statute. In Florida, for example, a guardian tops the list, if the patient already has one. If not, the patient's spouse should be asked to help with decisions. If there is no spouse, then we turn to the majority of adult children, and so on.[4,5] The hierarchy used in Florida is not standardized across states, so you would need to check the statute in the state where you practice.

Sometimes, no relatives are available. In such cases, guardianship is typically sought so that there will be someone to advocate for the incapacitated patient's interests. Some states, again using Florida as an example, bypass recourse to guardianship by allowing a licensed clinical social worker to serve as a proxy decision-maker for the patient. Another alternative to guardianship is to locate a close personal friend who is familiar with the patient's values to serve as a proxy decision-maker. Again, health professionals need to become familiar with the law in their state to see if similar alternatives to guardianship exist.

2. Can a Patient Refuse Any Treatment?

The answer is almost always yes, if the patient is an adult with decisional capacity, who has made the decision after giving informed consent. (See Chapter 7.) Concern naturally arises when the treatment

2 Jonsen, AR. *Bioethics Beyond the Headlines: Who Lives? Who Dies? Who Decides?* Lanham, Maryland: Rowman and Littlefield; 2005.

3 Eckland-Olson, S. *Who Lives, Who Dies, Who Decides? Abortion, Neonatal Care, Assisted Dying, Torture, and Capital Punishment.* 3rd ed. New York: Routledge; 2018.

4 Florida Statutes, Title XLIV, Chapter 765. Health care advance directives. http://www.leg.state.fl.us/statutes/index.cfm?App_mode=Display_Statute;URL=0700-0799/0765/0765ContentsIndex.html;StatuteYear=2019;Title=%2D%3E2019%2D%3EChapter%20765. Accessed June 26, 2020.

5 The Florida hierarchy:
- (a) The judicially appointed guardian of the patient or the guardian advocate of the person having a developmental disability, if such guardian has previously been appointed; however, this paragraph shall not be construed to require such appointment before a treatment decision can be made under this subsection;
- (b) The patient's spouse;
- (c) An adult child of the patient, or if the patient has more than one adult child, a majority of the adult children who are reasonably available for consultation;
- (d) A parent of the patient;
- (e) The adult sibling of the patient or, if the patient has more than one sibling, a majority of the adult siblings who are reasonably available for consultation;
- (f) An adult relative of the patient who has exhibited special care and concern for the patient and who has maintained regular contact with the patient and who is familiar with the patient's activities, health, and religious or moral beliefs; or
- (g) A close friend of the patient.
- (h) A clinical social worker licensed pursuant to chapter 491, or who is a graduate of a court-approved guardianship program. Such a proxy must be selected by the provider's bioethics committee and must not be employed by the provider.

being refused is one that might help restore a patient to health and without which the patient will likely die. Such treatment is commonly referred to as life-saving treatment and would include antibiotics, transfusions, short-term mechanical ventilation, and so on. There were many early court cases that established the right of a competent patient to refuse unwanted treatment even if life-saving.[6,7] Legally, it doesn't matter if the treatment is refused in advance or refused after treatment has already been started. A member of the Jehovah's Witnesses, for example, would typically refuse all blood products in advance via an advance directive document that specifies no blood products, even if those products are considered life-saving. Alternatively, a patient on a mechanical ventilator, while initially accepting it, could later decide to stop it even though that means that without it the patient will likely die. The right to refuse life-sustaining or life-saving treatment has been sloganized into the phrase "right to die." There is, of course, no legal right to die. The legal right is actually the right to refuse unwanted medical treatment, regardless of whether the patient will die without it. While there are cases where courts have forced treatment on patients over their objections, for example in forced cesarean section cases, their rarity precludes discussion here.

3. Can a Patient/Family Demand Treatment That Providers Think Is Medically Inappropriate or Futile?

The paradigm case for medical futility involves using cardiopulmonary resuscitation (CPR) and advanced cardiovascular life support (ACLS) at the end of life. CPR is often not effective in a terminal illness setting. While early guidelines for appropriate use of CPR advised against using it in cases of terminal illness,[8] subsequent common practice has been to provide CPR by default in all cases of cardiac or respiratory arrest, regardless of the patient's illness and prognosis. Thus the question about appropriate use of CPR/ACLS remains.[9] As it stands, CPR/ACLS must still be provided to a terminally ill patient unless there is an order countermanding it. These orders are called do-not-resuscitate (DNR) orders or do-not-attempt-resuscitation (DNAR) orders. The approach works well when the patient/family agree that resuscitation should not be attempted. It fails, however, when the patient/family insists that it be performed against medical advice to the contrary. Unfortunately, there is no consensus about how to respond to such demands. Some providers simply accede to them. Others, however, might seek to override this demand by withholding CPR/ACLS on the grounds that it medically futile, adding that in such cases there is no ethical obligation to provide futile treatment.[10] (See Chapter 2, section 1.5, *Medical Futility*.)

One might think that there would be a large number of legal cases on this issue, but unlike the right to refuse treatment, there is actually a dearth of legal backing on this topic. In the case of Karen Ann Quinlan, which involved a young woman in a permanent vegetative state, the issue of medical futility was dismissed as being within the competence of the medical profession.[11] In the Wanglie case, which similarly involved an older woman in a permanent vegetative state, the physician brought the matter to a Minnesota

---

6 Cantor, NL. *Legal Frontiers of Death and Dying*. Bloomington, IN: Indiana University Press; 1987.

7 Gostin LO. Deciding life and death in the courtroom. From Quinlan to Cruzan, Glucksberg, and Vacco: a brief history and analysis of constitutional protection of the "right to die." *JAMA*. 1997;278:1523–1528.

8 Anonymous. Standards for cardiopulmonary resuscitation (CPR) and emergency cardiac care (ECC). V. Medicolegal considerations and recommendations. *J Am Med Assoc*. 1974;227 (suppl):864–868.

9 Blackhall, L. Must we always use CPR? *N Engl J Med*. 1987;317(20):1281–1285.

10 Lantos JD, Singer PA, Walker RM, et al. The illusion of futility in clinical practice. *Am J Med*. 1989;87:81–84.

11 *In re Quinlan*, 70 NJ 10 (1976).

court to specifically gain legal clarity on the issue of physicians having no legal obligation to offer or provide treatment considered medically nonbeneficial.[12,13] The court, however, completely sidestepped the matter by limiting their ruling to confirming that Mrs. Wanglie's husband was the legally appropriate decision-maker. A similar sidestep occurred in the case of Baby K,[14] (see Case 10.C) with the court viewing the case with reference to the EMTALA law instead of in terms of medical futility.

In legislation, Texas is the only state that allows physicians to say no to patient/family demands for treatment the provider deems medically inappropriate.[15] As for the rest of the states, there is little or no legal backing for the ethical dictum that there is no obligation for physicians/PAs to offer or provide futile treatment. As a result, we are left with hospital policies on futility, most of which are drafted by each hospital's Institutional Ethics Committee (IEC). In most cases, these policies recommend IEC consultation and a process-oriented approach in which the medical team continues to work with the patient/family as the clinical situation evolves, hoping ultimately to achieve agreement.

When demands for futile interventions are considered more closely, it is important to see that they are not extensions of the right to refuse treatment. The right only allows the patient to veto one or all of the interventions offered by the provider. There is no correlate right to demand that specific non-offered treatments be provided. This leads to the question of whether it is ethical for a provider to not offer or even disclose the possibility of interventions the provider believes would be futile. As it turns out, leaving interventions off the table only works with lesser known interventions, for example, continuous renal replacement therapy (CRRT). Most patients/families are not aware of CRRT, and so if a physician does not offer it on the grounds of medical inappropriateness or futility, the patient/family will remain unaware. By contrast, most people without a medical background have heard of dialysis and would wonder about it once they learn that their loved one, for example, has kidney failure. Because interventions like dialysis and CPR are so widely known, they must enter the discussion if only for the physician/PA to discount them as options.

Leaving lesser-known medical options off the table and undiscussed might easily be interpreted as deceptive and perhaps paternalistic (see Chapter 1, section 3.2.3.1, *Paternalism*), so this is not a recommended approach. The best practice is to disclose all legitimate medical options whether they are recommended, disclosed but not recommended, or disclosed but not offered. Should a patient/family then demand that a non-offered intervention be provided, providers would be forced to consult the IEC and follow the process of continuing the discussion. Alternatively, if the health professional feels that providing the non-offered intervention would be a violation of conscience, then he or she would be free to withdraw from the case. The healthcare facility would then be in the position of finding another member of the staff who might be willing to provide the intervention.

Like most matters of ethics, there are no clear one-size fits all approach. Every case will have a different twist. Things will be messy. As Aristotle says, we must not assign more precision to ethics than it admits of. That is the nature of the beast. Nevertheless, there is collective experience, IECs, policies and protocols, and legal precedent to guide us, so that we don't have to reinvent the wheel every time we encounter a new ethics challenge.

---

12 Miles, SH. Informed demand for "non-beneficial" medical treatment. *N Engl J Med.* 1991;325:512–515.

13 Angell, M. The case of Helga Wanglie: a new kind of "right to die" case. *N Engl J Med.* 1991;325:511–512.

14 *In the Matter of Baby K*, 832 F.Supp. 1022 (U.S. District Court, Eastern District Virginia, 1993).

15 Tex. Health; Safety Code, § 166.046. Procedure if not effectuating a directive or treatment decision. https://statutes.capitol.texas.gov/Docs/HS/htm/HS.166.htm. Accessed June 29, 2020.

CASE 10.A

A 78-year-old man has been taking escalating doses of NSAIDs for his osteoarthritis and has recently become fatigued. He went to his primary clinic to see his PA, who had been treating him for arthritis, hyperlipidemia, mild carotid vascular disease, and benign prostatic hypertrophy. The PA orders labs and schedules a close follow-up appointment. The PA later calls the patient before his upcoming follow-up appointment to tell him he has go to the hospital because he is in renal failure. The patient was admitted to a general medical service, and a nephrologist was consulted about short-term dialysis. The nephrologist reviewed the chart and wrote that dialysis was not indicated on the grounds of medical futility. When the attending provider asked the nephrologist to explain why it was futile, since NSAID-nephropathy can be to some extent reversible, the nephrologist replied that in her review of the chart, the patient was noted to have carotid vascular disease, and that he therefore likely also had renal vascular disease, so dialysis would not be provided.

If you are the attending provider, what would you do?

Analysis: ________________________________

____

____

____

____

____

____

____

____

4. Is Tube Feeding a Medical Treatment or Basic Care?

The provision of artificial nutrition and hydration (ANH) can become a difficult issue at the end of life. This issue was most highlighted in the case of Terri Schiavo, which started in Florida and later became a global news story.[16] Terri was a young woman who suffered anoxic brain injury after a cardiac arrest. When she was finally resuscitated, the damage had already been done. Terri spent years in a permanent vegetative state.[17,18] At issue was a family dispute over tube feeding. Her husband sought to have the tube removed, saying this is not something Terri would have wanted. Her parents disagreed, arguing that nutrition and hydration are basic human needs that should always be provided regardless of one's medical condition. So the question boils down to this: Is nutrition and hydration provided via a medical tube a form of medical treatment, or are nutrition and hydration basic needs that must be provided by any means possible, including medical feeding tubes? The courts in the United States that dealt with this issue, including the U.S. Supreme Court,[19] have consistently ruled that tube feeding, or more accurately ANH, is a medical treatment and as such, it can be refused even though the envisioned outcome might include the death of the patient. It is analogous to a Jehovah's Witness refusing a life-saving blood transfusion. In the case of Terri Schiavo, her husband won the legal fight, and the feeding tube was ultimately removed. Terri Schiavo died 13 days later.

While the law is clear on the issue of tube feeding, many people continue to feel strongly about providing it. In individual cases, it all comes back to informed consent. Since tube

16 Walker, RM, Black J. Terri Schiavo and televised news: fact or fiction? In: Goodman KW, ed. *Ethics, Politics and Death in the 21st Century: The Case of Terri Schiavo*. New York: Oxford University Press; 2010:210–224.

17 The Multi-Society Task Force on PVS. Medical aspects of the persistent vegetative state—first of two parts. *N Engl J Med*. 1994;330(21):1499–1508.

18 The Multi-Society Task Force on PVS. Medical aspects of the persistent vegetative state—second of two parts. *N Engl J Med*. 1994;330(22):1572–1579.

19 *Cruzan v. Director, Missouri Dept. of Health*, 497 U.S. 261 (1990).

feeding is an established medical intervention, it must always be placed on the table of offered treatments, though the individual physicians and PAs may recommend against it.

CASE 10.B

An 86-year-old woman is suffering from end-stage Alzheimer disease. She is currently bedbound, nonverbal, incontinent of bowel and bladder, contracted, and totally dependent for her activities of daily living. She is hand-fed by the staff in her assisted-living facility. The patient has had increasingly impaired swallowing and has intermittent coughing during feeding. After developing a fever and a cough, she is transported to the hospital, where she is diagnosed with aspiration pneumonia. A swallow study is ordered, which reveals the aspiration. The hospitalist recommends that a g-tube be placed. The patient has an advance directive that names her daughter as the healthcare decision-maker. The patient's Living Will states that she would not want tube feeding if she were in a terminal condition and had no reasonable hope of regaining her decision-making capacity. The daughter is inclined to go along with the hospitalist's recommendation; however, a nurse checked the Living Will on file at the hospital and became concerned when she read that the patient did not want tube feeding. She consulted the IEC for help. As a member of the IEC, you are sent to discuss this with the daughter. What will you tell her?

Analysis: ______________________________

____

____

____

____

____

____

____

____

____

5. Must Advance Directives Be Followed?

In general, the answer is yes, although states may vary on this. Advance directives are witnessed statements about medical care preferences made by an adult patient of sound mind in advance of permanent loss of decision-making capacity. As such, these documents legally control what should happen in regard to end-of-life treatment when a person loses the capacity to make decisions. The job of the surrogate or substitute decision-maker is to ensure that the patient's prior written wishes prevail. If the substitute decision-maker feels unable to participate in decisions, or disagrees with the patient's prior decisions, then the only appropriate action is to withdraw from the substitute decision-maker role, in favor of a named secondary decision-maker, if one exists. If there is no one, then the state hierarchy of preferred decision-makers should be followed. Health professionals again should check the specific laws in their states.

CASE 10.C

An 80-year-old retired nurse suffers a pontine bleed and is currently in the intensive care unit (ICU). She is completely unresponsive and has a blown pupil. The advance directive on file is unusual in that it is highly specific, listing multiple medical interventions that the patient would not want should she become terminally ill without any reasonable probability of regaining her ability to make decisions for herself. She had seen so much as a nurse that she made a concerted effort to list all of the specific medical interventions she wouldn't want. Her daughter, who is a respiratory therapist, is named in the document as the substitute decision-maker.

The patient has been in the ICU for 2 weeks with no improvement. The daughter, because of her respiratory therapist background, asks the medical team about the need for tracheostomy placement. The nurses on the unit become concerned because one of the specific refusals in the patient's advance directive is tracheostomy. A consult to the IEC is placed.

You respond to the consult, review the chart, talk with the nurses and others, then arrange for a meeting with the daughter. What questions would you ask?

Analysis: ______________________________

____

____

____

____

____

____

____

____

____

6. Is There a Difference Between Withholding and Withdrawing Treatment?

Is there a difference between withholding and withdrawing treatment? Many have felt that there is a difference between withdrawing a treatment and not starting it in the first place.[20] However, there is no legal difference. From a legal perspective, the core right is to be free of unwanted medical intervention by being able to refuse it. It doesn't matter if one has already started the intervention and now wants to stop, or if one has never started it. In either case, if a person doesn't want the intervention, they can be free of it. From an ethical perspective, once a person decides against an intervention, the proper response is to honor their autonomous choice, whether that means that we don't start something, or stop something we've already started. The problem is that not starting something doesn't require an act on the part of the physician/PA, whereas stopping something, like a ventilator, does require action.

What has to be appreciated here is that in both cases, the natural forces of disease are allowed to continue unopposed. If a person refuses in advance to receive ventilator support, or if they receive it and then decide they no longer want it, in both cases their refusal is honored, and the natural forces of illness are allowed to proceed without our active resistance. The perceptual problem lies in choosing to focus only on the action of the provider in stopping something that is life-sustaining. All they see is that the patient is alive, then the provider stops the ventilator, and shortly afterward the patient expires. This leads some providers to conclude that the patient would still be alive but for their action. Now that the patient is dead, the provider is left to wonder, "Did I end the patient's life?"

Unfortunately, the narrow focus on provider action and immediate results ignores the clinical context. Just as words require context to convey meaning, so do actions. The word cervical, for example, has more than one meaning. We can only identify the word's specific meaning when it is used in a sentence. For example, "Mr. Jones has a cervical fracture." In this case it is clear that the word is referring to a broken neck bone. However, let us consider the follow sentence: "Mrs. Smith has cervical cancer." Here the exact same word refers to the female reproductive tract. So context determines specific meaning. Again, the same is true for actions. There can be no meaning or interpretation of actions when they are divorced from the context in which they take place.

Consider the following hypothetical situation: A previously healthy 78-year-old female is diagnosed with community-acquired pneumonia and is admitted to the hospital. She develops respiratory

20 Levin PD, Sprung CL. Withdrawing and withholding life-sustaining therapies are not the same. *Crit Care.* 2005;9(3):230–232

difficulty and is intubated and given appropriate sedation. She continues to receive antibiotics. On day 3 in the ICU, she is starting to improve, and her PA opines that she will probably be able to get off the ventilator in a few days. Later that evening, a man in a white medical coat, appearing to be a member of the medical staff, enters the room and turns off the ventilator, with the result that the patient almost immediately expires. It turns out that the man is not a health professional, but instead he is the patient's only living relative. He is due to inherit her estate, provided it is not squandered on medical expenses. The act of turning off the ventilator in this context is clearly homicide.

Let's take an alternative fact pattern in which the same act is performed: Here the woman is suffering from stage IV lung cancer that has progressed despite prior treatment. At this point, no further treatment is in view. The patient was at home and developed progressive respiratory distress. Her husband panicked and called 911. The patient was resuscitated and intubated in the field and transported to the hospital. After several days, she remained unresponsive on the ventilator without the need for sedation, implying deep brain damage. When her husband learned that his wife would not improve and that it was likely she would die despite ventilator support, he said, "She would never have wanted this." When he later brought her advance directive documents to the hospital, the PA saw that she had clearly written, "If I am in a terminal condition, and no longer able to make my own decisions, I do not want to receive life-sustaining treatment and would prefer instead to be kept comfortable." Later in the document, she specifically refused tube feeding, dialysis, and mechanical ventilation. So the medical staff decided that the only ethical and legal thing to do was to honor her wish by removing the ventilator that she clearly wouldn't have wanted. She expires shortly after the ventilator was stopped. In this context, the act of stopping the ventilator is clearly to remove an unwanted medical intervention and allow the forces of illness to continue unopposed. So the act in both cases is exactly the same—a person in a white coat stops the ventilator and the patient shortly thereafter expires. But because of context, in one case it is an act of homicide; in the other, it is an act of appropriate and ethical medical practice.

7. Should We Be Involved in Physician-Assisted Death?

Physician-assisted death (PAD) is defined as "the practice where a physician provides a potentially lethal medication to a terminally ill, suffering patient at his request that he can (or not) at a time of his own choosing to end his life. It is also called physician-assisted suicide, physician aid-in-dying, and patient administered hastened death."[21] The initial problem is that this goes against the traditional understanding of our Hippocratic heritage, which proscribes physician involvement in such a practice. The Oath reads, "I will neither give a deadly drug to anybody if asked for it, nor will I make a suggestion to this effect."[22] While the Hippocratic tradition is fading in modern medicine in the United States, many still have moral concern about the practice of PAD. As the practice becomes legalized in more states, each physician will be faced with the choice of whether to participate. The moral concern centers around whether it is ethical for a physician to provide the means and the instructions for a patient to take their own life, should the patient ultimately decide to do so. If the patient does take his or her life by filling

21 Quill TE, Sussman B. Physician-assisted death. Hastings Center Bioethics Briefings for Journalists, Policymakers, and Educators Web site. https://www.thehastingscenter.org/briefingbook/physician-assisted-death. Accessed June 21, 2020.

22 Kass LR. Is There a medical ethic? The Hippocratic Oath and the sources of ethical medicine. In: *Toward a More Natural Science: Biology and Human Affairs*. New York, NY: Free Press; 1985:228–229.

the prescription and taking the medication as instructed, the patient will have died, not by a natural cause, but by the successive actions of the physician and the patient. By prescribing the means of death, the physician is involved with the patient in bringing it about—a death not by nature but by human hands.

This is very different from the situation where a patient decides they no longer wish to receive a life-saving treatment and can be reasonably expected to die without it. In such a case, the patient dies of the natural forces of injury or disease, not by his or her own hand. The patient has not been killed; rather, natural death has been allowed to proceed with the removal of unwanted medical obstacles. With PAS, the patient and the physician hasten death together by introducing a new lethal agent. With natural death, the patient and the physician do not hasten death but cease forestalling it.

The mistake made by two federal circuit courts ruling on assisted suicide in the 1990s was their assertion that patients have a right to hasten death.[23,24] Such a right has never existed. Instead, patients have a right to refuse unwanted medical intervention, even if deemed life-saving. When it comes to life-sustaining treatment, where there is no hope of improvement, only maintenance on machines and technology, then it becomes a right to refuse death-forestalling interventions. Each physician and PA, in states that allow PAD, must ultimately decide whether they are willing or unwilling to participate in PAD based on conscience.

8. Is the Principle of Double Effect Just Another Form of Euthanasia?

Euthanasia means "good death." The term has been used imprecisely, so its use here will be defined. Euthanasia is an act whereby a physician administers a lethal dose of medication in order to cause a patient's death. Unlike PAD, euthanasia is currently illegal in all 50 states. An important difference between PAD and euthanasia is that in PAD the physician only provides the patient with lethal prescription; he or she does not administer it.

The principle of double effect, by contrast, can be used to justify the use of potentially lethal medication in order to treat distressing symptoms at life's end. (See Chapter 1 for earlier discussion of the rule or principle of double effect.) The principle has four components:

1. The act itself must be morally good or neutral.
2. Only the good effects of the action must be intended.
3. The good effect must not be produced by means of the bad effect.
4. There must be some weighty reason for permitting the bad effect.[25]

Let's apply this to the use of morphine at the end of life. Imagine we have a 54-year-old woman dying of cancer, who develops a pain crisis, despite the ongoing use of oral opioid medication that had previously controlled her pain. The physician/PA decides to switch the patient from oral medication to a morphine infusion via patient-controlled analgesia (PCA). In this way, the physician/PA can provide a continuous basal infusion, while giving the patient the ability able to press a button on a handheld device to receive additional boluses of medication if needed. These bolus doses are limited in amount and frequency in order to prevent overdose. Commonly, initial infusion dosing will help but not achieve full comfort. So the dosing will need to be carefully adjusted upward to attain the desired effect. This practice of careful upward titration to comfort minimizes the risk of respiratory depression associated with sudden, large dose increases.

Now let's look at this with the principle of double effect. (1) Providing pain relief for a suffering

23 *Quill v. Vacco*, 80 F3d 716 (2d Cir 1996).

24 *Compassion in Dying v. Washington*, 850 F. Supp. 1454 (D.C. 1994).

25 May WE. Double effect. In: Reich W, ed. *Encyclopedia of Biomedical Ethics*. New York, NY: Free Press; 1978:316–320.

cancer patient is undeniably a morally good act. (2) Only the good effects of the action, giving pain medication, are intended. By careful titration, the provider is deliberately avoiding the bad effect of morphine, which is respiratory depression and death from giving too much morphine at once. (3) The good effect, pain relief and comfort, is not produced by means of the bad effect. The provider is not ending the patient's suffering by ending her life. (4) There must be some weighty reason for permitting the bad effect. I would qualify this by saying that there must be some weighty reason for risking the bad effect, because with morphine titration, it is possible in many cases to avoid the bad effect entirely. The weighty reason for risking the bad effect is that without opioids, this patient with severe cancer pain would be denied relief and would needlessly suffer.

Some might criticize this practice as simply slow euthanasia. But this is not necessarily the case. If it were true that using morphine always resulted in the death from respiratory depression, then giving it fast or slow might reasonably be seen as a distinction without a difference, but the opposite is true. The proper use of morphine rarely results in death from respiratory depression.[26] Therefore, using morphine in accordance with the principle of double effect is not euthanasia because the physician never administers a lethal dose of the medication to cause a patient's death. In fact, this is what the physician is working so hard to avoid.

CASE 10.D

A 67-year-old female is in the hospital for dyspnea. She has stage IV lung cancer with no further disease-modifying treatment available. She also has end-stage chronic obstructive pulmonary disease from past cigarette smoking. She was placed on oxygen and nebulized pulmonary medication, but these did not adequately reduce her dyspnea.

Though the patient did not have any pain, morphine was started to further treat her dyspnea. It was carefully titrated upward until it reduced her sense of air hunger. The patient remained alert and oriented, despite the morphine. Goals of care had been discussed with her and her husband early in her hospitalization. She lost her first husband 9 years earlier to lung cancer. Her second husband is in good health. The patient said her goal was to be as comfortable as she can be, knowing that there is no cure for her cancer. She had earlier completed a Living Will and designated her current husband as her healthcare decision-maker. Both the patient and her husband were satisfied with the symptom relief provided by the morphine. On the day after morphine had successfully improved the patient's dyspnea, her oldest son from her first marriage visited her in the hospital and was upset that his mother was on morphine. He accused the attending physician, an internal medicine doctor, of trying to kill his mom by depressing her respiration and insisted that it be stopped immediately. Vitals an hour before his visits showed a heart rate of 88 and a respiratory rate of 24.

How should the physician respond to the son's demand?

Analysis: ______________________________

____

____

____

____

____

____

____

____

____

26 LeGrand SB, Khawam EA, Walsh D, Rivera NI. Opioids, respiratory function, and dyspnea. *Am J Hosp Palliat Care* 2003;20:57.

9. How Should We Act When Faced with Scarce Medical Resources at the End of Life?

One of the problems with new medical technology is that it is often creates a situation of scarce medical resources. For example, when dialysis was first introduced, it was direly scarce and expensive. Ethics committees were formed at the time to determine who would receive this new life-saving technology. Those who did not receive it, of course, died from their kidney disease.

When transplantation of vital organs became a reality, great efforts were made to get more people to designate themselves as organ donors, and committees were formed to determine which patients might be the best candidates to receive organ transplantation, whether heart, liver, kidney, or some other organ. Because of scarcity, the guiding principles shifted from medicine's traditional focus on treating the sickest patients first, to treating only those who were likely get the most sustained benefit from the transplant. While one could argue that all patients with organ failure might equally need a transplant to stay alive, it is clear that not all patients could be guaranteed to experience the same benefit in terms of survival. Because of this, the potential for organ survival has become the guiding principle. It is now considered a social responsibility and good stewardship of scarce and precious resources to ensure that we only put organs into those who could be expected to live the longest with those organs. As a counter example, we wouldn't transplant a liver into an active alcoholic. That would be regarded as wasteful and socially irresponsible because the patient would continue to drink, damaging and perhaps destroying the new liver.

Other situations that produce a situation of scarce medical resources include disasters, such as earthquakes and hurricanes, which may stress local healthcare resources to the extent that decisions will need to be made not on the basis of pure medical need or first-come first-served, but on the basis of optimizing the usefulness of the resource. If we are running short on ventilators, for example, would we use it on an elderly man dying of stage IV lung cancer, or would we use it on a young first responder with an inhalation injury that can be treated and potentially result in the responder being returned to the front lines to help others?

Another related example pertains to the COVID-19 pandemic. If a hospital is running short of ventilators and can't get more, it will have to make decisions about the most effective way to use them. Would it make sense to keep a person with multiple medical problems on a ventilator once it is clear that the patient has adult respiratory distress syndrome (ARDS) and is unlikely to survive? Would the hospital be justified in removing the ventilator from the patient they can no longer help in order to use it for a patient they can help? Considerations like these have led to thinking about how to ethically ration scarce resources, or at least provide recommendations for appropriate use. In sum, resource scarcity modifies the ethical basis on which we act. In times of no scarcity, we have the ability to treat according to medical need. However, in scarcity, we have an obligation to shift toward utilizing the resource in a way that maximizes the benefit for all affected.

WRAP-UP

Chapter Summary

Common ethical concerns are naturally framed as questions. In this chapter, we looked at questions regarding appropriate decision-makers and what kinds of decisions they can make. We examined whether patients/families have a right to demand medical interventions as much as they have a right to refuse them. We also explored medical futility, tube feeding, adherence to advance directives, the difference between withholding versus withdrawing treatment, participation in physician-assisted death, the principle or rule of double effect, and the ethical basis for acting appropriately during times of healthcare resource scarcity. While the list of questions in this chapter only scratches the surface of complex and deep subjects, they serve as a good overview and initial discussion for the health professional, who will enter a difficult and changing medical ethical world.

Review Questions

1. Explain the difference between causing death and allowing it to occur once medical obstacles are removed.
2. What is the difference between euthanasia and physician-assisted death (PAD)?
3. List a sample hierarchy of substitute decision-makers who are commonly turned to when a permanently incapacitated adult has not named a decision-maker in an advance directive.
4. Explain how medical futility can misused to mask biases, such as ageism.
5. Explain the difference between hastening death and not forestalling it.
6. Define advance directives and why they are important in end-of-life care.

Case Analyses

Case 10.A Analysis

In this case, renal function could potentially be improved with stopping NSAIDs and providing short-term dialysis. The nephrologist claims that it is futile on the grounds of a probable disease state in the renal vasculature; however, we don't actually know this. The provider challenges this claim but cannot force the nephrologist to provide dialysis. It would seem that a trial of therapy would be reasonable here, but the nephrologist seems unwilling to do this. The case points out that while a provider might claim that an intervention is futile, it is not necessarily so. Indeed, the possibility of ageism is active in this case. For all when know, the nephrologist may have an internal maxim to not dialyze anyone over 65, cloaking this under the notion that it is medically futile. This, of course, would be to misuse the concept of medical futility to conceal an age bias. The provider in this case consulted a second nephrologist, who agreed to initiate dialysis for the patient.

Case 10.B Analysis

First, the patient is in the terminal phase of Alzheimer disease. She has irreversibly lost her decision-making capacity. Her Living Will states that she would not want tube feeding. Though daughter is named as the substitute decision-maker for her mother, her role is to ensure that her mother's wishes are carried out, not to override them. The daughter states that her mother needs nutrition and hydration and that this seems like the only choice she can make. It might be helpful to recommend a palliative care consultation at this point. The palliative medicine specialist could discuss goals of care with the daughter and have an in-depth discussion of the benefits versus the burdens of invasive feeding. What is not commonly appreciated in end-stage Alzheimer disease is that feeding tubes not only do not prevent aspiration, they may make it worse because a foreign body in the stomach increases reflux, which increases aspiration.[27] Also, there can be complications with tube dislodgment and tube-site infections, both of which lead to increased hospitalization, use of restraints, and pressure sores.[28] Finally, research has not shown that tube feeding significantly improves outcomes in end-stage Alzheimer disease.[29] Hopefully, the daughter will see that continuing hand-feeding at her facility would be the option that most supports dignity and honors her mother's written wishes.

Case 10.C Analysis

The meeting with the daughter is initially tense because she has decided to bring her attorney. After exploring prognosis and the patient's stated wishes, the attorney states that the daughter is the legal decision-maker, so her decision would be controlling and final. The daughter, being a respiratory therapist, could not bring herself to forego tracheostomy tube placement, much less to stop the ventilator. Being familiar with the advance directive law in your state, you know that named decision-makers have no authority to override the written choices in valid advance directive documents. After reviewing this with the daughter and the attorney, both eventually acknowledged understanding.

The patient lost her husband to cancer 7 years ago and lived alone. Her daughter was her only child. Having no one else to help with the decision-maker role, the daughter said that she knows her mother wouldn't want this, but that she needed more time. You and the daughter agree to give it one more week, during which a tracheostomy would not be performed per her mother's wishes. Two days before the week was up, the daughter called and said she was ready to honor her mother's wishes. The patient expired peacefully shortly after her palliative extubation procedure.

Some might argue that each day the patient remained on the ventilator against her wishes was a violation of her rights. But the patient also clearly trusted her daughter with the hard decision, so the short time she needed to come to terms with her role and the difficult decisions she had to make could be seen as a reasonable accommodation that was needed to bring things to their proper end.

Case 10.D Analysis

The son appears to have some medical knowledge because he is aware of the potential for morphine to depress respiration. However, he appears to mistakenly believe that the mere use of any amount of morphine would necessarily clinically depress respiration. Not so. The definition of respiratory depression is a respiratory rate of 10 breaths per minute or less.[30] In this case, even after titrating the morphine to symptomatic relief, the patient is not sedated, which typically precedes respiratory depression, and her respiratory rate remains 20. So this patient is not showing any

27 Finucane TE, Christmas C, Travis K. Tube feeding in patients with advanced dementia: a review of the evidence. *JAMA*. 1999;282(14):1365–1370.

28 Shega JW, Paniagua MA, eds. UNIPAC 9. HIV, dementia, and neurological conditions. *Essential Practices in Hospice and Palliative Medicine*. 5th ed. Chicago, IL: American Academy of Hospice and Palliative Medicine; 2017:85–86.

29 Candy B, Sampson EL, Jones L. Enteral tube feeding in older people with advanced dementia: findings from a Cochrane systematic review. *Int J Palliat Nurs*. 2009;15(8):396–404.

30 Shega JW, Paniagua MA, eds. UNIPAC 3: Pain assessment and management. *Essential Practices in Hospice and Palliative Medicine*. 5th ed. Chicago, IL: American Academy of Hospice and Palliative Medicine; 2017:72.

sign of respiratory depression. Instead, her symptoms are being appropriately managed with morphine, which is an important medication for the treatment of dyspnea in terminally ill patients.[31] The best approach would be to educate the son regarding morphine.

Though one could take the approach of dismissing the son's concern, by pointing out that he is not the decision-maker here, because the patient is competent, and her second husband is her named surrogate, this would be counterproductive and likely worsen the conflict level already present. The best approach is to be inclusive by acknowledging the son's concern and allaying it through education. If the son rejects the education of the attending physician, options would be to obtain a Palliative Medicine consult, or perhaps an IEC consult.

31 Shega JW, Paniagua MA, eds. UNIPAC 8: COPD, heart failure, and renal disease. *Essential Practices in Hospice and Palliative Medicine.* 5th ed. Chicago, IL: American Academy of Hospice and Palliative Medicine; 2017:17–18.

CHAPTER 11

Medical Malpractice and Health Professionals

LEARNING OBJECTIVES

1. Define *health law*, *medical malpractice*, *negligence*, and *torts* and explain how they relate to each other.
2. List, recognize, and explain the elements of *medical malpractice*.
3. Understand and explain the legal distinction between *nonfeasance* and *malfeasance* and how they relate to the *no-duty rule*.
4. Know and recognize the exceptions to the *no-duty rule*.
5. Explain how good Samaritan laws relate to the *no-duty rule*.
6. Understand and apply the *standard of care* concept as it relates to *medical malpractice*.
7. Explain how the *standard of care* is established in *medical malpractice* cases.
8. Define the *best judgment rule* and recognize situations implicating the rule.
9. Explain the *standard of care* as it relates to PAs.
10. Understand and distinguish *causation-in-fact* and *legal causation*.
11. Apply and distinguish the various tests for *causation-in-fact* and *legal causation*.
12. Understand, explain and apply the concepts of *economic* and *noneconomic damages*, damage limitations, and the *loss of a chance* doctrine.

Frank Galvin: *[after the church has offered a check for $210,000 to settle the case] How did you settle on the amount? Because it struck me, um, how neatly "three" went into this figure: 210,000. That means I would keep seventy. . . .*

Bishop Brophy: *Nothing we can do can make that woman well.*

Frank Galvin: *And no one will know the truth.*

Bishop Brophy: *What is the truth?*

Frank Galvin: *That that poor girl put her trust... into the hands of two men who took her life. She's in a coma. Her life is gone. . . She's tied to a machine. And you and me—have been bought off to look the other way. . . . I came here to take your money. . . . I can't do it; I can't take it. Cause if I take the money I'm lost. I'll just be a... rich ambulance chaser. . . .*[1]

1 Reed, Barry. The Verdict. New York: St Martin's Press, 1992.

In this chapter we take up medical malpractice law as it relates to health professionals.[2]

1. What Is Medical Malpractice Law?

Health law is "law as it affects the professionals and institutions that deliver health care."[3] Health law concerns itself with access to health care, the cost of health care, the quality of health care, and respect for the interests of the patient.[4] *Medical malpractice law* is a branch of health law focusing on the liability of health professionals.

Most medical malpractice cases are brought under the legal doctrine of *negligence* (i.e., as cases of medical negligence). Negligence is a kind of *tort*. A tort, in turn, is "a legal wrong committed upon the person or property of another independent of contract."[5] If a patient sues you in tort, that person is alleging that you violated some noncontractual duty that you owed him or her. Other categories of torts include *intentional torts* and *strict liability* torts. Battery, which we discussed in Chapter 7 in our discussion of consent, is an example of an intentional tort. Strict liability imposes liability on a party without a finding of fault. For example, a product manufacturer is liable if the product is defective, even if the manufacturer was not negligent in the product's manufacture.

2. Medical Negligence

Negligence is conduct that falls below the standard of care established by law for the protection of others against an unreasonable risk of harm. In order to prevail in a medical negligence action, a plaintiff must establish (1) that the defendant provider owed him or her a duty; (2) that the defendant provider breached that duty (i.e., that the defendant's conduct fell below the *standard of care*); (3) that the defendant provider's conduct caused some harm or damage to the plaintiff; and (4) that the plaintiff suffered some harm or damage against which the law provides protection. To reiterate: a duty owed; a breach of duty; causation; and damages.

2.1. Duty

The question of whether a defendant (e.g., a health professional) owes a legal duty to a plaintiff (e.g., a patient) is a question of law decided by the court (i.e., the judge), not a question of fact for the jury.[6]

2.1.1. The No-Duty Rule

Regarding duty, American law distinguishes between acts (*feasance*) and omissions (*nonfeasance*). Once a person acts, he or she has a duty to act reasonably. In contrast, the law does not require (with a few exceptions that we shall discuss later) a person to act, even when inaction might seem unreasonable. In other words, no general duty of due care applies to instances of nonfeasance. This is the so-called *no-duty rule*.

> Suppose A, standing close by a railroad, sees a two-year-old babe on the track and a car approaching. He can easily rescue the child with entire safety to himself, and the instincts of humanity require him to do so. If he does not, he may, perhaps, justly be styled a ruthless savage and a moral monster; but he is not liable in damages for the child's injury, or

---

2 Much of this chapter is adapted from Chapter 15, Health law and medical malpractice. In: Paola FA, Nixon LL, Walker RM, eds. *Medical Ethics and Humanities*. Sudbury, MA: Jones and Bartlett Publishers; 2010.

3 Furrow BR, Greaney TL, Johnson SH, Jost TS, Schwartz RL. *Health Law*. Vol. 1. St. Paul: West Publishing; 1995:vii.

4 Furrow BR, Johnson SH, Jost TS, Schwartz RL. *Health Law: Cases, Materials and Problems*. 2nd ed. St. Paul: West Publishing; 1995:viii–ix.

5 *Black's Law Dictionary*. Abridged 6th ed. 1991:1036.

6 Franklin MA, Rabin RL. *Tort Law and Alternatives: Cases and Materials*. 4th ed. Mineola, NY: Foundation Press, 1987:117–201, at 128.

indictable under the statute for its death. . . . The duty to do no wrong is a legal duty. The duty to protect against wrong is . . . excepting certain *intimate relations* . . . a moral obligation only, not recognized or enforced by law.[7] (italics added)

"Intimate relations," of course, lie at the very heart of medical practice. Let's consider, therefore, exceptions to the no-duty rule.

2.1.2. Exceptions to the No-Duty Rule

There are five such exceptions, and *they create duties to act when not acting would be unreasonable.*

2.1.2.1. Special Relationships. The first exception is the existence of a special relationship between the plaintiff and the defendant. For our purposes here, the most important such special relationship is the provider-patient relationship. Once a provider-patient relationship has come into existence and before it is lawfully terminated, the provider is legally obligated to behave reasonably vis-à-vis his or her patient. Thus, if a PA's patient suffers a cardiac arrest in the waiting room and the PA fails to attend to the patient because it was not that patient's turn, the law will not accept the PA's argument that because this was an instance of nonfeasance, no legal duty was owed. Because of the special relationship existing between the patient and the PA, the law imposes on that PA an affirmative duty to act reasonably. Were I instead to have witnessed the cardiac arrest of a nonpatient in the street, my argument would have legal merit.

2.1.2.2. Rescue Statutes. The second exception to the no-duty rule is that sometimes a statute can create an affirmative duty to act. An example of such a law is the Vermont rescue statute, the text of which reads as follows:

§ 519. Emergency medical care

(a) A person who knows that another is exposed to grave physical harm shall, to the extent that the same can be rendered without danger or peril to himself or without interference with important duties owed to others, give reasonable assistance to the exposed person unless that assistance or care is being provided by others.

(b) A person who provides reasonable assistance in compliance with subsection (a) of this section shall not be liable in civil damages unless his acts constitute gross negligence or unless he will receive or expects to receive remuneration. Nothing contained in this subsection shall alter existing law with respect to tort liability of a practitioner of the healing arts for acts committed in the ordinary course of his practice.

(c) A person who willfully violates subsection (a) of this section shall be fined not more than $100.00. (1967, No. 309 (Adj. Sess.), §§ 2-4, eff. March 22, 1968.)[8]

2.1.2.3. Contract Creating Duty to Act. The third exception to the no-duty rule is that sometimes contracts create an affirmative duty to act. This exception is illustrated by the case *Hiser v. Randolph.*[9] In that case, the defendant, Dr. Randolph, was one of seven area physicians who took turns manning the emergency room as the "on-call physician" for a 12-hour period at the Mohave County General Hospital in Kingman, Arizona. The on-call physician was paid $100 for each shift served. The patient Mrs. Hiser, a brittle insulin-dependent diabetic, presented to the emergency room (ER) in a semi-comatose condition. Dr. Randolph was on call, but when he learned that Mrs. Hiser had been treated in the ER on the preceding day by her regular physician Dr. Arnold,

---

7 *Buch v. Amory Mfg. Co.*, 69 N.H. 257 (1897).

8 The Vermont Statutes Online. Vt.Stat.Ann., tit. 12, section 519. https://legislature.vermont.gov/statutes/section/12/023/00519. Accessed June 17, 2019.

9 *Hiser v. Randolph,* 126 Ariz. 608, 617 P.2d 774 (Ariz.App.1980).

Dr. Hiser refused to attend to her and said that the ER nurse should call Dr. Arnold. When the nurse called Dr. Arnold, he said that he would not come to the hospital and that the on-call physician should attend Mrs. Hiser. The nurse communicated this to Dr. Randolph, who again refused to attend Mrs. Hiser. Ultimately, the hospital chief of staff arrived and attended Mrs. Hiser throughout the night, but she died the following morning. Dr. Randolph was sued by Mrs. Hiser's widower. Dr. Randolph's legal defense was that because he had not acted (nonfeasance) and because there was no preexisting physician-patient relationship between himself and Mrs. Hiser, he was under no obligation to attend her (i.e., he argued that the no-duty rule should apply). The court refused to apply the no-duty rule, finding a contractual exception.

> In our opinion, Dr. Randolph, by . . . accepting payment from the hospital to act as the emergency room doctor "on call" personally became bound "to insure that all patients . . . treated in the Emergency Room receive the best possible care," . . . .
>
> . . . Under these circumstances, the lack of a consensual physician-patient relationship before a duty to treat can arise has been waived . . . .[10]

2.1.2.4. Voluntary Assumption of Duty. The fourth exception to the no-duty rule concerns the voluntary assumption of duty by the defendant. Once the defendant voluntarily begins to act (for example, to render assistance to the plaintiff), he or she must proceed with reasonable care and may not discontinue efforts *if doing so would leave the plaintiff worse off than when assistance was begun.*[11] If you think about it for a moment, you will see that technically speaking this exception isn't really an exception to the no-duty rule. The no-duty rule applies to instances of *nonfeasance*, but when a defendant voluntarily begins to act, he or she leaves the world of nonfeasance and enters the world of feasance, in which a general duty of due care is owed (i.e., he or she has a duty to act reasonably).[12]

Good Samaritan laws exist to encourage bystanders (and health professionals in particular) to stop and help persons to whom they owe no legal duty. They do so by shielding such good Samaritans from liability in negligence. These laws do not shield the Samaritan whose behavior is reckless or intentionally tortious (e.g., performing chest compressions as a part of CPR by jumping up and down on the chest of a cardiac arrest victim who, it so happens, I am not fond of).[13] As such, Good Samaritan laws may be thought of as being an exception to this fourth exception.

2.1.2.5. Defendant Responsibility. The fifth exception to the no-duty rule is the defendant responsibility exception, under which the defendant owes a duty of warning or assistance if the plaintiff's danger or injury is the result of the defendant's conduct.

Originally, this exception applied only when the plaintiff's danger or injury was the result of the defendant's wrongful conduct (*misfeasance* or *malfeasance*). When the danger or injury resulted from the defendant's innocent conduct, the exception did not apply. The more modern view holds that the defendant owes a duty of care to the plaintiff whenever defendant's conduct—even if innocent—results in danger or injury to the plaintiff. Thus, state "hit-and-run" statutes routinely require drivers involved in an accident in which another is injured to stop and render reasonable assistance.[14]

---

10 *Hiser v. Randolph,* 126 Ariz. 608, 617 P.2d 774 (Ariz.App.1980).

11 Franklin MA, Rabin RL. *Tort Law and Alternatives: Cases and Materials.* 4th ed. Mineola, NY: Foundation Press, 1987:117–201.

12 *Zelenko v. Gimbel Bros,* 287 N.Y.S. 134 (N.Y. Sup. Ct. 1935).

13 New York Good Samaritan Act, NYS Public Health Law, Article 30—Emergency medical Services; 3000-a.1. https://www.nysenate.gov/legislation/laws/PBH/3000-A. Accessed March 5, 2020.

14 Leaving the Scene of an Accident/Hit and Run: State Laws. https://traffic.findlaw.com/traffic-tickets/leaving-the-scene-of-an-accident-hit-and-run-state-laws.html. Accessed March 5, 2020.

CASE 11.A

Consider the following case:

> On July 9, 2017 in Cocoa, Florida, Jamel Dunn drowned while five teenagers looked on while laughing and filming the incident. A family friend of Dunn notified law enforcement of a video of his death after seeing it on social media. Dunn's body was discovered three days after the incident.
>
> According to the authorities, the teens were smoking marijuana at a park. They saw Dunn, a disabled man who used a cane, and advised him not to go into the retention pond. They then observed him enter the pond. The video, which shows Dunn screaming for help and struggling in the water, was filmed by the teens. They did not call 911. One teen joked that Dunn had just died, resulting in laughter from the group. According to the police, the teens did not appear to show any grief.[15]

Did the teens owe Dunn a legal duty to rescue or summon help?

Analysis: ______________________________

CASE 11.B

Consider the following scenario:

> Suppose A, standing close by a railroad, sees a two-year-old babe on the track and a car approaching. He can easily rescue the child with entire safety to himself, and the instincts of humanity require him to do so. If he does not, he may, perhaps, justly be styled a ruthless savage and a moral monster; but he is not liable in damages for the child's injury, or indictable under the statute for its death.[16]

What facts, if changed, would render A legally liable for the child's injury?

Analysis: ______________________________

2.2. Standard of Care

Once it is established that the defendant medical practitioner owed the plaintiff a legal duty, the issue becomes, "Did the defendant's conduct fall below the standard of care?" If the answer is "yes," the defendant is said to have breached his or her duty. For reasons

15 Salo, J. (2017, July 20). 'Oh, he just died': Teens mock drowning man in disturbing video. *New York Post*. https://nypost.com/2017/07/20/oh-he-just-died-disturbing-video-shows-teens-mocking-drowning-man/. Accessed June 17, 2019.

16 *Buch v. Amory Mfg. Co.*, 69 N.H. 257 (1897).

that will become clear later on, we shall first discuss the standard of care as it relates to physicians.

2.2.1. Standard of Care of Physicians

A superb enunciation of the standard of care as it relates to medical practice dates to the 1898 New York case *Pike v. Honsiger*:

> The physician is under an obligation to exercise the same degree of knowledge, skill, diligence and care that the ordinary competent practitioner would exercise under the same or similar circumstances. The physician is under the further obligation to use his best judgment in exercising his skill and applying his knowledge.[17]

Generally, juries decide whether or not the standard of care has been met as a question of fact by deciding whether the physician behaved as an "ordinary competent practitioner" would have under the same or similar circumstances.

2.2.1.1. The Rule: The Ordinary Competent Practitioner. How are nonphysician jurors supposed to decide whether a physician behaved as an "ordinary competent practitioner"? Traditionally, they employed the so-called *custom-based standard of care*. Under that standard, the jury determines—based on the testimony of medical experts—how "ordinary competent practitioners" customarily behave under circumstances similar to the case in question and uses that as the standard of care.[18]

More recently, there has been a retreat from the custom-based standard of care to a so-called *reasonable physician standard*. Under this standard, proof that a physician behaved as is medically customary does not equate to proving that he or she behaved reasonably (i.e., as an ordinary competent practitioner). Under the *reasonable physician standard*, "the jury decides whether the physician behaved reasonably, not whether she complied with custom. Although experts still battle in the courtroom, they argue about what physicians *should* do, not what physicians *ordinarily* do."[19]

2.2.1.2. Exceptions to the Rule. The general rule that the standard of care for physicians is established by the *ordinary competent practitioner* has several exceptions. Here we discuss five such exceptions.

2.2.1.2.1. Statutes and the Standard of Care. The first exception is that a statute[20] may establish the standard of care. The *Baby K* case[21] illustrates this exception.

CASE 11.C

Baby K was a female anencephalic born in October 1992 in Virginia. She required intubation and mechanical ventilation because of perinatal respiratory distress. The treating physicians informed Baby K's mother that continued mechanical ventilation was not medically indicated (i.e., that the standard of care did not demand it) because it furthered no legitimate medical goal; nevertheless, the mother refused to consent to a do-not-resuscitate (DNR) order. The treating physicians consulted the institutional ethics committee, which agreed that mechanical ventilation was medically futile and should be stopped. Baby K's mother rejected the committee's recommendation. In November 1992, during a period in which she was not

17 *Pike v. Honsiger*, . . .
18 Peters PG. The role of the jury in modern malpractice law. 87 *Iowa L. Rev.* 909 (2002).
19 Peters PG. The role of the jury in modern malpractice law. 87 *Iowa L. Rev.* 909 (2002).
20 A statute is "an act of the legislature declaring, commanding, or prohibiting something." *Black's Law Dictionary*. Abridged 6th ed. N St. Paul, MN: West Publishing, 1991:981.
21 *In the Matter of Baby K*, 832 F.Supp. 1022 (U.S. District Court, Eastern District Virginia, 1993).

ventilator-dependent, Baby K was transferred to a nursing home. Alas, Baby K required readmission to the hospital in January and again in March 1993. Because it was expected that she would continue to experience episodes of respiratory distress requiring admission, intubation, and mechanical ventilation, the hospital commenced legal action, requesting a declaratory judgment that withholding of ventilatory support would not be illegal. The hospital asserted that "the prevailing standard of medical care for infants with anencephaly is to provide only warmth, nutrition, and hydration."[22] A guardian was appointed to represent Baby K, and the guardian agreed with the hospital's position. In July 1993, the U.S. District Court for the Eastern District of Virginia held that under the federal anti-dumping law (the Emergency Medical Treatment and Active Labor Act, or EMTALA) "the hospital would be liable . . . if Baby K arrived there in respiratory distress . . . and the hospital failed to provide [the] mechanical ventilation . . . necessary to stabilize her acute medical condition." The court reasoned that EMTALA requires that hospitals provide stabilizing treatment to any person who comes to an emergency department in an "emergency medical condition" and that apnea and bradypnea are emergency medical conditions under the EMTALA statute. Explain how the outcome of this case relates to the standard of care.

Analysis: ____________________________________

____

____

____

____

____

____

____

____

When the law in question exists for the protection of persons, its unexcused violation may be "treated as negligence without any argument or proof as to the particular surrounding circumstances."[23] This is known as *negligence per se*.[24]

CASE 11.D

Consider the following excerpt from the Baby K opinion:

> Despite EMTALA's clear requirements and in the face of the Hospital's admissions, the Hospital seeks an exemption from the statute for instances in which the treatment at issue is deemed "futile" . . . by the hospital physicians. . . . The statute does not admit of any "futility" [exception] . . . . Even if EMTALA contained the exception[] advanced by the Hospital, [the] . . . exception[] would not apply here. The use of a mechanical ventilator to assist breathing is not "futile" . . . in relieving the acute symptoms of respiratory difficulty which is the emergency medical condition that must be treated under EMTALA.[24]

Recall our discussion of medical futility in Chapter 2. Which subtype of medical futility does the court adopt in this case?

Analysis: ____________________________________

____

____

____

____

____

____

____

____

____

22 *In the Matter of Baby K*, 832 F.Supp. 1022 (U.S. District Court, Eastern District Virginia, 1993).

23 *Black's Law Dictionary*. Abridged 6th ed. St. Paul, MN: West Publishing; 1991:719.

24 *In re Baby K*, 832 F. Supp. 1022, at 1027.

2.2.1.2.2. Judicial Risk-Benefit Balancing. A second exception to the general rule that the standard of care for physicians is established by the ordinary competent practitioner is that case law or precedent can establish the standard of care when judges engage in risk-benefit balancing. Probably the most cited example of this exception is *Helling v. Carey*.[25] In that case, a 38-year-old plaintiff who suffered visual loss as a result of undiagnosed open angle glaucoma sued defendant ophthalmologists in negligence. At trial, the plaintiff's medical experts did not dispute the assertion of the defendants' medical experts that the "standards of the profession for that specialty [ophthalmology] in the same or similar circumstances do not require routine pressure tests for glaucoma upon patients under 40 years of age."[26] Under the *custom-based standard* that prevailed at that time, the verdict in the trial court was, as expected, for the defendants. On appeal, the Supreme Court of Washington overruled the trial court:

> The issue is whether the defendants' compliance with the standard of the profession of ophthalmology . . . should insulate them from liability . . . . Justice Holmes stated in Texas & Pac. Ry. v. Behymer, 189 U.S. 468, 470, 23 S. Ct. 622, 623, 47 L. Ed. 905 (1903): "What usually is done may be evidence of what ought to be done, but what ought to be done is fixed by a standard of reasonable prudence, whether it is usually complied with or not." In The T.J. Hooper, 60 F.2d 737, on page 740 (2d Cir. 1932), Justice Hand stated: "[I]n most cases reasonable prudence is in fact common prudence; but strictly it is never its measure; a whole calling may have unduly lagged in the adoption of new and available devices. It may never set its own tests, however persuasive be its usages. *Courts must in the end say what is required* . . . . We therefore hold, as a matter of law, that the reasonable standard that should have been followed under the undisputed facts of this case was the timely giving of this simple, harmless pressure test to this plaintiff and that, in failing to do so, the defendants were negligent . . . .[19]

Essentially, the Supreme Court of Washington was saying two things: (1) that the traditional *custom-based standard* is useful only as a rough surrogate for the *reasonable physician standard*, which is the more fundamental standard, and (2) that based on the Court's own balancing of the costs and benefits of pressure testing, the standard of care for ophthalmologists required the defendants to give the pressure test to the plaintiff.

2.2.1.2.3. Informed Consent, Sometimes. The third exception to the general rule that the standard of care for physicians is established by the ordinary competent practitioner involves the standard of care in informed consent cases in those states that employ the *reasonable patient standard (see Chapter 7)*.[27] That standard, you will recall, requires "disclose of risks that a reasonable patient would consider to be material in making a medical treatment decision."[28]

2.2.1.2.4. *Res Ipsa Loquitur.* The fourth exception to the rule that the standard of care for physicians is established by the ordinary competent practitioner is the doctrine of *res ipsa loquitur*, Latin for "the thing speaks for

25 *Helling v. Carey*, 519 P.2d 981 (Wash. 1974).

26 *Helling v. Carey*, 519 P.2d 981 (Wash. 1974).

27 It goes without saying that states that follow the professional disclosure standard (see Chapter 6, section 2.2.1.1) follow the rule rather than the exception, since they require that physicians disclose to patients that information that would have been disclosed by an ordinary competent physician.

28 Hall MA, Bobinski MA, Orentlicher D. *Health Care Law and Ethics*. 7th ed. Austen: Aspen Publishers; 2007:203–204.

itself."[29] More precisely, the doctrine is actually an exception to the rule that medical expert witnesses must be employed to establish the standard of care in medical malpractice cases. *Res ipsa loquitur* creates a "[r]ebuttable presumption or inference that [the] defendant was negligent, which arises upon proof that [the] instrumentality causing injury was in the defendant's exclusive control, and that the accident was one which ordinarily does not happen in the absence of negligence."[30]

CASE 11.E

Consider the following case.

> The patient suffered a severe cut to the top of her right foot and she was taken to the hospital to receive an operation to repair nerve and tendon damage. The surgeon performed the operation while the patient was unconscious. After the operation, the surgeon put a plaster of paris [*sic*] cast over the patient's lower leg, almost to the top of her calf. After the patient regained consciousness, it was discovered that she had sustained third degree burns on her upper right calf, just under the cast. No one seemed to know the cause of the burns. The trial court granted the surgeon's motion for summary judgment[31] because there was no proof of negligence. The appellate court reversed.[32]

Why did the appellate court reverse in the absence of any testimony by a medical expert that the surgeon was negligent?

Analysis: ______________________________

____

____

____

____

____

____

____

____

____

2.2.1.2.5. Contract and the Standard of Care. The fifth exception to the rule that the standard of care for physicians is established by the ordinary competent practitioner is in medical cases involving breach of contract. These actions arise when health providers make promises to patients regarding treatment outcomes.

> Thus in Hawkins v. McGee, 84 N.H. 114, 146 A. 641 (1929), the defendant doctor was taken to have promised the plaintiff to convert his damaged hand by means of an operation into a good or perfect hand, but the doctor so operated as to damage the hand still further. The court . . . asked the jury to estimate and award to the plaintiff the difference

29 *Black's Law Dictionary*. Abridged 6th ed. 1991:905.

30 *Black's Law Dictionary*. Abridged 6th ed. 1991:905.

31 A party, such as the defendant surgeon in this case, may move for a summary judgment "when he believes that there is no genuine issue of material fact and that he is entitled to prevail as a matter of law." See *Black's Law Dictionary*. Abridged 6th ed. 1991:1001.

32 *Graham v. Thompson*, 854 S.W.2d 797, 1993 Mo. App. LEXIS 416 (Court of Appeals of Missouri, Western DistrictMarch 23, 1993, Filed). https://advance-lexis-com.ezproxylocal.library.nova.edu/api/document?collection=cases&id=urn:contentItem:3RX4-6RG0-003F-C53H-00000-00&context=1516831.

> between the value of a good or perfect hand, as promised, and the value of the hand after the operation.[33]

In essence, when a health provider promises a particular outcome to a patient, he is setting the standard of care for himself—to meet it, he must behave not as an ordinary competent practitioner, but in such a way so as to produce the promised result.

2.2.1.3. The Best Judgment Rule. Before turning specifically to the standard of care of PAs, there is one more issue to address. Look again at the formulation of the medical standard of care as cited previously:

> The physician is under an obligation to exercise the same degree of knowledge, skill, diligence and care that the ordinary competent practitioner would exercise under the same or similar circumstances. *The physician is under the further obligation to use his best judgment in exercising his skill and applying his knowledge.* (emphasis added)[34]

What, you might ask, is the effect of including this second sentence in the formulation of the medical standard of care? Consider the following case.

CASE 11.F[35]

Plaintiff Daniel Burton was born 6 weeks prematurely on July 3, 1953, at Brooklyn Doctors Hospital. He was transferred the next day to New York Hospital.

Just two days earlier, "a national human research study known as the Cooperative Study of Retrolental Fibroplasia [RLF] and the Use of Oxygen was undertaken to determine the role of oxygen in RLF and the effect of its withdrawal or curtailment." The Cooperative Study would go on to find that "the prolonged liberal use of oxygen was the critical factor in the development of RLF, and that curtailing oxygen to premature infants after 48 hours to clinical need decreased the incidence of RLF without increasing the risk of death or brain damage." The Cooperative Study's conclusions were announced on September 19, 1954, and published in October 1956, 1 year and 3 years, respectively, after the events in question.

While at the time of Daniel Burton's admission to New York Hospital "liberal exposure to oxygen continued to be routine treatment for premature babies . . . , the view that more oxygen was better had already become suspect. In fact, New York Hospital "had, from January 1952 to June 1953, conducted its own study and concluded that 'prolonged oxygen therapy may be related to the production of RLF.' The results of that 18-month study were announced by the hospital on June 16, 1953 [over two weeks before Daniel Burton's admission] at a meeting attended by its pediatricians and ophthalmologists." Because the results of its own study were deemed preliminary and insufficient, the hospital decided to become a participant in the Cooperative Study. This was the situation that existed on July 4, 1953, when plaintiff entered New York Hospital.

Upon Daniel Burton's arrival, Dr. Lawrence Ross, a pediatric resident, ordered that the plaintiff be placed in an incubator with oxygen to be delivered at 3 to 4 liters per minute. That same evening, Dr. Ross, aware that oxygen had been implicated as a cause of RLF, ordered that oxygen be "reduced as tolerated."

On July 6, Dr. Mary Engle, an instructor in pediatrics and coauthor of the New York Hospital study mentioned previously, on instructions from Dr. Levine [the chairman of the Department of Pediatrics] and without ever examining the plaintiff or speaking to his parents, entered the following order in his medical record: "Oxygen study: In

---

33 *Sullivan v. O'Connor,* 296 N.E.2d 183 (Mass. 1973).

34 *Pike v. Honsiger,* 155 NY 201 (1898).

35 *Burton v. Brooklyn Doctors Hosp.*, 452 N.Y.S.2d 875 (N.Y. App.Div. 1982). Case 10.F is taken from case 15-A in Chapter 15, Health law and medical malpractice. In: Paola F, Walker RM, Nixon L, eds. *Medical Ethics and Humanities.* Sudbury, MA: Jones and Bartlett; 2010:350–352.

prolonged oxygen at concentration greater than 50%." As a result of Dr. Engle's order the concentration of oxygen to which the plaintiff was being exposed was increased over a span of 28 days from 30% to a high of 82%. "Except for faint light perception in his left eye plaintiff is totally blind and, because his eyes are shrinking, will require enucleation and replacement with plastic ones."

In a lawsuit brought against Drs. Ross and Engle, how should the case be decided?

Analysis: ______________________________

____

____

____

____

____

____

____

____

____

2.2.2. Standard of Care of Nonphysician Health Professionals

In general, health professionals are held to the standard of other ordinary, competent health professionals acting under the same or similar circumstances. This is analogous to the rule that holds physicians to the standard of other ordinary, competent physicians acting under the same or similar circumstances. As you shall see momentarily, though, the standard of care of at least one type of health professional—the PA—is a bit more complicated.

2.2.3. Standard of Care of PAs

What is the standard of care applicable to PAs? Should the PA be held to the same standard of care as his or her supervising physician? The PA is, after all, practicing medicine, right? Or should the PA be held to the same standard of care as other PAs?

2.2.3.1. The General Rule. As a general rule, PAs are held to the standard of other ordinary competent PAs—or as the Supreme Court of Tennessee has put it, "to the 'recognized standard of acceptable professional practice in the profession' of physician assistants and any specialty thereof."[36]

2.2.3.2. Exceptions to the Rule. Several states, on the other hand, require that PAs meet the standard of care required of physicians. Thus, under Michigan statutes a "physician's [*sic*] assistant shall conform to minimal standards of acceptable and prevailing practice for the supervising physician or supervising podiatrist."[37] Similarly, under the Wyoming Board of Medicine Rules and Regulations, "a physician assistant is expected to perform with similar skill and competency and to be evaluated by the same standards as the physician in the performance of assigned duties."[38] Additionally, case law suggests that PAs are held to the standard of care of physicians in Louisiana[39] and South Carolina[40] as well.

36 *Cox v. M.A. Primary and Urgent Care Clinic,* 313 S.W.3d 240 (Tenn. 2010).

37 Mich. Comp. Laws Ann. § 333.17078 (2). http://www.legislature.mi.gov/(S(lz0rwi1ygm1omv4xodcmw0w3))/mileg.aspx?page=GetObject&objectname=mcl-333-17078. Accessed March 7, 2020.

38 Wyo. Bd. of Med. R.& Regs., ch. 5 § 4(d). https://rules.wyo.gov/. Accessed March 7, 2020.

39 *Cleveland v. United States,* 457 F.3d 397, 2006 U.S. App. LEXIS 18120, 88 Empl. Prac. Dec. (CCH) P42,479, 70 Fed. R. Evid. Serv. (Callaghan) 776 (United States Court of Appeals for the Fifth Circuit, July 19, 2006, Filed). https://advance-lexis-com.ezproxylocal.library.nova.edu/api/document?collection=cases&id=urn:contentItem:4KFM-8350-0038-X17H-00000-00&context=1516831.

40 *Andrews v. United States,* 548 F. Supp. 603, 1982 U.S. Dist. LEXIS 14955 (United States District Court for the District of South Carolina, Charleston Division, September 30, 1982). https://advance-lexis-com.ezproxylocal.library.nova.edu/api/document?collection=cases&id=urn:contentItem:3S4N-9HX0-0039-S35D-00000-00&context=1516831.

2.3. Causation

The third element in a medical malpractice case is causation: Did the defendant provider's conduct cause the damages that the patient alleges? There are two parts to the causation inquiry, involving two kinds of causation: *causation-in-fact* (i.e., *scientific causation*) and *proximate causation* (i.e., *legal causation*). The plaintiff must prove both by a *preponderance of the evidence* (i.e., that it is *more likely than not*) that the defendant's conduct caused the injury alleged.[41]

2.3.1. Causation-in-Fact (Scientific Causation)

Scientific causation, or causation-in-fact, is a question of fact for the jury (or the judge when he or she acts as the finder of fact in a trial without a jury). It is causation as most people understand the term intuitively.

The test most commonly used to establish causation-in-fact is the *but for* test. Under this test, the defendant's conduct is the cause-in-fact of the plaintiff's injury *if the injury would not have occurred but for the defendant's conduct*. Consider, for example, a case in which a passing motorist throws a lighted cigarette into plaintiff's parched front lawn, which ignites into flames that consume the plaintiff's house. The plaintiff identifies and sues the motorist in negligence. Was the motorist's conduct the cause-in-fact of the homeowner's injury? Clearly yes.

Now imagine that the property of the above plaintiff lies between two parallel roads, one running past the front yard and another running past the backyard. Suppose that two passing motorists (defendants A and B) simultaneously flick lighted cigarettes onto the plaintiff's arid property (defendant A into the front yard, defendant B into the backyard). Two separate fires result and simultaneously consume the plaintiff's house; either fire alone would have been sufficient to destroy the plaintiff's house and property. Is defendant A's conduct the cause-in-fact of the homeowner's injury? Under the "but for" test the answer would be no because the plaintiff's injury would have occurred even without defendant A's conduct. Neither is defendant B's conduct the cause-in-fact under this test for the same reason. Employing the *but for* test of causation-in-fact in this scenario leaves the unfortunate plaintiff without any remedy and unjustly allows both negligent defendants to escape liability.

In order to avoid such an unjust outcome in cases where joint causes are involved, the law uses a different test of causation-in-fact—the *substantial factor* test. Under this test, the defendant's conduct is the cause-in-fact of the plaintiff's injury *if defendant's conduct was a substantial factor in causing the injury*. Under this test, the conduct of defendant A was a cause-in-fact of the plaintiff's injury, as was the conduct of defendant B.

A third test of causation-in-fact is presented in the following case.

CASE 11.G

Summers v. Tice[42]

Defendants Tice and Simonson were quail hunting. Both fired their shotguns in the direction of the plaintiff, who was struck in the eye with a single shotgun pellet. Because both defendants used the same gauge shotgun and the same size shot, it could not be determined which of the two had fired the shot that struck the plaintiff. In a trial without a jury, the trial judge found the plaintiff blameless and found both defendants negligent. The judge awarded judgment against both defendants. How was causation-in-fact established against the defendants?

Analysis: ______________________________

____

____

41 Prosser, Law of Torts, sec. 41 (4th Ed. 1971).

42 *Summers v. Tice*, 33 Cal.2d 80, 199 P.2d 1 (1948 Cal.). I have modified the facts slightly for the sake of simplicity.

2.3.2. Legal Causation (Proximate Causation)

Legal causation is best thought of as a means of limiting liability in the interest of fairness. The test of legal causation is the *foreseeability* test, under which a defendant is liable for all the harmful results that fall within the increased risk caused by his acts. Stated otherwise, if defendant's act increases the likelihood that a particular harm would result, and that harm does result, the defendant's act is the legal cause of the harm. Consider the following.

> A chauffeur negligently collides with another car which [*sic*] is filled with dynamite, although he could not know it. An explosion follows. *A*, walking on the sidewalk nearby, is killed. *B*, sitting in a window of a building opposite, is cut by flying glass. *C*, likewise sitting in a window a block away, is similarly injured. And a further illustration. A nursemaid, ten blocks away, startled by the noise, involuntarily drops a baby from her arms to the sidewalk. We are told that *C* may not recover while *A* may. As to *B* it is a question for court or jury. We will all agree that the baby might not. Because, we are again told, the chauffeur had no reason to believe his conduct involved any risk of injuring either *C* or the baby. As to them he was not negligent.[43]

The chauffeur's act (negligently colliding with another car) was the legal cause of *A*'s injury because it foreseeably increased the risk that nearby pedestrians would be harmed. The chauffeur's act was NOT the legal cause of either *C*'s injury or the baby's injury because it did NOT foreseeably increase the risk that persons a block away or ten blocks away would be harmed. As regards *B*, whether or not the chauffeur's act was the legal cause of *B*'s injury depends on whether the finder of fact (jury or judge acting as jury) believes it increased the risk that persons "sitting in a window of a building opposite" would be harmed.

The *egg-shell skull rule* is an exception to the foreseeability test. The rule refers to a hypothetical plaintiff wrongfully struck on the head by a defendant unaware of the fact that plaintiff's skull is as thin as an eggshell, a la Humpty Dumpty.[44] Under the rule, the defendant is liable for all damages resulting from the wrongful contact, even those (unforeseeable) damages that would not have occurred if the plaintiff's skull were normal. Stated otherwise, defendants must "take their victims as they find them."[45]

43 *Palsgraff v. Long Island Railroad Co.*, 248 N.Y. 339 (N.Y. 1928).
44 Carroll L. *Through the Looking-Glass*. https://www.gutenberg.org/files/12/12-h/12-h.htm. Accessed April 26, 2020.
45 Emanuel S. *Torts*. 3rd ed. Larchmont: Emanuel Law Outlines; 1988:98–120.

CASE 11.H

Consider the following case.

> The parents of deceased infant Arielle Irizarry . . . brought this medical malpractice action against Children's Hospital . . . and Cross Country Travcorps (Cross Country) following Arielle's death. The parents claim that David Herbert, a respiratory therapist employed by Cross Country who was called in to the emergency room at Children's to administer oxygen to Arielle, negligently failed to suction her after she vomited through her mouth and nose as Mr. Herbert was administering the oxygen through a mask and bag. The parents claim that instead of suctioning the infant or otherwise clearing her airways after she vomited, in accord with the standard of care governing respiratory therapists in Washington, Mr. Herbert merely stared at the baby for a moment and then continued to administer oxygen, thereby causing the baby to aspirate (inhale her own vomit). Whether Mr. Herbert timely suctioned the baby is . . . disputed . . . . Nevertheless, it is undisputed that the baby did inhale her own vomit in the emergency room that night, and that as a result she went into respiratory and cardiac failure, after which a code was called. It took about a half an hour to resuscitate her. While in the intensive care unit (ICU) following this episode, Arielle developed aspiration pneumonia and had to be placed on a mechanical ventilator 24 hours a day, 7 days a week, in order to breathe. After some four months, when it became apparent to her doctors that she could never be weaned from the ventilator, her grieving parents agreed to have the machine turned off. Arielle died a few moments later, at the age of 8 months.[46]

Recall that to make a prima facie case for medical negligence, the plaintiff must show *duty*, *breach*, *causation*, and *damages*. How would you go about proving that the respiratory therapist (RT) breached the standard of care?

Analysis: ______________________________

____

____

____

____

____

____

____

____

____

2.4. Damages[47,48]

A breach of one's medical duty is not actionable unless it results in some damage that is legally compensable. "He broke my arm" describes a legally compensable damage; "he made faces at me" does not.[49]

In general, in medical malpractice actions, plaintiffs who prevail may recover *actual* or *compensatory damages*, which "replace the loss caused by the . . . injury. . . . The rationale behind compensatory damages is to restore the injured party to the position he or she was in prior to the injury."[50]

46 *Hinkson-Irizarry v. Children's Hosp. & Reg'l Med. Ctr.*, 2004 Wash. App. LEXIS 964 (Court of Appeals of Washington, Division One, May 10, 2004, Filed). https://advance-lexis-com.ezproxylocal.library.nova.edu/api/document?collection=cases&id=urn:contentItem:4CC2-DJ20-0039-42DY-00000-00&context=1516831.

47 Emanuel S. *Torts*. 3rd ed. Larchmont: Emanuel Law Outlines; 1988:164–175.

48 Furrow BR, Greaney TL, Johnson SH, Jost TS, Schwartz RL. *Health Law*. Vol. 1. St. Paul: West Publishing; 1995:vii.

49 As the children's nursery rhyme goes, "Sticks and stones may break my bones but names will never hurt me." The Phrase Finder. https://www.phrases.org.uk/meanings/sticks-and-stones-may-break-my-bones.html. Accessed April 13, 2020.

50 *Black's Law Dictionary*. Abridged 6th ed. 1991:270.

These damages include *economic damages* (which include lost wages and medical expenses, both past and future[51]), and *noneconomic damages* (e.g., pain and suffering). The plaintiff bears the burden of proving these damages by a preponderance of the evidence (again, proving that it is *more likely than not* that he suffered damages and that the defendant's negligence caused them). In contrast, neither *nominal damages*[52] nor *punitive damages*[53] are generally available to plaintiffs in medical negligence cases.

2.4.1. Damage Innovations: Damage Limitations (e.g., MICRA)

The Medical Injury Compensation Reform Act of 1975 (MICRA) was a California statute enacted to lower medical malpractice premiums. One of its provisions—Civil Code Section 3333.2—limited *noneconomic damages* in medical malpractice cases to $250,000 or less. This limitation on damages attributable to pain and suffering prevents juries from awarding exorbitant sums—such as the $9.6 million awarded by a New York jury to a 42-year-old contractor who sustained a debilitating stroke and was left permanently paralyzed after a brain aneurysm was not properly diagnosed or treated and thereupon ruptured in a massive bleed.[54] Such verdicts raise the cost of medical malpractice insurance and, indirectly, the cost of health care.

CASE 11.1

Herskovits v. Group Health[55]

Mr. Herskovits presented to Group Health Hospital in early 1974 with complaints of pain and coughing. Rales were heard, and chest x-rays revealed a left-sided infiltrate. Though his complaints persisted, no further diagnostic steps were taken except for an occasional chest x-ray, and he was treated only with cough medicine. In 1975, Mr. Herskovits saw Dr. Jonathan Ostrow privately for a second opinion and within 3 weeks was diagnosed with lung cancer. In July 1975, Herskovits' lung was removed, but he died 20 months later at the age 60.

> At [trial] . . . plaintiff was unable to produce expert testimony that the delay in diagnosis "probably" or "more likely than not" caused her husband's death. . . . [P]laintiff's expert witness, Dr. Jonathan Ostrow . . . indicated that had the diagnosis of lung cancer been [timely] made . . . the patient's possibility of 5-year survival was 39 percent. At the time of [the actual] . . . diagnosis of cancer . . . the possibility of a 5-year survival was reduced to 25 percent. . . . Thus, the delay in diagnosis may have reduced the chance of a 5-year survival by 14 percent.[56]

Assuming Group Health breached its duty to timely diagnose Mr. Herskovits' lung cancer (i.e., that its conduct fell below the standard of care), did Group Health cause Mr. Herskovits' injury?

---

51 Because a plaintiff may sue a defendant only once for the same injury, he or she generally asks not only for damages that have already occurred, but also for damages that will occur in the future as a result of the defendant's negligence.

52 Nominal damages are "a trifling sum awarded to a plaintiff in an action, where there is no substantial loss or injury to be compensated, but still the law recognizes a technical . . . breach of the defendant's duty . . . ." *Black's Law Dictionary.* Abridged 6th ed. 1991:272.

53 Punitive damages (aka exemplary damages) "are awarded to the plaintiff over and above what will . . . compensate him . . . . [and] are based upon an entirely different public policy consideration—that of punishing the defendant or of setting an example for similar wrongdoers . . . . In cases in which it is proved that a defendant has acted willfully, maliciously, or fraudulently, a plaintiff may be awarded exemplary damages in addition to compensatory or actual damages." See, *Black's Law Dictionary.* Abridged 6th ed. 1991:271.

54 *Oakes v. Patel,* 87 A.D.3d 816, 928 N.Y.S.2d 795 (2011).

55 *Herskovits v. Group Health,* 664 P.2d 474 (Wash. 1983).

56 *Herskovits v. Group Health*, 664 P.2d 474 (Wash. 1983).

Analysis: ______________________________

____

____

____

____

____

____

____

____

____

CASE 11.J

Reread Case 11.I. Consider that on appeal the Supreme Court of Washington held in a six to three split that the case should not have been dismissed, that the jury should have been allowed to reach a verdict. The case is remanded (sent back to the lower court) for a trial on the merits, implying that Mr. Herskovits' estate could prevail on the causation issue. How could the estate possibly prevail on causation?

Analysis: ______________________________

____

____

____

____

____

____

2.4.2. Damage Innovations: "Loss of a Chance" Doctrine

Let's conclude our discussion of medical malpractice by examining another damage innovation—the *loss of a chance* doctrine.

The *loss of a chance* doctrine vindicated in *Herskovits v. Group Health* holds that where a provider's negligence reduces the plaintiff's chance of survival—even though the chance of survival was less than 50% before the negligence—the provider is liable for the value of the lost chance. In reaching its verdict, the Court wrote, "To decide otherwise would be a blanket release from liability for [providers] any time there was less than a 50% chance of survival, regardless of how flagrant the negligence."[57]

2.5. Procedural Innovations: Safeguarding the System

Negligence law furthers important public interests. One might think of these as goals of negligence law.

First it acts as a *specific deterrent* of future malpractice on the part of the wrongdoer. Having been made to pay a judgment, he or she is less likely to behave carelessly in the future.

Second, it acts as a *general deterrent* of future malpractice on the part of other would-be wrongdoers. Having learned that a wrongdoer has been made to pay a judgment, other potential wrongdoers are more likely to exercise care in their own professional matters.

57 *Herskovits v. Group Health*, 664 P.2d 474, at 477 (Wash. 1983).

CASE 11.K

Consider the following case:

> Plaintiff . . . Patricia Jackson . . . filed suit in the circuit court of Cook County against defendants Chicago Classic Janitorial & Cleaning Service (Chicago Classic) and Maximum Rehabilitation Services (Maximum) alleging that Chicago Classic negligently maintained a window of plaintiff Patricia Jackson's employer, causing it to crush her fingers while performing her duties. Plaintiff[] also allege[s] that [she] was referred to Maximum for a functional capacity evaluation (FCE) by her treating physician and that she suffered injuries to her back as a result of maximum's improper administration of the FCE. Defendant Maximum moved to dismiss plaintiffs' complaint . . . claiming that plaintiffs failed to file a certificate in compliance with section 2-622 of the Code . . . . [which] provides in pertinent part:
>
> "In any action, whether in tort, contract or otherwise, in which the plaintiff seeks damages for injuries or death by reason of medical, hospital, or other healing art malpractice, the plaintiff's attorney or the plaintiff, if the plaintiff is proceeding pro se, shall file an affidavit, attached to the original and all copies of the complaint, declaring one of the following:
>
> 1. That the affiant has consulted and reviewed the facts of the case with a health professional who the affiant reasonably believes: (i) is knowledgeable in the relevant issues involved in the particular action; (ii) practices or has practiced within the last 6 years or teaches or has taught within the last 6 years in the same area of health care or medicine that is at issue in the particular action; and (iii) is qualified by experience or demonstrated competence in the subject of the case; that the reviewing health professional has determined in a written report, after a review of the medical record and other relevant material involved in the particular action that there is a reasonable and meritorious cause for the filing of such action . . . .
>
> (g) The failure to file a certificate required by this Section shall be grounds for dismissal . . . . "
>
> The circuit court denied Maximum's motion; however, it certified the following question to this court . . . :
>
> "Whether it is necessary for a plaintiff to attach a certificate from a health care professional . . . where the Complaint alleges negligent conduct by a licensed occupational therapist during the performance of a Functional Capacity Evaluation which was ordered by plaintiff's treating physician and used to determine the vocational suitability of plaintiff."
>
> We answer the certified question in the affirmative.[58]

How does this case relate back to *What Is a Health Professional?* To the concept of professionalism discussed in Chapter 2? Why do you think the court decided as it did?

Analysis: ______________________________

____

____

____

____

____

____

____

____

____

58 *Jackson v. Chi. Classic Janitorial & Cleaning Serv., Inc.*, 355 Ill. App. 3d 906, 823 N.E.2d 1055, 2005 Ill. App. LEXIS 54, 291 Ill. Dec. 469 (Appellate Court of Illinois, First District, First Division, January 31, 2005, Opinion Filed). https://advance-lexis-com.ezproxylocal.library.nova.edu/api/document?collection=cases&id=urn:content Item:4FCS-KP10-TVTV-62C3-00000-00&context=1516831.

Third, it provides *compensation* of sorts to the victim of the wrongdoing, attempting to the extent possible to make him or her whole again.

Finally, it exacts *retribution* from the wrongdoer—a proverbial "pound of flesh."

Of course, the existence of a legal remedy creates incentives to sue. In order to protect the system from frivolous lawsuits, various procedural safeguards have been developed. Consider the following case, which illustrates one such procedural innovation in action.

WRAP-UP

Chapter Summary

Medical malpractice is a subset of *health law*, and most medical malpractice cases are brought as *negligence* cases. *Negligence* is conduct that falls below the standard of care established by law for the protection of others against an unreasonable risk of harm. Along with *intentional torts* and *strict liability*, negligence is a *tort*. To prevail in a medical malpractice action against a health professional defendant, a plaintiff patient must prove that the defendant owed the patient a legal *duty*; that defendant's conduct fell below the *standard of care* (i.e., that defendant "breached his or her duty"; that the defendant's conduct was the *cause* of some injury to the plaintiff; and that the plaintiff suffered some *damage(s)* against which the law offers protection. Health professionals owe an affirmative duty of care to all patients with whom they have a provider-patient relationship and in some cases to third parties as well. The *standard of care* requires health professionals to exercise the same degree of knowledge, skill, diligence, and care that the ordinary competent practitioner would exercise under the same or similar circumstances, and to use their *best judgment* in exercising that skill and applying that knowledge. Proof of causation requires both proof that the defendant's conduct brought about the plaintiff's damages (*causation-in-fact* or *scientific causation*) and proof that the plaintiff's damages were *foreseeable* (*legal* or *proximate causation*). Plaintiffs prevailing in a medical malpractice action may recover for present and future damages, both *economic* (e.g., medical expenses and lost earnings) and *noneconomic* (pain and suffering). Modern damage innovations include limitations (caps) on noneconomic damages and the so-called *loss of a chance* doctrine.

Review Questions

1. What is *medical malpractice*, and how does it relate to *negligence*?
2. What is a *tort*? List some different categories of torts and give examples of each.
3. What is *negligence* and what elements does it comprise?
4. What is the *no-duty rule*? List five exceptions to that rule.
5. What is the *standard of care* in medical malpractice cases, as formulated in *Pike v. Honsiger*?
6. Explain how the *best judgment rule* influences the medical standard of care. Give an example.
7. How is the *standard of care* usually established in medical malpractice cases? List five other ways (five exceptions) in which the standard of care can be established.
8. Does the *standard of care* of PAs differ from that of physicians? Should it? Give reasons to support your answer.
9. Explain *scientific* and *legal causation* and their differences.

10. Explain the three tests used to establish *scientific causation*. Under what circumstances would each be used?
11. If *scientific causation* already exists as a concept, why is there a need for the concept of *legal causation*?
12. What are included in calculating *economic damages*? *Noneconomic damages*?
13. What is the *loss of a chance doctrine*, and how does it work?

Case Analyses

Case 11.A Analysis

The teens' failure to rescue or summon help (their inaction) was a case of nonfeasance. Recall that the law does not require that a failure to act be reasonable under the circumstances unless any one of five exceptions to the no-duty rule applies. Do any apply? Let's see. First, no special relationship existed between Dunn and the teens. Regarding the second exception, is there a rescue statute in Florida? Let's come back to that. Third, there was no contract creating a duty of rescue, as might have been the case had the teens been hired as lifeguards. Fourth, the voluntary undertaking exception is not applicable. Fifth and finally, the defendant responsibility exception does not apply since we are told "the teens told Dunn not to go into the murky waters" and that Dunn "walked in on his own." So, there was no legal duty to rescue unless there is a rescue statute in Florida. Is there?

No, there is not. In a follow-up news item, it was revealed:

> COCOA, Fla. – Florida prosecutors say they aren't charging a group of teens who taunted a drowning disabled man and recorded his death.
>
> State Attorney Phil Archer released a statement Friday announcing his office's decision not to criminally charge four juveniles and one adult for failing to help 31-year-old Jamel Dunn at a Cocoa retention pond last July.
>
> Archer pointed out that no Florida law requires a person to provide emergency assistance under the facts of this case. Such a law was proposed during this year's state legislative session but failed to pass.[59]

Therefore, there was no legal duty to rescue or summon help. The absence of any legal duty to rescue means only that those involved did not break the rule "Obey the law." From a moral standpoint, their behavior was appalling, reprehensible, and arguably sociopathic. Their behavior was callous and cruel but not illegal in Florida.[60]

Case 11.B Analysis

If a *special relationship* exists between A and the toddler (e.g., parent-child), then A may have a legal duty to rescue. If the episode takes place in a jurisdiction in which a *rescue statute* has been enacted, then A may owe a legal duty of rescue. If A owes some *contractual duty* to the toddler (e.g., if he is a babysitter who is being paid to watch the toddler), then he may have a legal duty to rescue. If two persons—A and let's say B—were in a position to rescue the child and A waved B off like an outfielder ("I got him, I got him!"), only to pull up at the last instant, leaving B

59 Teens who taunted drowning disabled man won't face charges. *New York Post.* June 23, 2018. https://nypost.com/2018/06/23/teens-who-taunted-drowning-disabled-man-wont-face-charges/. Accessed June 17, 2019.

60 The behavior of the teens was so disgraceful and the consequences so serious that the disconnect between law and morality in this case offends us. Such cases are not isolated. See, e.g., Murder of Kitty Genovese, https://en.wikipedia.org/wiki/Murder_of_Kitty_Genovese; for a more recent case, see Oceanside Stabbing: After a Brawl, Teenagers Gawked as a Boy Lay Dying. https://www.nytimes.com/2019/09/17/nyregion/ny-teen-murder-oceanside.html. Accessed March 5, 2020.

with no chance to rescue the child, it is likely that A will be found to have owed the child a duty of rescue under the *voluntary undertaking* exception. Finally, if A is responsible for the toddler being on the tracks to begin with (e.g., having placed him there), then A owes the child a legal duty of rescue under the *defendant responsibility* exception.

Case 11.C Analysis

In asserting that "the prevailing standard of medical care for infants with anencephaly is to provide only warmth, nutrition, and hydration," the treating physicians and the hospital were arguing that the medical standard of care did not require intubation and mechanical ventilation of anencephalic infants in respiratory distress. In other words, they were essentially arguing that *ordinary competent practitioners* did not (custom-based standard) or would not (reasonable physician standard) intubate Baby K if she were brought into the ER in respiratory distress. The effect of the court's holding, however, was to interpret the EMTALA statute as establishing for legal purposes the standard of care for the physicians and healthcare institutions involved in the case.

Case 11.D Analysis

The court seems to be equating medical futility with *physiologic futility* when it writes, "The use of a mechanical ventilator to assist breathing is not 'futile' . . . in relieving the acute symptoms of respiratory difficulty which is the emergency medical condition that must be treated under EMTALA."[61] The court does not consider whether mechanical ventilation benefits Baby K as a person (and so appears to reject the *qualitative* formulation of medical futility) or how likely mechanical ventilation is to produce its desired physiologic or personal benefit (and so appears to reject a *quantitative* formulation of medical futility as well). Interestingly though unrelatedly, because the wording of the EMTALA statute defines an emergency medical condition by the presence of *symptoms*,[62] and because anencephalics are incapable of experiencing symptoms,[63] a strict application of the EMTALA statute would suggest that there is no such thing as an emergency medical condition involving anencephalics.

Case 11.E Analysis

The appeals court reversed because it decided that the doctrine of *res ipsa loquitur* was applicable. The doctrine applies once the plaintiff establishes that the cause of her injury was in the defendant's exclusive control and that the accident was one that ordinarily does not happen in the absence of negligence. Here the patient was unconscious when the injury occurred, and so she and presumably whatever caused her third-degree burns was in the defendant surgeon's control at the time of the injury. Second, the injury was unusual—one does not expect to awake from anesthesia for an operation on one's foot to find a third-degree burn on the proximal calf, an area "wholly outside the area of operation."[64] Note that the decision of the

61 *In re Baby K*, 832 F. Supp. 1022, at 1027.

62 "The term 'emergency medical condition' means—(A) a medical condition manifesting itself by acute *symptoms* of sufficient severity (including severe pain) such that the absence of immediate medical attention could reasonably be expected to result in—(i) placing the health of the individual (or, with respect to a pregnant woman, the health of the woman or her unborn child) in serious jeopardy, (ii) serious impairment to bodily functions, or (iii) serious dysfunction of any bodily organ or part . . . ." 42 U.S. Code § 1395dd.Examination and treatment for emergency medical conditions and women in labor. Cornell Law School Legal Information Institute. https://www.law.cornell.edu/uscode/text/42/1395dd. Accessed March 27, 2020.

63 A symptom is defined as "any morbid phenomenon or departure from the normal . . . experienced by the patient and indicative of disease . . . ." Stedman's Medical Dictionary Illustrated, 23rd ed. Baltimore, MD: Williams and Wilkins; 1976:1376.

64 *Graham v. Thompson*, 854 S.W.2d 797, 1993 Mo. App. LEXIS 416 (Court of Appeals of Missouri, Western DistrictMarch 23, 1993, Filed). https://advance-lexis-com.ezproxylocal.library.nova.edu/api/document?collection=cases&id=urn:contentItem:3RX4-6RG0-003F-C53H-00000-00&context=1516831.

decision of the Court of Appeals does not mean that the plaintiff patient has won her case or even that she has prevailed on the standard of care issue. It merely creates a presumption—one that the defendant surgeon may rebut—that the patient's burns were the result of her surgeon's negligence.

Case 11.F Analysis

The issue here is whether each of the defendants met the standard of care. Did they "follow[] sound medical practice in 1953 in permitting plaintiff to be exposed to an increased oxygen environment for a prolonged period, even though it was common practice at the time, when they were aware of the possibility that RLF might result"? Let's consider each of the defendants in turn.

If you apply only the first sentence of the previous enunciation of the medical standard of care to Dr. Engle—"The physician is under an obligation to exercise the same degree of knowledge, skill, diligence and care that the ordinary competent practitioner would exercise under the same or similar circumstances"—the answer would have to be that yes, she met the standard of care, since there was at least a respectable minority of physicians, and quite possibly a majority, in July 1953 who were still proponents of oxygen use. However, once you apply the second sentence to Dr. Engle—"The physician is under the further obligation to use his best judgment in exercising his skill and applying his knowledge"—the conclusion you reach is that no, she did not meet the standard of care because even though use of oxygen in premature infants was medically customary at the time, she knew better. In other words, she didn't follow her best judgment. The appellate court found particularly illuminating the fact that in New York Hospital's involvement in the Cooperative study, two out of three babies were given curtailed oxygen—a tacit admission on the part of the hospital that it believed curtailment of oxygen was preferable.

Dr. Ross, on the other hand, whose order to reduce oxygen was countermanded, did not breach his duty of due care to the plaintiff. In ordering that oxygen be "reduced as tolerated," he was following both his best judgment (subjective standard) and the opinion of at least a respectable minority of "ordinary competent practitioners" (objective standard) who had come to believe that oxygen use in premature infants was detrimental.

The appellate court decided that Dr. Engle and the hospital had failed in their duty to plaintiff and that Dr. Ross was not liable.

Case 11.G Analysis

While each defendant, in firing in the direction of the plaintiff, breached his duty to act reasonably (i.e., the conduct of each fell below the standard of care), only one of them caused the plaintiff's injury, since only one shotgun pellet struck the plaintiff. To prevail the plaintiff must prove that it is more likely than not that the conduct of the defendant caused the result. Because we don't know which of the two defendants fired the shot that struck the plaintiff, applying either the *but for* test or the substantial factor test of causation-in-fact will result in an acquittal of both defendants, as there is no more than a 50% chance that either defendant fired that shot. But we do know that both defendants behaved unreasonably and that one of them caused of the plaintiff's injury. That being the case, a verdict for the defendants would allow one of them to unjustly avoid liability and would leave the plaintiff without a remedy.

In order to avoid this injustice, the court used a third test of causation-in-fact that we shall call the *Summers v. Tice* test. Under this test, employed when alternative rather than joint causes (see earlier "substantial factor" test) are involved, "where the plaintiff can show that each of two persons was negligent, [though] only one could have caused the injury, . . . [it is] up to each defendant to show that the other caused the harm." In other words, in such cases courts will shift the burden of proof from the plaintiff to the defendant in the interests of fairness and justice.

Case 11.H Analysis

In general, the standard of care is established by having expert witnesses testify as to how "ordinary competent practitioners" customarily behave under circumstances similar to the case in question. In this case the expert witness would have to be familiar with the standard of care of RTs. Indeed, in this case

> . . . the parents provided the declaration of Mr. Hirnle, a registered respiratory therapist [RRT], to set forth the standard of care. Mr. Hirnle had over 20 years of experience as a respiratory therapist and instructor and was qualified to testify on the standard of care of a respiratory therapist. Mr. Hirnle declared that general hospital protocols require immediate suctioning and/or repositioning of an infant who has vomited, and that any failure to engage in these actions would be a "gross departure from accepted standards of practice and below the degree of skill, care, and learning expected of a reasonably prudent respiratory therapist . . . acting in same or similar circumstances." This declaration was based on Mr. Hirnle's personal knowledge regarding the applicable standard of care for respiratory therapists. Mr. Hirnle also reviewed the medical records and specific depositions and opined that these records indicated to him that the suctioning of the child reflected in the records simply was not immediate enough.[65]

The standard of care can also be established by a number of other means (see section 2.2.3.2 *Exceptions to the Rule*, in this chapter), of which the one that might be applicable here is discussed in section 2.2.1.2.4 *Res Ipsa Loquitur*. Indeed, the court mentioned this possibility in its discussion:

> . . . expert testimony on the standard of care and breach . . . is not required . . . when medical facts are observable by a layperson's senses and describable without medical training. For instance, when a medical provider inadvertently leaves a foreign object in a patient's body during an operation . . . expert testimony is not required to establish that the standard of care required removal of the object. Here, whether Mr. Herbert promptly applied suction to clear the baby's airways after she vomited through her mouth and nose and before he continued to force air into her lungs is a medical fact that would be observable to a layperson's senses and describable without medical training. Where a prone individual is having problems breathing and then vomits through the mouth and nose while having air pumped into the lungs by mechanical means, the importance of clearing the airways of the vomit before continuing to force air into the lungs is easily grasped by laypersons who have no medical training. When that prone individual is a premature infant weighing less than five pounds, the logic is inescapable regardless of medical training: To continue to pump air into such an infant's lungs without first clearing the airways of the vomit necessarily and inevitably will force the vomit deep into the infant's lungs. This is a matter of elementary physics easily grasped by a trier of fact.[66]

So, the parents presented sufficient evidence regarding the standard of care using the *res ipsa loquitur* doctrine by providing the declaration of Arielle's mother, who was present in the emergency room during the entire incident. The declaration stated in part:

> In the examination room, the RT [respiratory therapist] began providing oxygen

---

65 *Hinkson-Irizarry v. Children's Hosp. & Reg'l Med. Ctr.*, 2004 Wash. App. LEXIS 964 (Court of Appeals of Washington, Division One, May 10, 2004, Filed). https://advance-lexis-com.ezproxylocal.library.nova.edu/api/document?collection=cases&id=urn:contentItem:4CC2-DJ20-0039-42DY-00000-00&context=1516831.

66 *Hinkson-Irizarry v. Children's Hosp. & Reg'l Med. Ctr.*, 2004 Wash. App. LEXIS 964 (Court of Appeals of Washington, Division One, May 10, 2004, Filed). https://advance-lexis-com.ezproxylocal.library.nova.edu/api/document?collection=cases&id=urn:contentItem:4CC2-DJ20-0039-42DY-00000-00&context=1516831.

> to Arielle through a bag and mask. Arielle was laying [*sic*] . . . on her back, on the . . . gurney. After a few minutes, Arielle vomited while the RT was still bagging her and while I was still present next to both of them. After Arielle vomited, the RT just stood there staring at Arielle, taking no action to prevent Arielle from aspirating. The RT did not reposition Arielle by turning her from her back onto her side or stomach. The RT did not use a suction catheter device that was present in the room to suction the vomit. The RT took no other action to clear Arielle's airway. The RT simply re-applied the mask and continued to bag Arielle. No other employee or agent for [Children's Hospital] attempted to use suctioning or attempted to reposition Arielle after she vomited and before she aspirated. [Internal citations omitted.][67]

Case 11.I Analysis

The answer would seem to be no. Under traditional evidentiary standards, Mr. Herskovits' "injury" is premature death, and his estate would have to prove that it is *more likely than not* that but for Group Health's delay in diagnosis he would have avoided dying prematurely. Since it was more likely than not that Herskovits would die prematurely (to be precise, probability of 61%) even before Group Health erred, Herskovits could not prevail under traditional evidentiary standards. Since the plaintiff cannot possibly prevail on the causation element, it would seem that the case should be dismissed.

Case 11.J Analysis

For the Herskovits estate to prevail on the causation issue, the traditional evidentiary standard (i.e., *more likely than not*) would have to be relaxed, or the compensable injury suffered by Mr. Herskovits (premature death under the traditional rule) would have to be redefined as the reduction of a chance (or loss of a chance) of survival. In fact, in *Herskovits v. Group Health*, two of the six Justices in the majority took the former route, identifying the compensable injury as premature death but requiring that the plaintiff prove only that the defendant's "negligence increased the risk of injury or death. The step from the increased risk to causation is one for the jury to make."[68] The remaining four Justices retained the traditional *more likely than not* evidentiary standard, but reasoned that the *reduced chance of survival*, rather than the premature death itself, was the compensable injury.

Case 11.K Analysis

This case demonstrates the special nature of the "healing arts," or the health professions. In essence, section 2-619 of the Illinois Statutes requires that a plaintiff in a suit alleging negligence on the part of a healing arts practitioner submit an affidavit affirming that he or she has reviewed the facts of the case with an expert witness (an appropriately qualified health professional) who has determined that filing the lawsuit is "reasonable and meritorious" under the circumstances. (Negligence suits against wrongdoers or tortfeasors who are not practicing the healing arts do not require such an affidavit.) The requirement for the input of experts at this pre-trial stage is separate from but related to the requirement for expert testimony in establishing the standard of care and the causation elements discussed previously. In both cases—that is, determining whether to allow a case to go to trial, and deciding that case on the merits at trial—laypersons (non-health professionals) are being asked to "apply[] distinctively medical knowledge or principles," concepts arguably

67 *Hinkson-Irizarry v. Children's Hosp. & Reg'l Med. Ctr.*, 2004 Wash. App. LEXIS 964 (Court of Appeals of Washington, Division One, May 10, 2004, Filed). https://advance-lexis-com.ezproxylocal.library.nova.edu/api/document?collection=cases&id=urn:contentItem:4CC2-DJ20-0039-42DY-00000-00&context=1516831.

68 *Herskovits v. Group Health*, 664 P.2d 474, at 478 (Wash. 1983).

"not within the grasp of the ordinary lay juror." The obligatory involvement of experts at the pre-trial stage promotes efficiency and protects the court system from having to decide frivolous cases. This also explains why the court decided in favor of the defendants in *Jackson*. The court found it telling that the occupational therapist who supervised the FCE was licensed by the State of Illinois and was subject to discipline through the Department of Professional Regulation as are medical doctors, and that "occupational therapists who conduct FCEs employ specialized knowledge and skill that is not within the grasp of the average lay juror."[69]

69 *Jackson v. Chi. Classic Janitorial & Cleaning Serv., Inc.*, 355 Ill. App. 3d 906, 823 N.E.2d 1055, 2005 Ill. App. LEXIS 54, 291 Ill. Dec. 469 (Appellate Court of Illinois, First District, First Division, January 31, 2005, Opinion Filed). https://advance-lexis-com.ezproxylocal.library.nova.edu/api/document?collection=cases&id=urn:contentItem:4FCS-KP10-TVTV-62C3-00000-00&context=1516831.

Glossary of Legal Terms

Battery Intentional harmful or offensive physical contact with the person of another without his or her consent.

Cause in fact The particular cause that produces a result and without which the result would not have occurred. Aka, scientific cause.

Common law A body of legal principles and rules of action that derive their authority from the judgments of the courts.

Confidential communication Statements made in confidence between two persons (e.g., physician-patient, attorney-client, priest-penitent, or between spouses) who believe that the communication will be held in confidence—i.e., that the communication is meant only for the ears of the other person. Such communications are said to be *privileged* and thus protected from forced disclosure on the witness stand.

Contract An agreement between parties that creates a legal obligation.

Damages Monetary compensation recovered in the courts by a person who has suffered a legally compensable injury as a result of the wrongful act or omission of another.

Declaratory judgment A declaration by a court concerning the rights/legal relations of a party to a legal case/controversy.

Defendant The party against whom legal relief is sought in a civil action, or the accused in a criminal case.

Duty A legal or moral obligation to do or refrain from doing something.

Executive The branch of government that is charged with carrying the laws into effect.

Feasance The doing of an act.

Federalism A system of government under which states unite under a federal (national) government while retaining autonomy over internal affairs.

Foreseeability The capability of being known in advance.

Good Samaritan doctrine Holds that one who, despite having no legal duty to do so, undertakes to rescue/aid another person in danger cannot be charged with negligence, so long as they do not behave recklessly.

Health law Law affecting the professionals and institutions responsible for healthcare delivery.

Informed consent A person's agreement to submit to some intervention (e.g., a diagnostic test or therapeutic intervention) following an adequate disclosure of facts relevant to the decision.

Intentional tort A wrongful act in which the actor is determined to have acted intentionally.

Judicial branch The branch of state and federal government tasked with interpreting, construing, and applying the laws of the land.

Judicial review Power of courts to determine the constitutionality of legislative or executive acts.

Justiciable controversy A matter that might properly come before a court for adjudication.

Legal cause Aka, proximate cause (see *Proximate cause*).

Legislative power The powers of a legislature to make new laws or to amend or repeal existing laws.

Malfeasance The performance an unlawful act.

Medical malpractice Medical conduct falling below the standard of care established by law for the protection of patients against an unreasonable risk of harm.

Misfeasance The improper or negligent performance of an otherwise lawful act.

Mootness doctrine Holds that when a matter is moot (i.e., if events have placed the matter beyond the reach of the law, or if the matter in dispute would not be affected by a judicial decision) the matter is nonjusticiable, and federal courts do not have jurisdiction over them. Along with the *political question* doctrine, the *standing* doctrine, and the *ripeness* doctrine, this doctrine is a fourth grounds for finding a matter nonjusticiable.

Negligence Conduct that falls below the standard of care established by law for the protection of others against an unreasonable risk of harm.

Negligence per se Negligence that results from violation of a statute. For example, when a defendant violates a statute meant to protect against a certain type of harm, and his or her violation causes that type of harm to a plaintiff, this is said to have occurred.

Nonfeasance Failure to perform an act that one had a duty to perform.

Police power The power of the state to enact laws to further public safety, health, morals, or general welfare.

Plaintiff The complainant in a civil action.

Precedent A court case that has already been decided and that, in common law legal systems, constitutes legal authority for a later identical or similar case.

Prima facie At first appearance, or at first glance.

Privacy, right of Actually, a bundle of rights, including (1) nonintrusion (the right to be let alone); (2) noninterference (the right to act in personal matters without unwarranted interference by others); and (3) protection of personal information from disclosure (confidentiality is related to this aspect of privacy).

Proximate cause If a defendant's act foreseeably increases the risk that a particular harmful result will occur and that harmful result does occur, the defendant's act is said to qualify as this. The doctrine serves as a limitation on liability.

Ratio decidendi The grounds or reason for the decision in a legal case; the reason that determines the outcome.

Rebuttable presumption A presumption that may be rebutted by evidence to the contrary.

Reckless Indifferent to consequences.

Res ipsa loquitur Latin for "The thing speaks for itself."

Respondeat superior Latin for, "Let the master answer." This doctrine or maxim means that a master is liable for the wrongful acts of his servant.

Ripeness doctrine Holds that the federal courts require an actual, present controversy, and therefore will not act when the issue is premature, hypothetical, or speculative. Along with the *political question* doctrine, the *standing* doctrine, and the *mootness* doctrine, this doctrine is a fourth grounds for finding a matter nonjusticiable.

Standard of care In tort law, the degree of care that a reasonably prudent person should exercise under similar circumstances. Conduct evincing a lesser degree of care is negligent.

Standing to sue doctrine Holds that a party must have a stake in an otherwise justiciable controversy in order to bring suit. Along with the *political question* doctrine, the *mootness* doctrine, and the *ripeness* doctrine, this doctrine is a fourth grounds for finding a matter nonjusticiable.

Stare decisis Latin, meaning "To adhere to decided cases." The doctrine holds that, in general, cases should be decided in accordance with legal precedent (see Precedent definition).

Strict liability Liability imposed without fault or intent on the part of the defendant.

Tort A legal wrong, other than breach of contract, committed upon the person or property of another. This type of law contemplates civil remedies, e.g., in the form of monetary damages.

Vicarious liability The doctrine under which, where person X is negligent and Y is not, the negligence of X is imposed upon Y solely based upon some relationship existing between X and Y. Aka, imputed negligence.

Waiver The voluntary relinquishment of a right, such as one's right to informed consent. In order to protect rights, the law requires that waivers be unambiguous.

Index